CHRISTMAS BEFORE
CHRISTIANITY

CONSTITUTIONAL HISTORY
The Articles of Confederation Explained: A Clause-by-Clause Study of America's First Constitution
The Constitution of the Confederate States of America Explained: A Clause-by-Clause Study of the South's Magna Carta

VICTORIAN CONFEDERATE LITERATURE
Rise Up and Call Them Blessed: Victorian Tributes to the Confederate Soldier, 1861-1901
The Old Rebel: Robert E. Lee As He Was Seen By His Contemporaries
Victorian Confederate Poetry: The Southern Cause in Verse, 1861-1901

ABRAHAM LINCOLN
Abraham Lincoln: The Southern View - Demythologizing America's Sixteenth President
Lincolnology: The Real Abraham Lincoln Revealed in His Own Words - A Study of Lincoln's Suppressed, Misinterpreted, and Forgotten Writings and Speeches
The Great Impersonator! 99 Reasons to Dislike Abraham Lincoln
The Unholy Crusade: Lincoln's Legacy of Destruction in the American South
The Unquotable Abraham Lincoln: The President's Quotes They Don't Want You To Know!

CIVIL WAR BATTLES
Encyclopedia of the Battle of Franklin - A Comprehensive Guide to the Conflict that Changed the Civil War
Nathan Bedford Forrest and the Battle of Fort Pillow: Yankee Myth, Confederate Fact

PARANORMAL
Carnton Plantation Ghost Stories: True Tales of the Unexplained from Tennessee's Most Haunted Civil War House!
UFOs and Aliens: The Complete Guidebook

FAMILY HISTORIES
The Blakeneys: An Etymological, Ethnological, and Genealogical Study - Uncovering the Mysterious Origins of the Blakeney Family and Name
The Caudills: An Etymological, Ethnological, and Genealogical Study - Exploring the Name and National Origins of a European-American Family
The McGavocks of Carnton Plantation: A Southern History - Celebrating One of Dixie's Most Noble Confederate Families and Their Tennessee Home

MIND, BODY, SPIRIT
Autobiography of a Non-Yogi: A Scientist's Journey From Hinduism to Christianity (Dr. Amitava Dasgupta, with Lochlainn Seabrook)
Britannia Rules: Goddess-Worship in Ancient Anglo-Celtic Society - An Academic Look at the United Kingdom's Matricentric Spiritual Past
Christ Is All and In All: Rediscovering Your Divine Nature and the Kingdom Within
Christmas Before Christianity: How the Birthday of the "Sun" Became the Birthday of the "Son"
Jesus and the Gospel of Q: Christ's Pre-Christian Teachings As Recorded in the New Testament
Jesus and the Law of Attraction: The Bible-Based Guide to Creating Perfect Health, Wealth, and Happiness Following Christ's Simple Formula
Seabrook's Bible Dictionary of Traditional and Mystical Christian Doctrines
The Bible and the Law of Attraction: 99 Teachings of Jesus, the Apostles, and the Prophets
The Book of Kelle: An Introduction to Goddess-Worship and the Great Celtic Mother-Goddess Kelle, Original Blessed Lady of Ireland
The Goddess Dictionary of Words and Phrases: Introducing a New Core Vocabulary for the Women's Spirituality Movement
The Way of Holiness: The Story of Religion and Myth From the Cave Bear Cult to Christianity

WOMEN
Aphrodite's Trade: The Hidden History of Prostitution Unveiled
Princess Diana: Modern Day Moon-Goddess - A Psychoanalytical and Mythological Look at Diana Spencer's Life, Marriage, and Death (with Dr. Jane Goldberg)
Women in Gray: A Tribute to the Ladies Who Supported the Southern Confederacy

Five-Star Books & Gifts From the Heart of the American South

SeaRavenPress.com

Warning: SEA RAVEN PRESS BOOKS WILL EXPAND YOUR ★ MIND!

CHRISTMAS BEFORE
CHRISTIANITY

How the Birthday of the "Sun"
Became the Birthday of the "Son"

ILLUSTRATED BY THE AUTHOR, "THE SOUTHERN JOSEPH CAMPBELL," COLONEL

LOCHLAINN SEABROOK

JEFFERSON DAVIS HISTORICAL GOLD MEDAL WINNER

Diligently Researched for the
Elucidation of the Reader

2018

Sea Raven Press, Nashville, Tennessee, USA

Published by
Sea Raven Press, Cassidy Ravensdale, President
PO Box 1484, Spring Hill, Tennessee 37174-1484 USA
SeaRavenPress.com • searavenpress@gmail.com

SEA RAVEN PRESS
SOUTHERN BOOKS, REAL HISTORY!

1st SRP paperback edition, 1st printing May 2010; 2nd printing January 2018: ISBN 978-0-9821899-8-6
1st SRP hardcover edition, 1st printing January 2018: ISBN 978-1-943737-61-1

ISBN: 978-0-9821899-8-6 (paperback)
Library of Congress Control Number: 2010922901

Christmas Before Christianity: How the Birthday of the "Sun" Became the Birthday of the "Son" - by Lochlainn Seabrook. Includes an index and bibliographical references.

Front and back cover design and art, book design, layout, and interior art by Lochlainn Seabrook
All images, graphic design, graphic art, and illustrations copyright © Lochlainn Seabrook
All images selected, placed, manipulated, and/or created by Lochlainn Seabrook
Cover image: Victorian Christmas card, circa 1900

The views on the American "Civil War" documented in this book are those of the publisher.

PRINTED & MANUFACTURED IN OCCUPIED TENNESSEE, FORMER CONFEDERATE STATES OF AMERICA

SEA RAVEN PRESS

DEDICATION

To my religion, Christianity,

which has kept the Pagan gods, goddesses, myths, customs, and beliefs of the ancient world alive for 2,000 years through the celebration of Christmas.

EPIGRAPH

The truth is that the greatest enemies to the doctrines of Jesus are those calling themselves the expositors of them, who have perverted them for the structure of a system of fancy absolutely incomprehensible, and without any foundation in his genuine words. And the day will come when the mystical generation of Jesus, by the supreme being as his father in the womb of a virgin, will be classed with the fable of the generation of Minerva in the brain of Jupiter. But we may hope that the dawn of reason and freedom of thought in these United States will do away with all this artificial scaffolding, and restore to us the primitive and genuine doctrines of this the most venerated reformer of human errors.

U.S. PRESIDENT

Thomas Jefferson

MONTICELLO, CHARLOTTESVILLE, VIRGINIA, APRIL 11, 1823

CONTENTS

Part Three
MODERN CONTRIBUTIONS

Keep Your Body, Mind, & Spirit Vibrating at Their Highest Level

YOU CAN DO SO BY READING THE BOOKS OF

SEA RAVEN PRESS

There is nothing that will so perfectly keep your body, mind, and spirit in a healthy condition as to think wisely and positively. Hence you should not only read this book, but also the other books that we offer. They will quicken your physical, mental, and spiritual vibrations, enabling you to maintain a position in society as a healthy erudite person.

KEEP YOURSELF WELL-INFORMED!

The well-informed person is always at the head of the procession, while the ignorant, the lazy, and the unthoughtful hang onto the rear. If you are a Spiritual man or woman, do yourself a great favor: read Sea Raven Press books and stay well posted on the Truth. It is almost criminal for one to remain in ignorance while the opportunity to gain knowledge is open to all at a nominal price.

We invite you to visit our Webstore for a wide selection of wholesome, family-friendly, well-researched, educational books for all ages. You will be glad you did!

Five-Star Books & Gifts From the Heart of the American South

SeaRavenPress.com

THE CHRISTIAN TETRAMORPH

The Christian iconography below, images still visible in various European churches (such as France's Chartres Cathedral), reveals the origins and evolution of the "Four Gospelers" of the New Testament. Starting out as the Pagans' Four-Compass Gods (representing north, south, east, and west), these eventually became the four astrological star-signs that form the Galactic Cross (or Cosmic Cross) in a horoscope: Aquarius, Leo, Taurus, and Aquila (now known as Scorpio). Hence its Pagan name: the Tetramorph ("four bodies").

Some 150 years after Jesus' death, based on these four Pagan star-signs, the Christian Church appended the artificial names "Matthew," "Mark," "Luke," and "John" to the four accepted (canonical) Gospels, all important elements in the development of Christmas. Henceforth the Church called it the "Christian Tetramorph." These facts, once well-known and accepted by both the Christian clergy and the Christian laity, are today kept carefully hidden from the masses. [1]

Matthew as Aquarius, the Pagan zodiacal Waterman; represents the Winter Solstice.

Mark as Leo, the Pagan zodiacal Lion; represents the Summer Solstice.

Luke as Taurus, the Pagan zodiacal Bull; represents the Spring Equinox.

John as Aquila, the Pagan zodiacal Eagle (now Scorpio); represents the Fall Equinox.

NOTES TO THE READER

SCRIPTURE
☞ All biblical scriptures and references are from the King James Version of the Bible (KJV), named after my cousin, King of Scotland, James (Stuart) the 6th (1566-1625).

ON THE MEANING OF "MYTH"
☞ Unless indicated, throughout this book I do not use the words myth or mythology to mean something fabricated, unreal, false, imaginary, unfounded, or unverifiable, their more commonly held meanings. Rather, I use myth, in Webster's original and most important sense, to mean a traditional and historical story, event, trait, or figure that either embodies or explains a people's belief or practice, or a natural phenomenon of some kind.

Thus, when I make reference to the "Jesus myth," or to "Christian mythology," I do not mean to imply that Jesus or Christianity are fake or not real. I am commenting on a particular story or characteristic that I believe personifies Jesus and Christianity. See following note.

A PRO-CHRISTIAN BOOK
☞ Because much of this book views Christmas, and by association Jesus and Christianity, through the lenses of mythology, folklore, and legend, there will be those who consider it an anti-Christian, or even an atheistic, work. To them my words may seem to repudiate Christmas, while calling into question not only the divinity of Jesus, but His very existence as a historical person as well.

A careful reading of this book will prove otherwise, however, for I am a lifelong Christian, one who worships, not the *crucified* Jesus (in the Pagan manner), but the *living* Christ (in the original Christian manner).[2]

The living Christ was a historical man who walked the Earth 2,000 years ago, teaching radical spiritual laws and principles,[3] such as the "mysteries of the kingdom of heaven,"[4] the Golden Rule,[5] the Law of Attraction,[6] reincarnation,[7] the Law of the Third Eye,[8] the Law of the Third Ear,[9] the Law of Spiritual Rebirth,[10] the idea of spiritual food,[11] the notion that all humans are gods and goddesses in their own right,[12] the Law of Universal Salvation,[13] the oneness of God, Jesus, and humanity (theosis),[14] the complete and utter rejection of formal, organized religion[15] (new wine cannot be put into old bottles, said the Master),[16] and the reinstatement of the Divine Feminine (that is, love) back into patriarchal (male-dominant) religion.[17]

At the same time, however, it is important we acknowledge that Jesus was not the first to teach such things; nor was He the first savior, the first to be born of a virgin under a heraldic star, the first infant messiah to be wrapped in swaddling clothes, the first to perform miracles, to have twelve disciples, to hold a last supper, to establish a sacrament, to be crucified and laid in a cave, or to be resurrected three days later.

Irrefutable evidence for these facts derives from the historical record, and from centuries of exhaustive work by archaeologists, anthropologists, and various academicians and scholars, and even from the Bible and other early Christian works themselves.

What has been uncovered is inescapable confirmation that other crucified saviors born of virgin mothers, other "sons of God," other "Lambs of God," preceded Jesus; that Christmas is almost entirely rooted in Pagan myth, ritual, and belief; and that Christianity itself owes most if not all of its many accouterments to Paganism.

Such accouterments would include: baptism, prayer, ritual human sacrifice, the Eucharist, the sacrament, hymns, choirs, religious art, prophecy, sacred literature, miracles, the pope, priests, nuns, seminaries, monasteries, nunneries, atonement, redemption, the laying on of hands, heaven, hell, purgatory, the Way, the Trinity, the virgin mother or Madonna, the dying-and-rising savior-son, the nativity, the holy family, sin, the Sabbath, communion, absolution, ablution, revelation, resurrection, the parousia, salvation, priestly offices, ascension, transubstantiation, the cult of relics, assumption, celibacy, thank-offerings, confession, penance, extreme unction, agape, sacred architecture, the tonsure, the sistrum, the procession, sacred numerology, religious astrology, the Mysteries, the Logos, the Lamb of God, the second coming, supernaturalism, martyrdom, exorcism, the Last Judgement, the end times, and the use of churches, chapels, vestments, the rosary, bread, wine, incense, candles, holy water, bells, and catacombs.

Every one of these beliefs, concepts, customs, and items can be found in Pagan religions that predated Christianity, in particular Hinduism—which may be between 5,000 and 10,000 year old. Even the idea of monotheism (one God) is unarguably Pagan (Egyptian) in origin.

Does this disprove Christianity? Do these facts make Christ's divinity a sham? Is Christmas less meaningful because of these facts?

Just as early Christians did, I believe modern Christians must resolve these issues for themselves.

Speaking for myself as a Christian (and an indifferentist), there is nothing in the following pages that detracts from or even threatens my convictions. Not even the lack of a single authentic eyewitness account of Jesus has ever shaken my belief in His historical reality.[18]

Why? Because my beliefs are not based on the faulty writings of ancient Christian scribes, the politically-calculated editing of ancient Catholic priests, the sinister scripture-twisting of many of today's so-called "Christian" preachers, or the religion-loathing claims of modern scientists. Here, I walk by faith, not by sight.[19]

When it comes to Christmas, however, the mind justifiably seeks rational answers to its many obvious ties to pre-Christian spiritual belief systems. For those who choose to knock, this book will open the door.[20]

LEARN MORE

☛ Christmas, and the religion that celebrates it, can never be fully understood without a knowledge of comparative religion and comparative mythology. As this book is only meant to be an introductory guide to these topics, one cannot hope to learn the complete story here. For those who are interested in gaining a greater understanding of original (pre-Catholic) Christianity, see my books:

- *Seabrook's Bible Dictionary of Traditional and Mystical Christian Doctrines*
- *Christ Is All and In All: Rediscovering Your Divine Nature and the Kingdom Within*
- *Jesus and the Gospel of Q: Christ's Pre-Christian Teachings As Recorded in the New Testament*
- *Jesus and the Law of Attraction: The Bible-Based Guide to Creating Perfect Health, Wealth, and Happiness Following Christ's Simple Formula*
- *Britannia Rules: Goddess-Worship in Ancient Anglo-Celtic Society - An Academic Look at the United Kingdom's Matricentric Spiritual Past*
- *The Bible and the Law of Attraction: 99 Teachings of Jesus, the Apostles, and the Prophets*
- *The Book of Kelle: An Introduction to Goddess-Worship and the Great Celtic Mother-Goddess Kelle, Original Blessed Lady of Ireland*
- *The Goddess Dictionary of Words and Phrases: Introducing a New Core Vocabulary for the Women's Spirituality Movement*
- *The Way of Holiness: The Story of Religion and Myth From the Cave Bear Cult to Christianity*

CHRISTIANITY HAS ALWAYS EXISTED AND CHRISTMAS HAS ALWAYS BEEN CELEBRATED

"That, in our times, is the Christian religion, which to know and to follow is the most sure and certain health, called according to that name, but not according to that thing itself, of which it is the name; for the thing itself which is now called the Christian religion really was known to the ancients, nor was wanting at any time from the beginning of the human race until the time when Christ came in the flesh, from whence the true religion, which had previously existed, began to be called Christian; and this in our days is the Christian religion."[21] — SAINT AUGUSTINE (Church Father)

"The names of Jesus and Christ were both known and honored by the ancients [that is, pre-Christian peoples]. . . . That which is called the Christian religion is neither new nor strange, but—if it be lawful to testify the truth—was known to the ancients."[22] — EUSEBIUS (Church Father)

"Not only did the Christ exist from the very beginning [of time], but so did the Church."[23] — THE GNOSTIC CHRISTIAN CHURCH

INTRODUCTION

In considering the origins of Christmas, we are immediately confronted with a series of heavily documented unavoidable facts:

- No one knows when (or where) Jesus was born.
- Jesus' birth on December 25 specifically was not mentioned by any writer, scholar, or historian during the first thirty years of the 1st Century, the period in which Jesus lived.
- The word Christmas appears nowhere in the Bible.
- Not one person in the Bible celebrated Christmas.
- As such, there is no biblical injunction to celebrate Christmas, and in fact, many of the early Church Fathers prohibited it.
- Because early Christians believed that Jesus only became divine after His baptism (at age thirty), they did not think it important to celebrate His birth. Indeed, the belief that Jesus Himself was a deity (God) was not even officially accepted by the Christian Church until the year 325, at the Council of Nicaea.
- December 25 was not officially and lawfully established as Christmas until the year 534. And even then, it was not because Jesus was actually born on that day, but rather because the Christian masses overwhelmingly identified Jesus with the Pagan Roman sun-god Mithras, as well as with numerous other pre-Christian solar deities, all whose birthdays fell on December 25. (It was because of this that many Church Fathers, like Saint Augustine, opposed the decision due to the date's overt Pagan associations.)
- Before December 25 was chosen, many other dates were suggested by the Church Fathers as the probable day of Jesus' birth, among them January 6, March 28, April 24, and May 25. But even these dates all had Pagan foundations.
- Nearly everything we consider "Christmas tradition" (for example, the Virgin Birth, the Nativity, the Star of Bethlehem, the Three Wise Men, Christmas trees, gift-giving, the turkey dinner) was brought along from Paganism at the adoption of the date December 25.
- In short, Christmas was not directly, or even indirectly, originally connected with Christianity.

As shocking as these facts will be to some, a study of authentic history has unfailingly and repeatedly shown them all to be valid.

Anthropologists, archaeologists, and comparative mythologists have, of course, known about them for many decades, even centuries. Unfortunately, this knowledge is rarely disseminated to the Christian laity, which has long been taught the falsehood that Christmas marks Jesus' authentic birthday. This is an insult to the Church and a mockery of our Lord, for the truths He taught as a mortal man can never be understood if He is viewed as a Pagan god—as He is by so many modern Christian denominations, groups, and organizations.

In order to discover the true meaning of this syncretistic holiday then, we must go beyond so-called "Christian tradition." We must objectively examine the magico-religious cosmologies, the astrotheologies, the cultural mythologies, and the occult ideologies of both paleoanthropic and ancient cultures that pre-dated Christianity by millennia.

In doing so, the wonderful holy day we now call Christmas will take on a new spiritual significance, one with the power to both strengthen the beliefs of all Christians and further ennoble the religion of Christ and His true nativity: the birthday of the Sun.

Lochlainn Seabrook
Franklin, Tennessee, USA
May 2010
Luke 17:21 KJV

PART ONE

AN INTRODUCTION TO COMPARATIVE CHRISTMAS STUDIES

1

THE PREHISTORIC MATRIARCHATE AND THE GREAT VIRGIN-MOTHER

MYTHOLOGY IS NEVER "just a myth," as many like to refer to things they regard as fanciful. Everything derives from something. In the case of religious mythology, one of those "somethings" is the human psyche, some of the earliest traces which have been found in the fossil remains of a people who lived in Europe during the Upper Paleolithic Period between 40,000 and 10,000 years ago: the Cro-Magnons.

The artistic images they left behind, cave paintings, engravings, reliefs, and statuettes of both animals and deities, prove that mythology was an integral aspect of Cro-Magnon culture.

Among the deity category were figurines of pregnant females with emphasized physical features (large breasts and buttocks, swollen abdomens and vulvas, and wide flaring hips) who were often represented as faceless, or even headless women. These are none other than the earliest known depictions of the great Virgin-Mother-Goddess.[24]

Who was this deity and where did she come from?

As prehistoric societies had no conception of the biology behind sexual reproduction—that is, of paternity (the male's contribution to conception)—they believed that all females were parthenogenic; that is, that they were virgin mothers who created life inside their "magical" wombs autonomously and asexually. The sacrality surrounding the supernatural life-giving powers of the human female gave rise to humanity's earliest known religion: the cult of the great Virgin-Mother-Goddess, Divine Creatrix of the Universe and All Life.

From this time period, hundreds of her images, the absurdly misnamed "Venus" statues,[25] have been found. Revealingly, however, not a single corresponding artistic image of a male god has ever been discovered from the same period. For this was the age of the Matriarchate, in which Goddess-worship and the Female Principle dominated human society, embodied in each town as a head Mother and her Twelve Priestesses[26]—a female-centric way of life that would later reach its pinnacle among the Minoans of ancient Crete.

This is not to say that *all* human societies were once matriarchal, but rather that many of them passed through one kind of matriarchal phase or another at some point in their development. This is particularly true of European peoples dating to before 6000 BC, the region we are most familiar with archaeologically.

From the Matriarchate's central figure, the great Virgin-Mother-Goddess, would descend nearly all of the worlds hundreds of thousands of religions.[27] And it is from here, tens of thousands of years ago, in the fossil remains of prehistoric peoples, that we find the first traces of what would one day become Christmas.

2

The Mother Figure And The Original Nuclear Family

WHY WAS A belief in the great Virgin-Mother-Goddess so important to early humans? One reason is biological instinct: modern studies show that very young children all over the world, no matter what their culture or nationality, regard the mother as the primary, or more often, the sole parent. This sentiment continues into adulthood, as most are aware.[28]

The father, who Nature designed to be a hunter not a parent, and who thus has no innate paternal feelings, is correctly seen by children as a secondary, or even a nonessential member of the family.[29] (We are speaking biologically here, apart from modern social constructs concerning the human family.) This is why the earliest artistic depictions of families among prehistoric peoples were of a mother and child, not of a mother, child, and father. The mother-child unit *is* the original nuclear family.

This is also why, among many living archaic peoples to this day, men often live completely separate and apart from the women, with villages divided in half: the female section on one side, the male section on the other. And it is for this same reason that modern courts intuitively continue to award the custody of children of divorce almost solely to their mothers, rarely to their fathers.

It is also why a majority of Catholics prefer the worship of the Virgin Mary to that of her Son (much to the dismay of Church authorities), and it is why you are more likely to see a statue of Mary outside a Catholic Church than one of Jesus.

With such a powerful, built-in instinct for the parthenogenic maternal figure, it is little wonder that the first religions, and even the first human societies themselves, known as matriarchies ("rule by mothers"), were built around mothers.

There is another reason, however, why early humans were so drawn to the great Virgin-Mother-Goddess: psychology. As Carl Jung pointed out, the collective unconscious of humanity seems to contain "essential archetypes" which, out of psychological and biological necessity, exhibit themselves in every known religion, both prehistoric and contemporary.

Among these archetypes we have the warrior/warrioress, the hunter/huntress, the healer, the joker, the trickster, the athlete, the hermit, the king, the queen, the priest/priestess, the angel, the sinner, the witch (or wise woman), the wizard (or wise man), the hero, the criminal, the coward, the father, the mother, the son, the daughter, the grandfather (Sage), the grandmother (Crone), and so on.[30]

For us, the most pertinent ones concern the virgin-mother and the sun/son/savior archetypes, for being the core of the original nuclear family, it is these two images which long ago formed the basis of both ancient and modern religions.

Of the modern ones, some 40,000 separate Christian denominations now exist, all founded on and around the figures of the Virgin-Mother Mary and her Savior-Son Jesus, whose birth is said to have occurred on December 25. From the Catholics, Mormons, and Baptists to the Unitarians, Methodists, and Lutherans, a third of the world's population each year celebrates the primitive ritual of Christmas in one form or another.

3

In Search Of
The Historical Jesus

DESPITE THE ENTHUSIASTIC worldwide celebration of Christmas, it must be regarded as more than passing strange that there is not a single *authentic* document dating from the first thirty years of 1st-Century Rome that makes note of the birth of Jesus. Not one mention of His miraculous nativity was recorded by anyone in the ancient world *while He was alive.*

And yet this was a time period when even the tiniest minutia concerning everyday Roman life was recorded in detail, including local news and gossip; even shopping lists and the names of people's servants and pets have survived in the archaeological record.

Still, somehow Jesus' Virgin Birth, the Star of Bethlehem, and the Three Wise Men, all escaped the notice of His fellow record-keeping Romans, including meticulous contemporary writers like Philo of Alexandria (c. 25 BC-AD 47) and Seneca the Elder (c. 55 BC-c. AD 39). Most did not even acknowledge the existence of Jesus, let alone His birth, miracles, earth-shattering death, and sensational resurrection.

Justus of Tiberias, for example, a historian who was born in Galilee shortly after Jesus died, makes no mention of anyone by that name, a fact that perplexed and shocked Photius, the Patriarch of Constantinople, when he read the works of Justus in the 9th Century.

The great ancient historian Pliny the Elder (23-79), who lived at the same time as Jesus, and who wrote his masterpiece *Historia Naturalis* a mere thirty years or so after Jesus' death, never once refers to any of the miracles ascribed to the Messiah or the many wonders surrounding His life.

Around the year 112 Pliny the Younger (c. 61-c. 113) speaks of the "early Christians" in a letter to Emperor Trajan, but the document is widely considered a forgery. And even if it is genuine, he does not mention a crucified man named Jesus.

The same must be said for Suetonius (b. 69) who, writing around the year 120, mentions a strange religious sect led by a man named *Chrestus*. Suetonius was not referring to Christ here, however, as many today believe. Chrestus (meaning "good") was then a common title not only for Gnostic high priests, but also for the Egyptian deities Osiris and Serapis, the latter who was enthusiastically worshiped by Syrian Gnostic-Christians as the "Good God."

Based on a brief reference to "Christus" and "Christiani" in his voluminous work *The Annals*, the Roman politician Tacitus (c. 60-117) is often cited as proof of Jesus' historical existence. However, there are so many problems with these passages that even many mainstream Christians dismiss them as counterfeits. (Some even question the authenticity of *The Annals* itself, claiming that the entire manuscript is the work of Medieval Catholic apologists.)

Then there are the two so-called "references" to Jesus by the famed Jewish historian Flavius Josephus (37-c. 101) in his *Antiquities of the Jews*.[31] Again, both statements are widely regarded in the scientific community, and even by many Christian scholars, as obvious late forgeries.[32]

In 1791, in his book *The Ruins*, French philosopher and historian, Constantin François de Volney, writes:

> There are absolutely no other monuments of the existence of Jesus Christ as
> a human being, than a passage in Josephus . . ., a single phrase in Tacitus . .
> ., and the [four canonical] Gospels. But the passage in Josephus is
> unanimously acknowledged to be apocryphal, and to have been interpolated
> towards the close of the third century, and that of Tacitus is so vague, and so

evidently taken from the deposition of the Christians before the tribunals, that it may be ranked in the class of evangelical records. It remains to inquire of what authority are these records. "All the world knows," says Faustus, who, though a Manichean, was one of the most learned men of the third century; "All the world knows that the Gospels were neither written by Jesus Christ, nor his Apostles, but by certain unknown persons, who, rightly judging that they should not obtain belief respecting things which they had not seen, placed at the head of their recitals the names of contemporary apostles" . . . [thus] the existence of Jesus is no better proved than that of Osiris and Hercules, or that of Fot or Beddou [i.e., Buddha], with whom . . . the Chinese continually confound him, for they never call Jesus by any other name than Fot.[33]

Not even Saint Paul, the most important figure of early orthodox Christianity next to Jesus Himself, mentions any of the most miraculous events of Jesus' life in his authentic letters, and he began writing just twenty-seven years after the Savior's death.[34]

How do we today rationalize these apparent inconsistencies?

4

THE PROBLEM OF
THE FOUR JESUSES

ONE ANSWER IS to be found in the Bible itself, which, problematically, presents us with at least four different Jesuses: 1) *The Historical Jesus*—a brilliant, pacifistic,[35] wandering "Jewish Plato," who was born of earthly parents, and lived, married,[36] bore children,[37] and died as a normal human being.[38]

2) *The Mythological Jesus*—a fusion of a myriad of improbable miracle-working,[39] dying-and-resurrecting Pagan vegetation-gods,[40] son-gods,[41] sun-gods,[42] and savior-gods,[43] dating back to prehistoric times.

3) *The Theological Jesus*—the aggressive, tough, intolerant, meat-eating, wine-swilling, all-powerful political Messiah of the early orthodox Christian Church, that is, the Catholic Church.[44]

4) *The Cosmic Jesus*—the cryptic but gentle,[45] ascetic, celibate, bachelor,[46] and vegetarian[47] of the first Christians, the Gnostics,[48] many who did not view Jesus as a historical living human being,[49] choosing instead to see him as an arcane symbol of theosis ("God in man") and also of Christ Consciousness; that is, spiritual enlightenment (self-actualization), a state of mind symbolized by the solar halo, foliage crown ("crown of thorns"), radiate crown, or Divine Crown.[50] In Eastern religions, the Christian halo or "Crown of Life,"[51] is known as *Sahasrara*,

or the Crown Chakra, symbolized by a thousand-petaled lotus flower.

(We will note here that the above list only takes into account the various canonical versions of Jesus. There are dozens more different versions of Jesus to be found in the non-canonical material, all which, unfortunately for Christianity, was rejected early on by the orthodox Catholic Church as "heretical." Around the year 450 Saint Theodoret of Cyrrhus, Syria, states that he was aware of at least 200 different non-canonical Gospels in his diocese alone.)

By all outward and inward appearances, the four canonical Jesuses were overlaid one upon the other, and all have been confusingly inseparable ever since. As is the nature of the life stories of popular figures and deities, as the centuries have passed, this baffling amalgamation of widely varying influences has only accreted more myths, legends, miracles, and conflicting traits, not to mention words, many which Jesus almost certainly never uttered.

We can rest assured then that Jesus' authentic words, as they have been handed down to us, were actually very few, and that the four canonical Gospels contain very little of His genuine statements. Of the manner in which the four Gospel authors (whoever they were)[52] compiled Jesus' words, the 1st-Century clergyman, Bishop Papias of Hierapolis (Turkey), wrote:

> Mark, having become the interpreter of Peter, wrote down accurately, though not indeed in order, whatsoever he remembered of the things done or said by Christ. For he neither heard the Lord nor followed him, but afterward, as I said, he followed Peter, who adapted his teaching to the needs of his hearers, but with no intention of giving a connected account of the Lord's discourses, so that Mark committed no error while he thus wrote some things as he remembered them. For he was careful of one thing, not to omit any of the things which he had heard, and not to state any of them falsely. So then Matthew wrote the oracles in the Hebrew language, and every one interpreted them as he was able.[53]

Despite his great authority, many contemporary mainstream biblical scholars dismiss Bishop Papias' statement because it does not conform to their own subjective opinions and narrow belief systems. However, the more objectively-minded not only accept it, they agree with it, and it is from this conclusion that an interesting theory has emerged.

After decades of careful research of the four canonical Gospels, it is now believed by many that Jesus' true words are all contained in what impartial scholars call *The Book of Q,* "Q" deriving from *quelle,* the German word for "source."[54] While no such actual source book has yet been found, the Bible itself strongly suggests that it once existed, and that it was used by various religious writers, both canonical and non-canonical.

Assuming Q did exist (and Saint Luke himself implies that it, or variations of it, did),[55] it would have been a collection of Jesus' oral sayings, gathered during and shortly after His life.

The Jesus of Q, that is, the authentic Jesus, was a simple historical man with a simple but radical message; one, He often stated, that could even be understood by children.[56] The entirety of His unpretentious Gospel can be pared down to the following:

• Love and bless your enemies.[57]
• Be merciful.[58]
• Do not judge others.[59]
• Be humble.[60]
• Strive to be good.[61]
• Spread peace.[62]
• Lend money without expecting to be repaid.[63]
• Do not worry as God will provide for all of your needs.[64]

According to the *Book of Q* theory, nearly everything else accredited to Jesus would have to be late and spurious paganistic accretions, nefariously appended to him by Catholic priests, scribes, and mythographers, largely for political purposes. Of this terrible deed, Thomas Jefferson , American Founding Father and "a real Christian," as he called himself, correctly observed (in 1816) that the so-called orthodox preachers of the Gospel

> draw all their characteristic dogmas from what its author never said nor saw. They have compounded from the heathen mysteries a system beyond the comprehension of man, of which the great reformer of the vicious ethics and deism of the Jews, were he to return on earth, would not recognize one feature.[65]

Volumes have been written by religious scholars on the subjects of the historical Jesus versus the mythological Jesus, the theological Jesus versus the cosmic Jesus—all without consensus. No one view or theory has been accepted by everyone, because none can adequately explain *all* of the various contradictions involved in the portrayals of Jesus as found in the many dozens of existing Gospels, both canonical and non-canonical.

For example, in one canonical scripture Jesus says:

> For God commanded, saying, Honour thy father and mother: and, He that curseth father or mother, let him die the death.[66]

Yet in another, He states:

> If any man come to me, and hate not his father, and mother, and wife, and children, and brethren, and sisters, yea, and his own life also, he cannot be my disciple.[67]

Clearly, these are two completely different Jesuses speaking here. Did the real Jesus utter the first or the second statement? He cannot be the author of both.

There are similar problems with Jesus' family tree as shown in the New Testament. For one thing, the two genealogies provided by Matthew and Luke both trace Jesus' lineage through Joseph, not Mary. If the Virgin Birth was an authentic historical event, then Jesus was conceived by an angel and Joseph was merely Jesus' foster father. Why then do the Gospels clearly state that Jesus descended through Joseph, with no mention of Mary?[68]

Even more strangely, Matthew and Luke each give Jesus different genealogies. Matthew states that His father was Joseph,[69] while Luke holds that His father was both the Holy Ghost[70] *and* Joseph: after telling the story of Jesus' "virgin birth," Luke goes on to assert that both Joseph and the general public believed that he was the natural father.[71] (Saint Paul adds to the mystery by ignoring the virgin birth story completely. Instead, he reaffirms that Jesus was the natural human son of Joseph, and was only made the Son of God "according to the spirit of holiness.")[72]

Furthermore, Matthew states that Jesus' paternal grandfather was

Jacob,[73] while Luke says his name was Heli.[74] In other words, the New Testament tells us that Jesus had two different fathers and two different grandfathers. Even acknowledging that "anything is possible with God," why would God want to confuse us with such biological impossibilities?

Just as perplexing, while Matthew and Luke provide both Jesus' genealogy and His nativity story, Mark and John mention neither. Mark begins with Jesus already a grown man,[75] as does John.[76] Even Matthew and Luke's nativity stories (Chapters One and Two in both books) are not what they seem: these were, in fact, later additions, for both the Gospel of Matthew and the Gospel of Luke originally began with Chapter Three.[77] The two sole nativity stories themselves are jumbled, the result of subsequent unnecessary meddling and clumsy interpolations by slipshod, unenlightened editors.[78]

Matthew and Luke cannot even agree on where Jesus' parents were from, or where Jesus was born. The former says Bethlehem,[79] the latter Nazareth.[80] Mysteriously, Mark and John disregard the entire matter.

Early Christians, however, decided that Jesus was born in Bethlehem on the same spot as a shrine of the pre-Christian dying-and-rising god Tammuz (Adonis)—which only further reinforces our theory that the ancients viewed Jesus, not as unique, but as just another in a long line of savior-gods stretching back thousands of years.[81]

Jesus' Betrayal and Resurrection present us with more incongruities and biblical mayhem. Matthew, Luke, and John each state that Peter would deny Jesus three times before the cock crowed *once*.[82] Mark, however, the earliest of the four canonical Gospels, asserts that Peter would betray his Lord three times before the cock crowed *twice*.[83] For unknown reasons, this particular detail was tampered with and edited down over time.

As for the Resurrection, Matthew reports that there were two women and one angel present,[84] while Mark holds that there were three women and one angel.[85] Luke states that there were three women and two angels,[86] while John maintains that only Mary Magdalene and two angels were on the scene.[87] Furthermore, the four Gospels deviate on *where* Jesus was crucified. Matthew,[88] Mark,[89] and John say Golgotha,[90] while Luke says Cavalry.[91] How could four alleged "eyewitnesses" (or their sources) disagree so profoundly about such a world-altering event?

Finally, not only do the books of the New Testament disagree on who Jesus' Twelve Apostles were (John, as if not knowing their names, does not even try to identify all twelve),[92] but all differ wildly on exactly how long the Resurrection process took—that is, the time from when Jesus rose from the dead to when He finally returned to Heaven. Matthew and Luke maintain that it took only one day,[93] John says over a week,[94] Mark gives an indeterminate amount of time,[95] while the book of Acts declares that it took forty days (including Saint Paul's sighting of the Gnostic Cosmic Christ on the road to Damascus) before Jesus was "taken up."[96]

Clearly, the biblical record has left us with an error-ridden muddle of confusion concerning the life story of the man Jesus, one than can never be fully recovered or described accurately.

In his seminal work *The Quest of the Historical Jesus*, after reviewing dozens of detailed volumes on "The Life of Jesus" that span several centuries, Dr. Albert Schweitzer came to the same conclusion: based on what we know from our meager sources about Christ the Master Healer, Teacher, and Prophet, it is impossible to piece together even a minute sketch of His life. The biographical facts have been forever lost behind an impenetrable shroud of myth, legend, symbolism, mysticism, deception, inaccuracies, misinterpretation, misunderstanding, falsehood, distortions (purposeful and accidental), endless redaction, and time.[97]

5

THE PAGANIZATION AND
DEIFICATION OF JESUS

WITH SUCH PROBLEMS permeating not only the New Testament but the Old Testament as well, one might be forgiven for wondering how the Bible can be called the "infallible Word of God," as many claim. If it is, why then did God introduce so many blatant mistakes into it? If God and only God is the true author of the Bible, why did He portray Jesus as at least four dissimilar and very distinct individuals, then add dozens of obvious mistakes and discrepancies to the Savior's New Testament biography?

These questions have vexed all thinking people for thousands of years, even the most faithful.

Incredibly, when confronted with these often very different and conflicting Jesuses, many Christians simply dismiss the entire issue as unimportant, while brushing aside Bible critics as nothing more than atheists, skeptics, and humanists who "hate religion."

But not only are such charges often wrong,[98] ignoring the problem, or offering implausibly convoluted explanations, does not make it go away.

For us to truly understand Christmas and unravel the mystery of how the Birthday of the "Sun" became the Birthday of the "Son," we must not be afraid to question, even if we are steadfast Bible-believers. As the Christian astronomer and philosopher Galileo once remarked: "I do not feel obliged to believe that the same God who has endowed us with sense, reason, and intellect has intended us to forgo their use." Jesus himself questioned His native religion, Judaism. If He had not, what we call Christianity would not exist today.

In short, only a childlike, open-minded inquiry will reveal the truth.[99] To this end, we will turn to a branch of sociocultural anthropology perfectly suited to solving this uniquely Christian conundrum: comparative religion and comparative mythology.

Here, we can accept the historical reality of Jesus as a great spiritual teacher and divine human being, while at the same time acknowledging that countless Pagan myths, stories, and powers were affixed to His human life story during the initial development of the Church. This view has much to commend it.

Throughout history, for example, just as with Jesus, many deities and heroes were said to have been born of the union between a Pagan god and a mortal woman. Among them were earthly men like Amenophis III, Cyrus, Julius Caesar, Apollonius of Tyana, Lao-Kium, and Zoroaster. Gods too, such as Apis, Hercules, Ra, Attis, and Perseus, were all said to have come from the consummation of a heavenly being and an earthly mother. This theme even shows up in the Hebrew mythology of the Old Testament.[100]

Is it possible this same Pagan motif was later appended to the biography of Jesus?

Yes. In fact, irrefutable evidence from the Bible itself reveals that the story of Jesus' Virgin Birth was not known before the year 100, for none of the New Testament books written prior to that year mention the Virgin Birth story. The earliest canonical Gospel, Mark, written between the years 70 and 100, does not mention it, and neither does John, written shortly thereafter (probably about 100). The story only appears with the writing of Luke, written about 105,[101] and later in Matthew, written about 110, where it is more fully developed.

Why was this done? Why deify Jesus and paganize His birth story? Why create a wholly "fabricated Christianity," as America's third president, Thomas Jefferson, called it?

It was an attempt by the early Church Fathers to both suppress Paganism *and* draw new Pagan converts into the Christian fold.

From the Church's perspective, since the Pagan religion could not be fully stamped out, this syncretizing process made good sense. For the existence of hundreds of Pagan-like beliefs, rituals, figures, and myths (like the Virgin Birth) in the new Christian faith made this transition much easier and more comfortable for Pagans who were loath to give up the Old Religion.

It was this very process that caused Jefferson to write that he one day hoped to rescue Christ from

> the imputation of imposture, which has resulted from artificial systems (that is, the immaculate conception of Jesus, his deification, the creation of the world by him, his miraculous powers, his resurrection and visible ascension, his corporeal presence in the Eucharist . . .), invented by ultra-Christian sects, unauthorized by a single word ever uttered by him . . .[102]

Jefferson had good reason to complain about the paganistic deification of Jesus and the resulting corruption of the pure moral teachings He had preached during His short ministry on Earth. For this act had far reaching consequences, consequences that have degraded Christianity to a level completely unintended by the man for whom this religion was named. In the process, for example,

- the Pagan virgin-mother Meri became the Christian Virgin-Mother Mary.
- the Festival of the Pagan moon-goddess Diana (on August 13) became the Festival of the Assumption of the Virgin Mary.
- the ancient Egyptian serpent-god Sata became the Christian devil-god Satan.
- the Hindu goddess Devi became the Christian Devil.
- the Pagan underworld-goddess Hell became the name for the Christian underworld, Hell.
- the Hindu Law of Karma became the Christian Golden Rule.
- the Pagan Spring festivals became both the Christian Easter and the Christian Lent.
- the Egyptian Feast of Lamps became the Christian Festival of All Souls.

- the Pagans' harvest festival Samhain became the christianized (and demonized) holiday Halloween.
- the title of the Pagan high priest, *Pontifex Maximus*, became one of the titles for the Catholic pope .
- the Mithraic sacrament, with its cross-embossed bread, became the Christian Sacrament.
- the universal ancient Pagan flood myth became the Judeo-Christian flood myth of Genesis.
- the Roman city-god Petra became the Christian Saint Peter.
- the Pagan gateway-god Janus became the Christian Saint Januarius.
- the Pagan Buddha became christianized as Saint Josaphat.
- the Pagan goddess Juno Lucina became the Christian Saint Lucy.
- the Pagan goddess Aphrodite (after whom Africa is named) became the Christian Saint Afra.
- the Pagan god Mars became the Christian Saint Martin.
- the Pagan goddess Viviane became the Christian Saint Viviana.
- the Pagan goddess Venus Rosalia became the Christian Saint Rosalia.
- the ancient Egyptian god Osiris became the Christian Saint Onuphris.
- the Pagan Sabbat became the Christian Sabbath.
- the Egyptian monster-slaying god Horus became the Christian Saint George.
- the ancient Roman Parilia was made into the Festival of Saint George.
- the sacred Dove of the goddess Aphrodite became the sacred Christian symbol of the Holy Ghost.
- the Pagan Roman festival of the virgin-mother Juno Februata became the Christian holy day Candlemas.
- the Pagan Koreion or Epiphany (on January 6) became the Christian Twelfth Night or Epiphany.
- the Pagans' Midsummer water festival became the Festival of John the Baptist.
- the Pagan harvest festival known as *Hlafmæsse* ("Bread Mass") became the Christian Lammas.
- and most importantly for us, the Pagans' birthday of the Sun on December 25 became the Christian Christmas, birthday of the Son.[103]

While a few Churchmen were against the practice of borrowing and assimilating Pagan ideas, they were in the minority. It had the full support of most others, including, in some cases, the highest earthly authority, the Pope. Among them was Pope Gregory I who, in 601, wrote the following to an abbot named Mellitus, one of the Church's missionaries in England:

After the departure of our congregation which is with you, we were rendered very anxious because it happened that we heard nothing concerning the success of your journey. When, therefore, the omnipotent God shall have brought you to that most reverend man, our brother Bishop Augustine, tell him what I have a long time thought over with myself, concerning the case of the English—to wit, that the temples of the idols in that nation ought not to be destroyed; but let the idols themselves that are in them be destroyed. Let water be consecrated, and sprinkled in the same temples; let altars be constructed, relics deposited: because if these temples are well built, they ought of necessity to be converted from the worship of devils to the service of the true God, that whilst this nation sees that its temples are not destroyed, it may put away error from its heart, and acknowledging and adoring the true God, may the more familiarly meet at its accustomed places. And because they are wont to kill many oxen in sacrifice to devils, some solemnity ought to be specially appointed for them on this account, as, that on the day of the dedication, or on the birthdays of holy martyrs whose relics are there deposited, they may make for themselves huts of the boughs of trees, around the same churches which have been altered from temples, and celebrate a solemnity with religious feasting, and no longer immolate animals to the devil, but kill them for their own eating, to the praise of God, and return thanks for their satiety to the Giver of all things; to the end that, whilst some outward joys are reserved for them, they may more easily be able to consent to inward joys. For, without doubt, it is impossible to cut off all things at once from their rough minds, because also he who endeavours to ascend to the highest place, is elevated by steps or paces and not by leaps. So, indeed, the Lord made Himself known to the Israelitish people, in Egypt, but reserved to them, in His own service, the use of the sacrifices which they were wont to offer to the devil, and charged them to immolate animals in His sacrifice, to the end that, changing their hearts, they might let go one thing with respect to the sacrifice and retain another; so that although they were the same animals as they were wont to offer, yet being immolated to God and not to idols, they were no longer the same sacrifices. These things therefore it is necessary that you, well-beloved, should yourself say to the aforesaid brother, that he at present being there placed, may consider how he ought to order all things.[104]

Not surprisingly, some of the early Church Fathers were actually proud of their accomplishment of absorbing the Pagan religion, such as Saint Theodoret of Cyrrhus, who bragged of the many saints and martyrs who had started off as Pagan deities, and of the numerous Pagan temples and shrines that had been converted into Christian churches.

As many, like Alan Watts, Arthur Weigall, and others have pointed out, deifying Jesus was also the preference of ordinary everyday Christians, most who found it much easier to worship Him rather than to obey Him and follow His example. If Jesus were merely a man, albeit divine, as nearly all Christians in the 1ˢᵗ Century believed, His followers would have had no excuses for their moral failures, for Jesus proved that He, as a mere mortal, could achieve perfection.

By turning Him into a Pagan-like deity, however, Christians could take the less demanding path of simply revering, adoring, and idolizing Him, for as a supernatural figure, He had all the advantages of being the Son of God and none of the weaknesses of being human. He need not be obeyed then, for no mere mortal could ever begin to hope to accomplish what He did. Sadly, this attitude continues among many Christians to this day.

It is important to note here that Jesus would have energetically disapproved of the paganization and deification of His life and figure. In the canonical Gospels, for example, He not only plays down His divinity,[105] He tries repeatedly to discourage those who would worship Him as a god, as anything more than a spiritually enlightened man—a level of consciousness, He affirms, that anyone can attain.[106]

After healing someone, for instance, He would not take credit for the "miracle." Instead, He says to them: "It is *thy* faith that has made thee whole,"[107] always being careful to point out that the healing took place "according to one's faith," not His personal powers.[108]

To emphasize this view (that it was not Jesus, but the individual who healed himself through fearless belief),[109] Saint Mark makes note of the fact that in Christ's hometown He could not perform any great miracles, such as raising the dead. Why? Because His family and friends were nonbelievers.[110]

Jesus tried other methods of deterring His deification. When the healed evinced a desire to shout His name from the rooftops, He would say, "go thy way and tell no one what was done."[111] When the adulation of His adoring followers reached fever pitch, He did not wallow in narcissism and vainglory, as some popular religious leaders do today. Instead, He retreated to the wilderness to be alone.[112]

So against His deification was Jesus that He even tried to prevent the masses from knowing that He was Jesus the Christ.[113] When this failed, in public He repeatedly referred to Himself not as the "Son of God," but as the "Son of Man," the everyday Aramaic phrase for a mortal human.[114]

How different is the authentic historical Jesus from the paganized one portrayed by orthodox fundamentalist Christianity today![115]

Despite all His efforts, once He had ascended back up to Heaven there was nothing Jesus could do to prevent the inevitable. And so His deification and paganization process has continued unabated into the present day, with evermore wild and fanciful tales and attributes being affixed to Him and His life story on an almost daily basis. This may be the Jesus that many contemporary Christians now prefer, but it is not the Jesus who lived in the 1st Century, and it is certainly not the person Jesus Himself wanted to be portrayed as.

The original Christian view that Jesus was both a mortal man and divine may be shocking to some. But it was not shocking to the Church Fathers, and it is has never been shocking to Christian mystics, all who embrace the doctrine of theosis as laid down by the great spiritual teachers, including Jesus, that God—as the Christ—not only dwells in us[116] (making us individual gods and goddesses),[117] but that we are each a piece of God (portrayed as "light"),[118] made in his image.[119]

Yet, for those who do not accept authentic history or scripture, it will be, no doubt, even more appalling to learn that Jesus has absorbed many of the characteristics and myths of dozens of pre-Christian Pagan deities, none which existed in the earliest portraits and biographies of Him—where He was depicted as a humble blue-collar worker (carpenter) from an everyday middle-class Jewish family.[120]

To ancient peoples, however, the practice of borrowing and adopting the figures, myths, and concepts of other religions, known as syncretism, was not the alien idea that it is today. Indeed, the ancients were quite comfortable with it. Thus, the Greek god Zeus was borrowed by the Romans, becoming Jupiter; the Greek Poseidon became Neptune; the Greek Aries became Mars; Hephaistos became Vulcan; and Hermes became Mercury. This same process was at work when the Greek goddess Hera became the Roman goddess Juno; Athena became Minerva; Artemis became Diana; Aphrodite became Venus; Hestia became Vesta; and Demeter became Ceres, as just a few examples.

As we will see, this type of assimilation and cross-pollination of religious figures (and their myths) was extremely common among nearly all early religions, no more so than with the archetypal figure of the savior-sun-god.

Students of comparative mythology and comparative religion are well aware that there have been hundreds, if not thousands, of "saviors" and "messiahs" throughout human history. This is hardly surprising: our species has invented hundreds of thousands of religions over the millennia, nearly all originally built around the Sun, the Moon, the stars, agriculture, and the four seasons.

Indeed, as we will discuss, the savior myth, itself a product of prehistoric nature religions, has been found in nearly every culture around the world. Judaism, from which the Christian story of Jesus partially emerged, was no exception, the ancient Jews themselves having assimilated the idea from the Pagan religions of Egypt, Persia, Canaan, and Mesopotamia.

Numerous other religions as well, such as those of the Aztecs, Buddhists, and Hindus, have also created savior-gods who were born of virgins, died, and then rose into Heaven, promising eternal life to all faithful believers. What is the modern Christian to make of all this?

However one chooses to look at it, the question remains: if Jesus was, in fact, born of a virgin beneath the Star of Bethlehem, and if this amazing scene was actually witnessed by three wise men, where are the contemporary chronicles?

If Jesus performed the many miracles for which He is today so famous, why was nothing written about these fantastic events during the three decades He is said to have lived?

Why does early Christian literature, including the four canonical Gospels and the hundreds of banned Gnostic Gospels, all disagree with one another about who Jesus was, where, when, and how He was born, who His parents and grandparents were, what His true teachings were, what His life experiences were, and how and when He died—not to mention the events surrounding His resurrection and ascension?

Intelligent people must ask, if Jesus was the "only begotten son," why were millions of Pagans around the globe celebrating the virgin birth of hundreds of "only begotten sons" and "World Saviors" in late December, for thousands of years, long before the rise of Christianity?

Finally, just how, why, where, and when did the annual observance of the Savior's birth begin if not in 1st-Century Rome?

As with so many aspects of religion, and in particular Christianity, it all started with our neighborhood star: the Sun.

6

Birth Of The Idea
Of The Sun/Son~God

THE PROFOUND IMPORTANCE of the Sun to the diverse peoples of prehistory cannot be overstated. Quite understandably, it was regarded as the creator of all life and was worshiped as such by both hunting and cereal cultures. From the Greeks, Chinese, and Scandinavians, to the Irish, Haitians, and Amerindians, thousands of solar cults have come and gone in the vast panoply of our species' supernatural belief systems.

For the prescientific agrarians living ten thousand years ago, the difference between life and death was marked by the success or failure of their agricultural harvest. Through the use of magic, myth, fertility rites, and supplication rituals, they hoped to appease the sun-god who they believed controlled the planting, sprouting, growth, and harvesting of their crops.

Who was this universal sun-god, and how did he come to be the central figure in nearly all pre-Christian religions?[121]

In 1919, in his famous work *The Golden Bough*, Sir James George Frazer explains the process this way:

The spectacle of the great changes which annually pass over the face of the earth has powerfully impressed the minds of men in all ages, and stirred them to meditate on the causes of transformations so vast and wonderful. Their curiosity has not been purely disinterested; for even the savage cannot fail to perceive how intimately his own life is bound up with the life of nature, and how the same processes which freeze the stream and strip the earth of vegetation menace him with extinction. At a certain stage of development men seem to have imagined that the means of averting the threatened calamity were in their own hands, and that they could hasten or retard the flight of the seasons by magic art. Accordingly they performed ceremonies and recited spells to make the rain to fall, the sun to shine, animals to multiply, and the fruits of the earth to grow. In course of time the slow advance of knowledge, which has dispelled so many cherished illusions, convinced at least the more thoughtful portion of mankind that the alternations of summer and winter, of spring and autumn, were not merely the result of their own magical rites, but that some deeper cause, some mightier power, was at work behind the shifting scenes of nature. They now pictured to themselves the growth and decay of vegetation, the birth and death of living creatures, as effects of the waxing or waning strength of divine beings, of gods and goddesses, who were born and died, who married and begot children, on the pattern of human life. [122]

At one point in our species' evolution the idea arose that humanity could help expedite the Earth's natural processes by ritually killing one of their own, a so-called "sacrificial lamb," whose life-giving blood would spill upon the great Virgin-Mother-Earth-Goddess, (that is, the ground), and "fertilize" it.

In ancient Graeco-Roman astronomy, this goddess was personified in the constellation *Virgo* (meaning, the "Virgin"), while her son, the "sacrificial lamb," was embodied in the constellation *Orion* (meaning, the "Rising Sun").

More importantly for us, Pagan religions simply saw Goddess as the Earth (Mother-Earth or Earthly Mother), known globally as Ma, Ma Ma, Mar, Mare, Mari, Maya, Mer, Meri, Maria, Mariam, Myrrh, or Mary, due to her connection to water (marine).

As Mary was the Earth, to early agrarian peoples her divine son naturally came to be seen as the Sun (Father-Sky or Heavenly Father). In societies around the world this mythic sacrificial archetype was given a variety of names ending in *os* (for example, the Greek sun-god Helios), *is* (for example, the Phrygian sun-god Attis), or *us* (for example, the Druids' sun-god Hesus).

Why the intense prehistoric focus on Goddess and her son, the sun-god? Because, as we will recall, to the ancients it was the mother and child, not the father, mother, and child, who formed the nuclear family. And it was this pair who symbolized the sacred union (Hieros Gamos) between the spiritual plane (the male sun-god) and the material plane (the female earth-goddess), believed to aid humanity in creating abundant harvests (fecundity) and large healthy families (fertility).

Such ideas did not spring from the ancients' imagination. They were evident in the natural world around them, both in the four seasons here on Earth and in the many celestial changes that took place in the sky above. The most noticeable of these, of course, were the movements of the Sun, the great Heavenly Father-God, and how they affected life (mainly vegetation) on Earth.

As the sun/son-god journeyed through his yearly cycle in the sky, it was believed that he passed through four distinct stages, correlating with the four seasons:

1) At the start of Spring, the Sun was seen to reach the halfway point (Spring Equinox) between the beginning of its ascension (Winter Solstice) and the beginning of its descent (Summer Solstice).

2) At the start of Summer, the Sun was seen to reach its highest point of strength (Summer Solstice), after which it began to descend.

3) At the start of Fall, the Sun was seen to reach the halfway point (Fall Equinox) between the beginning of its descent (Summer Solstice) and the beginning of its ascension (Winter Solstice).

4) At the start of Winter, the Sun was seen to reach the bottom of its descent (Winter Solstice) and begin its ascension back upward.

Interpreted through the eyes of prehistoric and ancient peoples, this was nothing less than a celestial passion play, for the sun/son-god appeared to all the world to be annually "conceived" (or "reborn"), after which he passed through childhood into adulthood ("maturation"), was weakened ("betrayed"), killed off ("ritually sacrificed"), and "resurrected," finally "ascending" back into Heaven. The entire cycle then began again.

It was this last day, when the sun/son-god was "born again" and began to rise back up into the heavens at the Winter Solstice (near the end of December), that agricultural societies worldwide joyously celebrated the "birth (or rebirth) of the sun-god," the Holy Son of the Virgin-Mother Mer, Meri, or Mary. For it was exactly nine months between his conception (at the Spring Equinox) to his birth (at the Winter Solstice). It was from out of this dramatic, all-important nine-month astronomical event that the first passion plays and gospels surrounding the first savior-gods developed.

Thus, through the astrotheology of the ancients, the Virgin-Mother (the Earth) and her divine Savior-Son (the Sun) became the two most significant figures in religions all around the globe.

Eventually, as part of the natural evolution of spiritual ideas, the sun/son-god of the prehistoric passion play was replaced by a human stand-in, usually the real son (a prince) of a king (that is, "God"). Prior to his ritualized murder, the son-prince was imbued with the sins of the people, after which his bloody death was believed to purify the community.

Among ancient Pagans, this figure was transformed into the holy "Son of God," or "Prince of Peace," the titles of dozens of pre-Christian saviors. Among the Jews, this human victim was eventually substituted with an actual lamb, as the Bible tells us,[123] an idea, no doubt, borrowed from both the Persians, whose Mithraic sacrificial lamb was a member of the ancient Iranian Zodiac, and the Canaanites, one of whose gods, Mot-Aleyin, was known as the "Lamb of God." And so was created the Semitic title for the sacrificial savior-son-god, the Lamb of God.[124]

The popularity of the idea of the sacrificial prince or son-god can be seen in the historical record itself. According to Carthaginian tradition, for example, the son of General Hamilcar Barca was sacrificed at the Battle of Agrigentum (Sicily, 262 BC), while another Carthaginian general, Maleus, is said to have hung his son on a cross as a sacrifice to the Pagan god Baal. The Canaanites, Babylonians, and the Phoenicians are all well-known to have sacrificed the sons of kings. Myth too records the sacrifice of royal sons, such as the ritualized murder of Ieoud and

Sadid, two of the sons of the great Greek god Kronos.[125]

Nowhere, however, was this practice more popular than among the ancient Jews known as the Israelites, where the sacrificial son-god became the "scapegoat," killed to atone for the sins of the community.[126] In fact, it was quite customary during various periods of Hebrew history for kings, leaders, and fathers to sacrifice their sons for this reason, and in this manner, as the prophet Micah noted:

> Will the Lord be pleased with thousands of rams, or with ten thousands of rivers of oil? Shall I give my firstborn for my transgression, the fruit of my body for the sin of my soul?[127]

The best known biblical example of the sacrificial son is Abraham, who was ready and willing to put his beloved boy Isaac to death for his religion.[128] Both King Manasseh[129] and King Ahaz[130] threw their sons into a sacrificial fire to appease the Pagan god Baal. King Mesha ritually murdered his oldest son,[131] as did King Hiel at Jericho.[132]

There is also the Old Testament story of King David, who sacrificed seven sons of King Saul in an attempt to prevent a famine.[133] So common was this custom, in fact, that, according to the Bible, nearly all of "the children of Israel" at one time or another seemed to have practiced "passing their sons through the fire."[134]

Often, these "son-gods," human representatives of the sun-god (that is, the son of the great Father-God), were ritually killed during the Summer Solstice, the moment when the Sun reached its zenith in the sky, then began its long, slow, steady decline into the Underworld.

The "death" of the mighty sun-god at the Summer Solstice, however, was only temporary. He was always "born again" six months later at the Winter Solstice,[135] returning to save humanity by giving his warmth and light for another season of planting and harvesting. It was for this reason that he was called "Savior," "Sun of Righteousness," and *Sol Invictus*; that is, the "Invincible Sun," for his seemingly supernatural warmth and unconquerable light literally "saved" humanity each year from cold and starvation.

Thus, it was from out of the annual life and death cycles of domesticated vegetation and the changing seasons, along with the Pagan beliefs of highly superstitious people like the Israelites, that the gradual belief in a virgin-mother and a princely sun/son-god who governed these events (by dying and being resurrected) quite naturally came into being.

Based on comparative mythology alone, it is apparent that the savior-son concept, on which the modern celebration of Christmas is based, originated from just such Neolithic vegetation and solar cults.[136]

7

THE SOLSTICES: LIFE AND
DEATH CYCLES OF THE SUN

S IX THOUSAND YEARS ago the Copper and Bronze Age peoples
of the Northern Hemisphere (Europe, northern Africa, North and
Central America, and nearly all of Asia) believed that the Sun
moved around the earth. Not knowing that the Earth rotates on its axis
around the Sun, it appeared to them that it was the Sun that slowly
changed its position in the sky as the seasons progressed. Once every six
months, around June 21 (the longest day of the year) and around
December 22 (the shortest day of the year), the Sun seemed to change
direction and move toward the equator.[137]

The ancient observers of this phenomena called these periods
"solstices," from the Latin word *soltitium,* meaning "Sun standing still,"
for it seemed to them that the Sun stopped momentarily on these two
specific days as it reversed direction (in actuality, this is a terrestrial
optical illusion).

Additionally, every other six months, the Sun seemed to reach its
zenith when it crossed the equator, making day and night of equal length.
These two days, about March 21 and September 23, were given the
name "equinoxes," from the Latin word *aequinoctium,* meaning "equal
night."

All four days, the Spring Equinox, the Summer Solstice, the Autumn Equinox, and the Winter Solstice, were highly sacralized, becoming what Pagans termed the Four Quarter Days, the four holiest days of the year. Their annual arrival was celebrated with an astonishing array of festivals, rituals, processions, plays, and songs. It was around just such astronomical phenomena that prehistoric and ancient peoples constructed thousands of Sun-based religions—and in fact, these would reach all the way into the 21st Century, for the Four Quarter Days were later adopted by the Catholic Church and christianized, becoming, respectively, Easter, Midsummer Day, Halloween, and Christmas.

In ancient Egypt, the primary solar cult surrounded the son-god Horus (early on identified with the Egyptian sun-god Ra), the Divine Child of the virgin-mother-goddess Isis and the great father-god Osiris. According to Egyptian mythology, Horus was born on December 25, the traditional day on which all saviors are born; a day of mystical sacrality already celebrated for millennia before the rise of Christianity.

By the time of the early Romans, several thousand years later (500 BC), the honoring of Horus's birthday had become one of the most popular traditions in the area of the Mediterranean basin. The Romans conveniently borrowed this ancient Egyptian custom and incorporated it into their own eschatologies and mythologies.

Such syncretic appropriation between cultures was, and still is, an extremely common practice among the world's religions, including Christianity, as we will explore in more detail shortly.

8

THE ROMAN SATURNALIA

L IKE THE EGYPTIANS, the Romans celebrated this particular
time of year because it meant the return of longer days, which
began on December 22, the Winter Solstice. To them the "return
of the Sun" represented a time of joy and feasting, for the great Fall
harvests were over and the storehouses were full. And because it was
the start of Winter, the lengthening days also marked what seemed to
them to be the "rebirth of the Sun" (later re-imaged as the "resurrection
of the Son"), and the anticipation of warmer weather ahead.

One of the many nature-deities worshiped by the Pagans of the Iron
Age (2000 BC) was Saturn, the Roman god of agriculture and the sowing
of seeds. Due to its horned leaves, the ever green holly was dedicated
to the horned Saturn, also known as "All Father." This is highly
significant, because this was the same title given to Old Nick, who
became Saint Nicholas, who became Santa Claus.

The ancient Hebrews—who referred to Saturn as the star
Kaiwan—worshiped the planet as the god *Chiun*,[138] identical to *Gian Ben
Gian*, the "Divine Being" who ruled the world during the Golden Age of
humanity. Already the ancient Jewish roots of Christmas are evident
here.

In pre-Christian Rome quite naturally a celebration arose around the
harvested crops that Saturn was believed to have dominion over.

Saturday, the seventh day of the week, would come to be named after him: Saturn's Day. To this day, the horned god's holy day, Saturday, remains the Sabbath of the Jews.

In Pagan Rome eventually an annual festival called Saturnalia was held in Saturn's honor every year around the Winter Solstice. Each December 17, the Saturnalia festivities began. The usually strict social rules of Roman conduct were loosened and a wild state of debauchery reigned.

The similarities between the Roman's Saturnalia and the American Mardi Gras can hardly be overlooked: both celebrations last for a week or so; schools, courts, and businesses close; parties are held, and gifts are exchanged; and drunken and promiscuous behavior abounds. In the case of the early Romans, they were not allowed to quarrel, the roles of slave and master were reversed, and the execution of criminals was temporarily stayed.

On December 25, however, all of the riotous activities of the former week would end, and on this, the final day of celebration, the *Natalis Solis Invicti,* or "Birthday of the Unconquered Sun" was celebrated. Though the Sun had reached its lowest point in the sky three days earlier on the Solstice, it was not until the 25th that it appeared to be rising again. It was this "dark" three-day period which became the "three days" between the death and resurrection of the universal sun/son-god, and which was later absorbed by Christianity for use in the mythic elements of Jesus' biography.[139]

At midnight Roman priests clad in long white robes would enter an underground cave sanctuary and ascend the steps of the temple of the god Mithras as altar boys lit candles and incense. A great feast, the Brumalia (from *bruma,* "shortest day") was prepared and presents were exchanged. The temple was the Roman center of worship and, after the earlier week of sensual revelry, religious celebration now began in earnest.

Mithras was the most widespread and popular god in the Roman Empire at this time. Thus, not surprisingly, Mithraism was also the predominant religion. Mithraism held such dominance that it reigned for many hundreds of years before the first Gnostic Jesus cults arose. Indeed, it endured well into the 4th Century,[140] nearly supplanting early mainstream Christianity (Catholicism), and only finally dying out because so many of its tenets, doctrines, customs, sacraments, traditions, ceremonies, sacred days, rituals, figures, hymns, and myths were taken over and absorbed by the Church.[141] As the French philosopher Ernest Renan once truthfully said:

> If Christianity had been arrested in its growth by some mortal malady, the world would have been Mithraist.[142]

Who was this powerful deity Mithras, who started out as the arch rival of the Christian Jesus, only to later be merged with Him?

9

MITHRAS, THE MOST POPULAR SAVIOR OF THE ANCIENT WORLD

LIKE THE SYMBOLS, gods, goddesses, and myths that accompany all religions, Mithras had his beginnings in the human psyche: the collective unconscious of an ancient culture. This culture was India, a civilization already well established by the year 2000 BC. One of the many Hindu deities who was honored and revered was Mitra, god of the Sun and caretaker of the World.

About 1,500 years later, in 450 BC, the Persian (Iranian) ruler Artaxerxes incorporated the Hindu god Mitra into his country's own religion, Zoroastrianism, where the solar deity became Mithra. His cult quickly spread across Asia, gaining in popularity as it went.

One of Mithra's minor characteristics was his role as a warrior-god, who hurled life-destroying arrows and incurable diseases at his enemies on the battlefield. Both the soldiers and the common people of Rome found this tough, violent god especially appealing, and by 100 BC, Mithra had joined the hundreds of other deities of the Roman Pantheon, now as the sun-god Mithras.

Mythologists have established that a number of supernatural elements of Jesus' biography were, in large part, based on the figure of Mithras. Since the emergence of Mithras predates the birth of Jesus by many centuries, it is vital to our knowledge of Christmas to understand the essence of the mythic story of this once immensely popular god and what he meant to the people who worshiped him.

At one time, Mithras, like any proper divinity, lived in the sky above; that is, in "Heaven." As he watched the travails of humanity far below, he was touched with compassion, whereupon his father, the great creator-god Ahura-Mazda, decided to send his son to Earth in order to help alleviate human suffering.

According to his pre-Christian birth story, it was on December 25 that Mithras, carrying a torch in one hand and a knife in the other, was born of a virgin in a cave, the *Petra Genetrix* (caves have long been seen as vulva-womb symbols of the great Virgin-Mother-Goddess). His birth was witnessed by numerous shepherds and Wise Men (Magi), who brought him gifts and who spread the word of his nativity far and wide.

Mithras's entire earthly sojourn thereafter was one of benevolent deeds and kindness towards his followers. With his Twelve Apostles (like those of Jesus, symbols of the 12 astrological signs of the Zodiac),[143] he roamed the Earth performing miracles, healing the sick, casting out devils, and raising the dead.

When he felt he had accomplished his life's mission, he held a last supper with the closest of his disciples, where the group ate specially baked bread with a cross on it called *Mizd*, that is, "Mass." (So began the custom of the Mithraic Mass, a sacramental meal in which followers were cleansed of sin by eating special cross-emblazened bread, a symbol of the sun/son-god's earthly body.)

Mithras then died a sacrificial death for the sake of humanity, an event said to have been accompanied by a solar eclipse. He was then buried in a rock tomb, the same cave he had been born in, earning him the sacred titles "rock-born" and "the god of the rock." Then, at the Spring Equinox (presided over by the Spring-fertility-goddess Eostre or Ostara, who gave her name to the Christian festival Easter), he rose from the dead and ascended back to Heaven, promising eternal life to true believers.

The followers of Mithras believed that he would return to Earth again near the end of the world, at which time he would judge the sins of humanity. After a ferocious battle with the evil god Ahriman (a forerunner of the Christian Devil),[144] Mithras would then lead his chosen people across a burning body of water to a life of immortality and joy.

As many Christians do today, Mithraists prepared themselves for their Lord's Second Coming by mastering different levels of spiritual initiation or attainment. These were later adopted by the orthodox Christian Church and renamed "holy orders." In the process the various Pagan levels were renamed with titles such as deacon, bishop, monk, nun, elder, priest, curate, and so on.

In addition to the yearly observance of the birth of Mithras, known variously as "Savior," the "Light of the World," and the "Sun of Righteousness," on December 25 there was also a weekly celebration in his honor as god of the Sun. As its name implies, Sol-day (i.e., Sun-day, the first day of the week) was the sacred day on which this service took place.

When Christians absorbed Mithras, they also adopted his sacred day, Sunday, known by Pagans as the Lord's Day (as Mithras was called *Dominus*, "Lord"). Before then early Christians had been observing the Sabbath on Saturday, the Jewish holy weekday. The Roman Catholic Church also adopted the Mithraic Mass, the sun-god's festival known as the Epiphany, his sacramental meal of holy bread, and even the clothing and title of Mithras' high priest, the *Pater Patrum* ("Father of Fathers"), who became known as *Papa*, that is, the Pope ("Father").

The Church also assimilated Mithras' titles "rock-born" and "the god of the rock," and gave them to Jesus. Thus Saint Paul could write:

> And did all drink the same spiritual drink: for they drank of that spiritual Rock that followed them: and that Rock was Christ.[145]

So powerful was the influence of the Pagan "Lord and Savior" and his religion, Mithraism, that by the decline of the western Roman Empire in the 3rd and 4th Centuries, it had migrated all the way to Northumberland, England (on the border with present-day Scotland), becoming a permanent part of the fabric of European spiritual thought.

To this very day, vestiges of a Mithraic temple can still be seen in downtown London, England, less than 2,000 feet from Saint Paul's Cathedral.

10

MANI, JESUS, AND
THE SUN OF RIGHTEOUSNESS

S WITH MOST other religious groups of the time, the Jews also
celebrated on December 25, for this was their Feast of Dedication
(Hanukkah). A spectacular banquet was held in honor of Judas
Maccabeus (middle 1st Century BC) who, it was said, conquered the
Pagan King Antiochus IV of Syria in 164 BC.

Historical records show, however, that even this celebration was
originally a Jewish holiday in observance of the Sun and the Winter
Solstice. As many of the followers of Jesus were Jews, this would have
a profound influence on the development of the legends and myths that
came to surround the historical Jesus.

Meanwhile, there were other influences at work, moving the Pagan
world ever closer to christianization and the emergence of the Christmas
holiday.

Around the year 240, Mani (c. 216-276), a Persian sage, founded a
religion, Manichaeism, based on ideas borrowed from Mithraism,
Christianity, Buddhism, and Zoroastrianism. Mani considered himself
the Paraclete or Comforter,[146] and with his Twelve Apostles, sought to
convert the Eastern world to his teachings. Such actions would later lead
outraged Zoroastrian priests to crucify the unorthodox spiritual leader.

Before Mani died, however, he left us with a very illuminating mystical teaching: the *sun-god* of Paganism is identical with the *son-god* of Christianity, the Iranian spiritual leader preached. Mani was entirely correct, of course, as most other early Christians too were keenly aware.

Not only was Jesus regularly referred to as both the "Sun of Righteousness"[147] and "the Sun" by leading Christian authorities such as Saint Cyprian and Saint Ambrose, He was also often depicted in early Christian art as the sun-god Helios, driving His fiery chariot through the heavens. An example of this exact image can still be seen on a 3rd-Century ceiling mosaic in a tomb under Saint Peter's Basilica in Rome.

Pope Leo I lambasted those who turned to bow to the Sun before entering Saint Peter's, but to no avail. Well into the 5th Century, those who would come to be known as Italian Christians were still openly venerating Jesus as the Roman solar deity Apollo, despite the Church's best efforts to put a stop to the Paganistic practice.

Little wonder that Jesus was literally worshiped as a sun-god by some Christians, such as the sect known as the Heliognosti—who named themselves not after Jesus, but after Helios. For even the New Testament has Jesus referring to Himself by Apollo's popular title: "Light of the World."[148]

Luke himself admits, though occultly, that Jesus descended from the Pagan solar-deity Helios;[149] Matthew openly hints at Jesus' associations with the Pagan sun-god;[150] while Mark unreservedly connects the risen Jesus with the rising Sun.[151] Jesus Himself makes this remarkable statement:

> Then shall the righteous shine forth as the sun in the kingdom of their Father. Who hath ears to hear, let him hear.[152]

The "ears" Jesus is speaking of here are not physical ears. They are spiritual ears; that is, intuition—a word meaning "to learn from within."

Though today's fundamentalist, orthodox Christian sects and denominations reject Mani's view that the Pagan sun-god was the original template for the Christian son-god, modern archaeology and comparative mythology and religion have thoroughly vindicated him. In fact, it was just such Manichaeistic thought that gradually helped smooth the way for the hundreds of thousands of Pagans who were now converting to Christianity.

As these newly baptized followers of Jesus exchanged religions, they brought with them thousands of years of traditional Pagan customs and practices. In this manner, the celebration of December 25 was gradually transformed from the birthday of the *Sun* to that of the *Son*.[153]

The festivities and rituals of Saturnalia and Mithraism, by now so familiar to them, were brought along as well and incorporated into the celebration of the birth of the Christian sun/son-god Jesus.

The first tentative observance of what would, centuries later, be called "Christmas" had begun.

11

PAGAN THEMES AND FIGURES
ADOPTED BY CHRISTIANITY

NUMEROUS OTHER SYMBOLS, rituals, and figures from the Pagan world were brought over to Christianity and to the development and commemoration of Christmas.

To the biography of the historical Mary and the suckling infant Jesus was appended a blend of two deities: the Roman goddess Diana, virgin-goddess of chastity, childbirth, and the Moon, and the Egyptian virgin-goddess Isis, mother of Egypt, who was depicted on ancient tomb walls nursing her young child the sun/son-god Horus.

The historical Joseph was patterned after Seb (both names have similar etymological origins), the Egyptian earth-god, protector of Isis, and foster father of Horus.

The Egyptian phallic sign of life, the ankh, became the basis for the Christian cross, while the legendary founders of Rome, Romulus and Remus, were transformed into the figures of Saint Peter and Saint Paul.

Constantine the Great's birthday, December 25, was incorporated, along with Saturnalia, Horus', and Mithras' birthday, into the observance of Jesus' birthday. An ancient Christian from Syria confirmed the process:

> ... it was the custom of the heathen to celebrate on ... December 25th the birthday of the sun, at which they lit lights in token of festivity, and in these rites and festivities the Christians also took part. Accordingly, when the doctors of the Church perceived that the Christians had a liking for this festival, they resolved that the true Nativity should be commemorated on that day.[154]

As we will see, the Three Kings, the stable, the crib, the manger, and the Star of Bethlehem all have obvious Pagan astrological origins; all are, in fact, deeply embedded in ancient Egyptian, Buddhist, Hindu, Babylonian, Chinese, Persian, Greek, and Jewish mythologies, predating Christianity by countless centuries.

The accouterments of animistic ritual, so familiar to those contemporary Christians who attend church services, were also brought along by the converting Pagans: prayer; baptism in water; the burning of incense and candles; the ringing of bells; the wearing of robes and vestments by the clergy; sacraments, in which the blood of the once sacrificed human or nonhuman animal is today replaced by bread or wafers (the "body of Christ") and wine or water (the "blood of Christ"); chants and hymns; and the giving of presents to the honored god or goddess (today known as church tithing).

Since Paganism could not be fully suppressed, it was simply easier to incorporate it into the Church and imbue it with Christian significance. In this way, so the Church Fathers believed, Paganism would diminish while Christianity would grow and flourish.

12

How Paganism Continues To Thrive Under Christianity

WITH THE ESTABLISHMENT of the Roman Catholic church by Emperor Constantine the Great (c. 280-387) in the middle of the 4th Century, the Pagan gods and goddesses of the Old Religion would seem to have met their final demise. But such was not to be the case. In fact, not only did Paganism not die out, it had a spiritual rebirth under the guise of Christian symbolism, doctrine, ritual, literature, architecture, belief, and myth.

As we have seen, it was the increasing numbers of Pagans converting to the early Jesus cults, bringing with them the old deities, that gave Christianity its solid Pagan foundation. The idea of "the Christ," the sacrificial savior-god, himself was, after all, of pre-Christian origins.

Here was an archetypal figure dating from prehistoric times, a folkloric deity who took on human form, was born of a virgin at the Winter Solstice, performed supernatural acts, and was crucified and resurrected at the Spring Equinox, identical in every respect to the many hundreds of other savior-gods from other cultures throughout history. Thus, the very foundation of Christmas—though a holy day known by many other names—was already in existence many thousands of years before Christianity.

Pope Julius I (c. 309-352) seems to have been the first to decree that December 25 be celebrated as the "Mass of Christ," for the earliest documented reference we have that this day was known by the word *Christmas* came in the year 354, shortly after Julius' death.

One hundred and fifty years later, Christmas was made an official Roman holiday by Emperor Flavius Justinian (483-565). By the 7th Century, the celebration had spread across the European continent.

Others, in particular the ancient Egyptians, Saxons, Celts, Druids, Scandinavians, and Germans, all contributed various legends, ideas, trappings, and rituals to the celebration of Christmas as the centuries passed:

- The Christmas tree, once an ancient Egyptian phallic symbol.
- Mistletoe, used in ancient European fertility rites.
- The Nativity, based on ancient Egyptian sun-god legends.
- The Star of Bethlehem, actually the star Sirius, known then as the "Herald of the Sun," used in a common Eastern Pagan passion play announcing the birth of gods, goddesses, and earthly rulers.
- The crib and manger, ancient Egyptian symbols for birthplaces.
- The stable and attending farm animals, Greek and Egyptian astrological myths connected with the star signs Capricorn (the goat), Virgo (virgin mother-goddess of fertility and agriculture), and Taurus (the bull), among others.
- The Three Kings, from an ancient Egyptian astronomical allegory concerning the three stars of Orion's belt.
- Holly, a Pagan symbol of immortality.
- Wreaths, mince pies, puddings, and the Yule Log, all Pagan Sun symbols.

We have a myriad of traditional holiday foods as well, such as goose, from the Egyptian word *sa,* which stood for both "goose" and "son," and turkey, a culinary descendant of the goose.

As we will discuss in more detail shortly, all found their way into the festivities of Christmas, each one firmly rooted in pre-Christian Pagan religions of great antiquity.

13

CHRISTMAS BANNED
IN EARLY AMERICA

IN THE 10th Century Vikings began arriving on the continent of North America, an area already inhabited by thousands of Amerindian cultures, peoples who had crossed the Bering Straits land bridge perhaps 40,000 years earlier.

By the 16th Century European explorers were forging permanent settlements on American soil. These early white colonists, however, were not as enthusiastic about celebrating Christmas as Christians are today. In fact, from 1659 to 1684, the leaders of the Massachusetts Bay Colony forbade the celebration of Christ's birth in any manner. Strangely, its official observance in North America was almost totally unknown until the middle of the 19th Century. Why?

The Christian Fathers of the Puritan colonies viewed the observance of Christmas as a sacrilegious English import for which there was no biblical injunction. But more importantly, they considered it a vain, heathenistic, and vulgar exercise. Indeed, they well knew that the idea of Santa Claus emerged from Pagan folk legends surrounding magic, the occult, and Winter Solstice celebrations.

This is why the English Puritans originally pushed through an Act of Parliament to have Christmas prohibited in what is now the United

Kingdom. In 1644, for example, while they managed for a time to outlaw the festival in Scotland, in England the ruling was overturned by King Charles II, much to the joy of the populace.[155]

14

PAGAN CHRISTS

THE PURITAN FATHERS were right. As we have seen, nearly every facet of Christmas is ultimately Pagan in origin, dating far back to the first civilizations and beyond into the mists of prehistory. For in reality Christmas is a combination of the birthday of hundreds of ancient sun-gods, assorted heathen deities, and historical Pagan rulers.

Still, there are those who believe that Paganism is dead, trampled into oblivion by the Holy Cross. But they are wrong.

As noted, the very essence of Christianity—including its teachings, myths, rituals, holidays, its many Pagan-like gods and goddesses, its angels and demons, its saints and symbols—is founded on concepts of non-Christian origin. The name "Christ" itself may be taken as an example.

The word finds it origins in ancient Egypt, where it evolved from the words *krs*, *krst*, and *karas* (all words related to mummies, mummification, and resurrection). The full name of the pre-Christian savior Osiris, in fact, was *Osiris the Karast*: "the Mighty Christ."[156] By 1000 BC, the word had made its way into Babylonia, at which time it was under Chaldean rule. Inevitably, one of the words the Chaldeans began to use for their sun-god was *Crs* or *Chris* (in Hebrew, the word for the Sun is *heres*—or, without vowels, *hrs*—a Jewish equivalent of the Chaldean *Chris*). The ancient Greeks borrowed this Chaldean title to use for their word for anointing: *Christos*. In the first English translations of the Bible, *Christos* was spelled Christ.

Placing olive oil on one's head was a common practice of consecration, used often in religious rites among ancient Pagan peoples.[157] Why? Because traditionally, the olive has long been associated with the Sun.

Its oil was used originally in connection with sacred rituals surrounding sun-gods and spiritual growth: the oily sheen of the anointed person's head was seen as an allusion to the brightness of the golden Sun, while the Sun itself is a symbol of the head, or occultly, spiritual enlightenment. In Eastern religions, this state of mind is represented as the Crown Chakra, which became known as the halo in Christian mythology.

We must also consider the obvious linguistic parallels between both the names "Jesus" and "Christ" and that of numerous other ancient Pagan deities. For example, we have the Greek wine-god Bacch*us*; the Greek fire-god Promethe*us*; the Roman sun-god Mithr*as*; the Hindu hero-god Chri*s*hna (*Kris*hna); the Babylonian savior-god Tamm*uz*; the Egyptian sun-god Hor*us*; the Greek king-god Ze*us*; the Greek savior-god Adon*is*; and the Jewish messiah Cyr*us*; to name but a few.

Even in the ancient languages we find associations between the name Jesus and Paganism. In Latin, for example, Jesus is *Iesus*, in Greek *Iesous*, and in Hebrew, *Ieshoua* (Yeshua or Joshua). These spellings show parallels with the names of such Pagan gods as Ieoud, Ieud, Ieu, Ieue, Iehu, Ieve, Ieuw, Iao, Iota, Iaove, Iovi, Iove (Jove), and Iupiter (Jupiter, that is, "Father Ieu").

We will note here that the name Jesus (also written Joshua, Jeshua, Yeshua, Jeud, Jehu, or Jose) itself was an extremely common name among the Jews of 1st-Century Rome. Besides the Christian Savior Jesus, the Bible lists at least ten other men by that name, all spelling variations which ring of the names of far older Pagan deities—such as the Greek hero-god Jason (also spelled Iasion or Iasus), whose name is a Grecian form of Joshua/Jesus.[158]

Jesus/Jason/Joshua is also the same name of the Jewish Father-God Yahweh (or Iu, Jah, Jeud, Yah, Ieu, Iao, Yahu, Yaho, Ieuw, Jahveh,

Jahi)—as Jesus Himself stated,[159] while the English translation of Yahweh's name, Jehovah, was formulated around the name of the Pagan god Adonis ("the Lord"),[160] the Greek savior who was born in a cave in Bethlehem to the virgin mother Myrrha. In Syria the pre-Christian solar-deity Adonis was said to have been sacrificed at the Spring Equinox (later Easter/Passover), then buried in a womb-cave, after which he was resurrected, returning to Heaven.

Jesus/Yahweh/Jehovah then is the same as Zeus/Jove/Jupiter, father-gods who are identical in name to such saviors and hero-gods as Adonis and Jason. All seem to derive their names from an even older Pagan deity, in this case the Canaanite moon-goddess Yareah (or Jarih), who appears in the Old Testament as the Hebrew word for Moon: *yareach*.[161] Yareah's cult was, no doubt, prehistoric, and so popular that it continued among ancient Jewish women well into the middle of the 1st Millennium BC, at which time they were condemned for wearing crescent Moon pendants in her honor.[162]

Even the word God comes from Paganism, in this case from the great Hindu mother-goddess Goda, who also gave her name to the Teutonic father-god Godan (Odin or Woden), to the Goths ("Gods"), and to Lady Godiva.[163]

Such linguistic derivations, associations, parallels, and similarities have been observed by archaeologists, hierologists, etymologists, mythologists, and Bible scholars for many centuries. It will be obvious to all but the most dogmatic biblical literalists that such closely corresponding names, all from widely dissimilar cultures and periods in history, have a common mythological origin.

That the Christ motif itself[164] is both archetypal and universal in nature can be seen from the following partial list of some of the better known pre-Christian Pagan and Jewish Christs. Many of these figures were sun-gods or sky-gods, born of a virgin at the Winter Solstice (Christmas), performed miracles, had twelve disciples, were crucified on a cross (or hung in a tree) at the Spring Equinox (Easter/Passover), and were reborn three days later:

Adad, the Assyrian Christ
Adonis, the Greek Christ

Attis, the Phrygian Christ
Baal, the Phoenician Christ
Baili, the Orissan Christ
Balder, the Scandinavian Christ
Bali, the Afghan Christ
Beddru, the Japanese Christ
Belenus, the Celtic Christ
Buddha, the Indian Christ
Bunjil, the Australian Aboriginal Christ
Chrishna (Krishna), the Hindu Christ
Christ, the Gnostic Christ
Criti, the Chaldean Christ
Cyrus, the Jewish Christ
Dionysus, the Greek Christ
Eros, the Druidic Christ
Glooskap, the Abnkaian Christ
Hesus, the Druidic Christ
Horus, the Egyptian Christ
Hyacinth, the Spartan Christ
Indra, the Tibetan Christ
Ieoud, the Greek Christ
Iva, the Nepalese Christ
Jao, the Nepalese Christ
Jason, the Greek Christ
Jesus ben Pandira, the Jewish Christ
Joshua, the Jewish Christ
Karast, the Egyptian Christ
Kukulcan, the Mayan Christ
Lleu Llaw Gyffes, the Welsh Christ
Lugh, the Irish Christ
Mahavira, the Jainist Christ
Marduk, the Babylonian Christ
Mikado, the Shintosian Christ
Mitra, the (East) Indian Christ
Mithra, the Persian Christ
Mithras, the Graeco-Roman Christ

Odin, the Germanic Christ
Orontes, the Egyptian Christ
Osiris, the Egyptian Christ
Prometheus, the Graeco-Roman Christ
Quetzalcoatl, the Aztec Christ
Sakia, the Indian Christ
Saoshyant, the Zoroastrian Christ
Shemesh, the Hebrew Christ
Son of Man, the Essenic Christ
Son of Righteousness, the Gnostic-Jewish Christ
Tammuz, the Babylonian Christ
Thor, the Scandinavian Christ
Thules, the Egyptian Christ
Witoba, the Telingoneseian Christ
Woden, the Scandinavian Christ
Zoroastra, the Persian Christ

15

THE HEAVENLY SUN
BECOMES THE EARTHLY SON

IT MUST BE quite evident to the open-minded student of religion and
mythology by now that the "Sun" in the sky above gradually came to be
the "Son" on the earth below. Though this process may seem
confusing, as it took many thousands of years to complete, we in the 21st
Century have the benefit of hindsight. In reviewing this intriguing
sequence of events, here is what we find.

Just as many of the Hebrew myths of the Old Testament are overt
copies of Pagan myths that long preceded them,[165] the supernatural
aspects appended to the biography of the historical Jesus are nearly
indistinguishable from those of the archetypal messiah-savior-sun-gods
worshiped by early Jewish and Pagan Gnostics, a mythic figure who in
turn arose from the far more primitive solar deities of humanity's oldest
civilizations.

In fact, at the foundation of every prehistoric and ancient Pagan
religion is a supernatural being who, from high above, controls the
events of human life; descends from heaven to aid humanity; is killed and
hung on a tree; is buried in a cave; and is resurrected after three days,
promising great rewards to those who "believe."

Christianity itself, as we have seen, is largely of Pagan origins, for the legend of the Christ has its earliest known roots in pre-Christian Africa. Here, the intensely spiritual ancient Egyptians created innumerable cryptic symbols, myths, and figures, religious archetypes so powerful that they have not lost their intrigue, appeal, or grandeur in sixty centuries.

With our brief introduction to comparative Christmas studies completed, we are now ready to explore the details of our topic: the manner in which Christmas, the Birthday of the "Sun," became the Birthday of the "Son."

Our journey begins in the country known as "the Gift of the Nile," of course, for it is in ancient Egypt where we find the mythological roots of Jesus' mother, the Virgin Mary. For the cradle of both Christianity and Christmas truly lies in the land of the pharaohs.

Part Two

Ancient and
Medieval Contributions

16

PAGAN ORIGINS OF THE CHRISTMAS IMAGES OF MARY AND JOSEPH

WHILE THE LEGENDS and characteristics of the Virgin Mary were woven over many centuries from the great tapestry of Pagan moon-goddesses and pre-Christian earth-mothers, her Christmas persona has more definitive roots.

It is a well established historical fact that, like so much of Christianity, the image of the Madonna suckling the infant Jesus was taken directly from Egypt; in this case from the Egyptian mother-goddess Isis, who gave her name to one-third of the word Israel, or Is-Ra-El, as it is more correctly written.[166] In fact, so closely interwoven are the two goddesses that scientists often have difficulty determining if an ancient image is supposed to be that of Isis or Mary.

Early Roman Christians, cognizant of the Isis-Mary connection, saw themselves as the shepherd-like "servants of Isis," and so referred to themselves as the *Pastophori*, a title later adopted by the orthodox Christian Church where it became *Pastors*. Early Christian writers themselves could scarcely conceal the integral link between the Egyptian Isis and the Semitic Mary, as they occultly admit in the book of Matthew.[167]

Thousands of years before the rise of Christianity, Isis, the myriad-named deity who was also called the "Immaculate Virgin," "Our Lady," "Queen of Heaven," "Star of the Sea," and the "Savior of Souls," was depicted on tomb walls as *Isis Lactans* ("milk-giving Isis"), nursing her child, the sun-god-savior Horus.

Portrayals of the two virgin mothers are so strikingly similar that even many Christian scholars have had to finally admit that the early images of Mary holding the son-god Jesus in her arms could only have been patterned on pre-Christian images of Isis cradling the son-god Horus in her arms. Isis and Horus were indeed the original "Virgin Mother and Child," later made famous in the popular song *Silent Night*. This is why early Christians showed little preference for Mary if a statue or image of Isis was at hand.

For skeptics this Pagan contribution to the Christian figure of Mary is made even more credible when we learn that Isis also went by the name of the cow-headed goddess of the Nile, *Meri*, actually a common appellation for virgin-goddesses and mother-goddesses of all kinds across the ancient world. Why?

Because the word *mar* means "sea," "ocean," or "water," as can still be seen in our word "marine." The prehistoric link between the feminine element *mer* (Meri) and water has also been retained in our modern English word "mermaid."

The cosmic connection between the Great Mother-Goddess and water comes from the fact that water, particularly the ocean, is an archetypal symbol of the pregnant female's amniotic fluid, the salty seawater-like liquid that sustains an infant in a soft underwater cocoon until it is ready for birth into the material world.

Thus we have an almost limitless list of names of goddesses—many of them virgin-mothers of various saviors, sun-gods, son-gods, and heroes—whose names begin with or contain the *ma*, *mar*, or *mer* elements. A few examples include:

Mariamne, the Semitic "Queen of Heaven"
Maya, the Asian virgin-mother
The Moerae, the Greek triple-goddess
Mara, the Buddhist triple-goddess
Mar, the Persian mother-goddess

Maria, the Roman mother-goddess
Mara, the Hebrew mother-goddess[168]
Maritala, the Hindu mother-goddess
White Mary, the Welsh triple-goddess
Miriam, the Jewish mother-goddess
Mariana or Mandane, the Persian mother-goddess
Maia, the Greek mother-goddess
Maid Marian, the English spring- and fertility-goddess
The May Queen, the European fertility-goddess
Mary Magdalene, the Gnostic-Christian mother-goddess
Mari-Anna-Ishtar, the Babylonian mother-goddess
Myrrha, the Semitic-Greek mother-goddess
And, as mentioned, Meri, the Egyptian river-goddess

Not only was Mar, Meri, or Mari a common name for goddesses, but also for female-based institutions. For example, the original meaning of the word marriage, or rather Mari-age, was: "union under the auspices of the great goddess Mari."

The Judeo-Christian Mary owes far more than just her Christmas persona to the Pagan virgin-mother Isis, whose name means "throne." Statues of Isis were believed by the early Egyptians to move, and her paintings were said to cry real tears. In addition, apparitions of Isis were said to regularly appear to true believers.

These attributes and others began to be officially assimilated into the Marian legend in the 4th Century when the Church of Saint Mary was erected next to the Temple of Isis in Alexandria, Egypt. So closely related were the two virgin-mother-goddesses that historians record that devotees of Isis and Mary moved freely back and forth, venerating uninhibitedly at both sanctuaries. With the passage of time, as Paganism weakened and Christianity strengthened, most of Isis' titles, such as Our Lady, Queen of Heaven, Immaculate Virgin, and Star of the Sea, were all transferred over to Mary.

By the year 400 Church authorities were reprimanding Christian women for worshiping Mary as if she were a Pagan goddess. When the idea of Mary's Assumption (not invented until the 2nd Century) was officially accepted by the Catholic Church in the 6th Century, it was decided that the festival created to honor the event would be held on August 13, the same day as the festival of the great moon-goddess Diana, who was known as Isis in Egypt.

The crescent Moon, the sacred symbol of Diana—variously identified with the Queen of Heaven Ashtaroth,[169] as well as with other goddesses, such as Artemis, Selene, Aphrodite, Astarte, Venus, Ishtar-Mari, Anath, and Asherah—was also adopted by the Church and appended to Mary. Such Pagan female deities were often portrayed standing on a crescent ("horned") Moon with an arch of twelve stars above their heads, as Mary herself would later be depicted in the book of Revelation.[170]

By the close of the 6th Century, the Cult of Isis had been fully absorbed by the Catholic Church: Isis' metamorphosis from Pagan virgin-mother to Christian virgin-mother was complete. This occurred on the Nile island of Philae, where the last standing Isisian Temple was seized and turned into a Christian church.[171]

All that was left was for the Catholic Church to accept Mary as a deity in her own right. This finally came to pass—albeit nearly 2,000 years later—on November 1, 1950 (when Pope Pius XII issued his *Munificentissimus Deus*, declaring the Assumption of the Virgin Mary to be an official dogma of the Church), and again at the Second Vatican Council (1962 to 1965), where it was announced that

> the Immaculate Virgin, preserved free from all stain of original sin, was taken up body and soul into heavenly glory, when her earthly life was over, and exalted by the Lord as Queen over all things.

Joseph, the patronymic husband of Mary and the foster father of Jesus, has his own mythological Pagan antecedents. Among them was the pre-Christian Nanda, the foster father of the Hindu son-savior Chrishna (Krishna), born of the virgin-mother Devaki.[172]

The primary legend on which Joseph's biography was designed, however, surrounds the Egyptian Earth-god Seb, with whom he shares common etymological roots: compare the name Jo-"Seph" (or in Hebrew, *Yo-sep*), with the name "Seb." Like Joseph, who was later modeled on him, Seb was also a foster father, in this case, of the virgin-born son-savior Horus.

Egyptian mythology tells us that Seb accompanied the virgin-mother Isis and her son, the divine sun-god Horus, in their flight out of Egypt in an attempt to escape the serpent-demon Herrut. Later, this ancient Egyptian tale was borrowed in its entirety by the Christian editors of the book of Matthew, who changed the name of Herrut to "Herod."[173]

17

Pagan Origins Of
The Star Of Bethlehem

L ET US NOW examine the Star of Bethlehem, which grew out of several pre-Christian myths and religious ideas.

One of these was the Graeco-Roman Cult of Sirius, a sect that was built around the veneration of the great dog-star Sirius, located in the constellation Canis Major ("Big Dog"), loyal companion of the Greek hunter-hero-god Orion. As the brightest star in the sky, it is not surprising that Sirius garnered such attention from the ancients, who often saw its movements as portents of great disasters or occasions of great auspiciousness.

The Star of Bethlehem has ancient African roots as well. The early Egyptians believed the constellation Canis Major to be a literal representation of Anubis, the dog-god of the dead, which is why the Anubian star Sirius took on such great sacrality. So important was Sirius to the Egyptians that they calculated their calendars by its movements.

According to ancient Egyptian mythology, Sirius had associations with elements of both water and solar-savior motifs as well, for the star rose just prior to the Sun during the flooding of Egypt's greatest river, the Nile, known to the Egyptians as Siris. Thus, the name of the river was appended to the star.

Sirius' connection with water, of course, also links it with the great Egyptian virgin-mother-goddess Isis, sometimes portrayed in Egyptian art as a mermaid, half woman, half fish. Other water-deities related to the worship of Sirius include Isis' neighborhood counterparts, the Babylonian merman-god Oannes, the Sumerian sea-god Enki, and the Accadian water-god Ea.

The Isis-Sirius myth truly bridges the past with the present: the modern Dogon people of Mali, West Africa (who are of Egyptian descent), maintain that thousands of years ago an amphibious Isis-like deity named Nommos came down to Earth and gave their Egyptian ancestors astronomical knowledge of both Sirius (also known as Sirius A) and its white-dwarf companion, Sirius B.[174]

Sirius was also called the "Sacred Star of Osiris" (after the Egyptian savior-god), known in ancient Egypt as Sothis. More significant to the early Egyptians, however, was the star's function as the "Herald of the Sun," or "Herald of the Son": every December 24, at 12:00 midnight, the exact moment of the Sun's "rebirth," Sirius attained its highest point in the night sky.

Also connected to Sirius was the mythology of the star-god Lucifer, the morning aspect of the planet Venus, the Roman goddess of love. According to Graeco-Roman legend, Lucifer, the son of Zeus and Eos,[175] was believed to announce the arrival of the sun-god Sol at dawn everyday.   As he rose each morning in the east, Lucifer's daily proclamation marked the birth (or rebirth) of the Sun, an event especially noted on or around December 25, the annual birthday of the great sun-god.

The star Sirius and the star-god Lucifer are facets of the much larger Pagan concept of heraldic stars. These were astronomical events which were said to announce the birth, death, or great deeds of deities and important human rulers.   The unknown author of the works of "Shakespeare"[176] makes reference to this ancient belief in the famed play *Julius Caesar*:

> When beggars die, there are no comets seen;
> The heavens themselves blaze forth the death of princes.[177]

In religious mythology heraldic stars are very common. Indeed, such heavenly bodies proclaimed the births of Chrishna, Abraham, Lao-Tsze, and Moses, among many others. At Buddha's birth to the virgin-mother Maya (Mary), for example, the event was announced to a group of wise men known as "Holy Rishis" by an unusual star moving across the horizon.[178]

It is apparent then that the Pagan heraldic star theme was adopted by the writers and editors of the New Testament for use in Jesus' nativity story.[179] This was done, no doubt, in an effort to assimilate the power and authority of the popular myths of Pagan saviors and their heraldic stars, as well as to correlate with a messianic prophecy found in the book of Numbers: "There shall come a Star out of Jacob."[180]

Indeed, in the minds of many ancients, Jesus, the Sun of Righteousness,[181] and Lucifer, the morning star-god, continued to be intimately linked well into the 2nd Century, as the Bible itself attests.[182]

18

PAGAN ORIGINS OF THE STABLE
AND THE MANGER MOTIFS

THE "STABLE" WHICH Jesus is said to have been born in was borrowed from pre-Christian Greek beliefs. In ancient times, the birth of the Sun, on December 25, fell under the sign Capricorn, while the constellation *Auriga*, also known as "The Stable of Augeas," stood nearby.[183] Thus, the Sun (Son) was widely held to have been born in a small barn or stable.

Yet, because Capricorn also symbolizes the spiritual cleansing of the lower nature, the Aurigan stable was believed to be polluted by the "sins of humanity" each year. Only the sun-god himself, in an annual ritual, could cleanse the stable. Thus, in the pre-Christian mythology of the Greeks, for example, the sixth labor of the sun-god Hercules was to purify the Augean Stables in one day.

This particular Grecian tale was appropriated by Christian mythographers in the 4th Century for use in the story of Jesus. Indeed, the great Church Father Justin Martyr (c. 100-c. 165) admitted as much when he declared that Jesus had been born at the same time as the Sun's birth in Augean Stable, descending to earth as a "new Hercules" to rid the world of its dirt and filth (sin).

Contemporary Christians writers, such as Weigall, also concede that the "stable" motif of the New Testament is purely Pagan in origin: when Saint Luke states that Mary swaddled the infant Jesus and laid him in a manger, he was using the Greek gods Hermes and Dionysus for his model, both who, according to myth, were wrapped in swaddling clothes and placed in mangers. These Grecian tales predate the rise of Christianity by many centuries.

There was another reason though that the connection between Dionysus and Jesus could not be ignored by early Christians. It was Dionysus who gave his name to December (the "tenth month"), the month of Jesus' "birth."[184]

In truth, neither of the two canonical Gospels which mention the Nativity directly state that Jesus was born in a "stable." On the contrary, the book of Matthew asserts that Jesus was born in a "house,"[185] while Luke makes no mention at all of Jesus' exact birthplace. A "stable" is insinuated, though not directly referred to, by the use of the word "manger,"[186] at the time a food bin or shelf from which farm animals ate. However, since stables as we know them today did not exist in the ancient Near East, it is obvious that Jesus had to have been born in some other type of shelter.

In fact, both Matthew's and Luke's stories contradict a third popular tradition that was circulating in the 2nd Century; namely that, like the Hindu savior Chrishna, the Greek logos-god Hermes, and the Persian-Roman savior Mithras (the "rock-born"), Jesus had been born in a cave.[187] Obviously then, the "manger" motif of the New Testament was borrowed from just such pre-Christian Pagan sources.

Another of the primary Pagan influences here came from the ancient Egyptians. According to early Egyptian mythology the summit of the Earth was called *Apta*, the Egyptian word for both "upper Earth" and "manger." Because this was the region from which the sun-god was said to have been born, *Apta*, or manger, became synonymous with "birthplace." Thus, Egyptian temples at the time displayed the solar-infant lying in a manger, an image worshiped specifically on the sun-god's birthday, December 25.

Again, artistic portrayals of this event are to be found on Egyptian tomb walls dating from long before the emergence of the Christian Church.

12

Ancient Egyptian Astrology: Pagan Origins Of The Three Wise Men

THE "THREE WISE Men," said to have visited the infant Jesus twelve days after His birth, is one of the more traditional themes of Christmas mythology.[188] Yet, on closer inspection we find that this too has been adapted from a host of earlier Pagan sources.

Indeed, not one of the canonical Gospels mentions either "three" wise men or their visiting Jesus in a "stable" specifically on the "twelfth" day following His birth.[189] Where did these particular legends arise from then?

Let us begin by reexamining the Star of Bethlehem, this time in more detail.

Many theories have been put forth as to what this phenomenon was: a comet, a meteor, a nova or supernova, or even the conjunction of two or more planets. But as astronomers well know, there is no object in the sky or in space that points to a specific place on the surface of the Earth.

The closest star to us (outside our own Sun) is Proxima Centauri, which is 4.22 light-years distant, or about 24 trillion miles away from Earth.[190] Most of the other stars in the night sky are much further away from us than even this. Obviously then, there is no connection whatsoever between stars outside our solar system and our planet.

Yet, there is one celestial phenomenon which, to the ancient mind, might have given the impression that it was indicating a certain direction or an exact point on Earth.

Prehistoric and ancient peoples believed that stars, planets, and comets, and other celestial bodies, were living beings, deities in fact. This was no doubt due to their awesome appearance, their unearthly light, their permanent nature, and their invariant nightly sojourn across the heavens. Quite naturally, these movements came to be seen as portents and oracles, indicators of when to sow and harvest crops, when best to take the throne, give birth, make war, get married, travel, or hold religious festivals.

In their attempt to understand and follow the workings of the stars and planets, along with the changing seasons associated with them, ancient peoples invented the Zodiac (Greek for a "circle of animals"), an imaginary belt in the sky that encompasses the paths of all the planets except Pluto (which was unknown until its modern discovery in 1930).

In its earliest form, the Zodiac had only four constellations. In Egypt these were known as the "Four Sons of Horus":

1) Amset: the man-god who ruled the Winter and the north.
2) Hapi: the ape-god who ruled the Summer and the south.
3) Tuamutef: the jackal-god who ruled the Spring and the east.
4) Gebhsennuf: the hawk-god who ruled the Autumn and the west.

One thousand years later these four Compass-deities were assimilated by the Greeks into their expanded version of the Zodiac as:

1. Aquarius: the Waterman who ruled the Winter Solstice and the north.
2. Leo: the Lion who ruled the Summer Solstice and the south.
3. Taurus: the Bull who ruled the Vernal Equinox and the east.
4. Scorpio (or Aquila the Eagle): the Scorpion/Eagle who ruled the Autumnal Equinox and the west.

Together, these four star-signs form a cross or crucifix (known variously as the Galactic Cross, Cosmic Cross, or Pagan Tetramorph) when seen in a natal horoscope. And it was partially for this reason that all four were later adopted—by way of the Jews[191]—for use by the orthodox Christian Father, Irenaeus (c. 130-c. 200), in assigning names of authorship to four anonymous Jewish-Christian books that he selected for placement in the New Testament. These were to become the four canonical Gospels of Matthew (Aquarius), Mark (Leo), Luke (Taurus), and John (Scorpio/Aquila). This version came to be called the Christian Tetramorph.

Evidence of the early Church's links with Pagan astrology and the Pagan Tetramorph can still be seen in Medieval Christian buildings all over Europe, one of the better examples being France's famous Chartres Cathedral.

Not only was this cathedral itself purposefully aligned to the Summer Solstice (on which day the sun-god is at its peak in the daytime sky), but astrological symbols, indeed, entire Zodiacs, can be seen scattered throughout the building's architecture, connecting Jesus with the Pagan sun-god Apollo (known by Pagans as "the Good Shepherd," a title later appended to Jesus), with the Pagans' great Virgin-Mother Goddess (often depicted symbolically as the Vesica Piscis), with the twelve star-signs of the Zodiac, and with the Pagan Tetramorph, the four compass-signs: Aquarius, Leo, Taurus, and Scorpio/Aquila.

Every year on the Summer Solstice, for example, the Sun shines through a window at Chartres. Not just any window, but one dedicated to "Saint Apollinaire," an overt christianization of the Roman sun-god Apollo. The Gothic church itself is still referred to as "the Cathedral of Our Lady of Chartres," the original "Lady" referred to here being, of course, the Pagan virgin-mother Meri (Isis), now masquerading as the Christian Virgin-Mother Mary.

Based on the most magical of all numbers, twelve (due to its many numerological and mathematical potentialities), the revised Greek Zodiac was divided into twelve constellatory houses, represented by twelve astral-deities: Aries, Taurus, Gemini, Cancer, Leo, Virgo, Libra, Scorpio, Sagittarius, Capricorn, Aquarius, and Pisces. Each house was given thirty degrees of longitude, all twelve equaling 360 degrees total.[192]

Naturally, numerous fables and legends grew up around the Zodiac, best epitomized in the epic yarns of Greek mythology, such as the Twelve Labors of Hercules.

Of most interest to us in our examination of the origins of Christmas, however, is the story of the "virgin birth of the sun-god," a pre-Christian nativity story that has its roots in the astrological myths of ancient Egypt.

In order to penetrate the symbolic veil of this legend, let us imagine that we are living between 2512 BC and 360 BC, the period when the Sun rose precisely in the constellation Capricorn on December 25. This will enable us to look at this magnificent celestial event as an ancient astronomer living then would have seen it.

Why is this necessary? Because the stars, and hence the constellations, have moved almost a full thirty degrees (due to the ongoing forces of the Big Bang) since the period when astrology first developed. In effect, this means that the Sun is now actually in the sign preceding the sign originally and traditionally assigned to it. Hence, on December 25 today, the Sun no longer rises in the constellation Capricorn, as it once did, but in Sagittarius. We want to go back to the era in which it rose in Capricorn.

In the northern hemisphere, early on the midwinter night of what would have been December 24, in the year 1500 BC, we can observe the constellation of Orion the Hunter rising in the east.[193] Most noticeable are the three stars which make up the great hunter's belt, called (from left to right), Alnitak, Alnilam, and Mintaka.[194]

As Orion rises higher in the night sky, to the earthly observer these three stars appear to point back to the eastern horizon where the constellation Canis Major (Orion's companion, the "Big Dog") and its brilliant star, Sirius, now begin to emerge. Across from Orion we can see the constellation Scorpio (the "Scorpion") and the constellation of Aquila (Latin for "eagle").[195]

Around midnight, with Canis Major moving upwards into the sky, the constellation Virgo (the "Virgin") soon appears on the eastern horizon. Nearby, the constellation Aries (the "Ram") may also be seen rising. At this time, too, the Sun reaches its lowest point in the constellation Capricorn (the "Goat"). Shortly after, at dawn on the following morning (December 25), the Sun rises in the east, still in the sign Capricorn.

Lastly, surrounding Orion, we see the constellations Taurus (the "Bull") and Ursus Major (known in ancient Egypt, not as the "Big Bear," or "Big Dipper," but as the "Ass of Typhon"). Below Orion is the constellation Columba (the "Dove"), while above Taurus is Auriga (Latin for the "Charioteer"), or, as it was also known in ancient times, the "Augean Stable."

It was this momentous yearly celestial event on December 24 and 25 from which arose one of the earliest known nativity stories. Remembering that the Pagans of antiquity viewed celestial bodies as living beings, let us now look at this astronomical event through the literalistic eyes of the ancient Egyptians.

The three stars of Orion's belt, Alnitak, Alnilam, and Mintaka, were believed to be of royal birth and so the Egyptians called them the "Three Kings," a name by which they are still known in various parts of Europe. Leading the "Three Kings" is the bright star Sirius which reached its zenith at midnight on this particular night—December 24, the eve of the birthday of the great sun-god Ra—and so was considered the messenger who announced the birth of the Supreme Solar-deity. Hence, Sirius was known as the "Herald of the sun-god,"[196] or the "Star from the East."

As Sirius rises into the night sky, he is closely followed by the great Mother-Virgin-Goddess (Virgo) who is now preparing to give birth to her son Ra, the sun-god-savior.[197] The Dove (Columba)—an ancient goddess symbol of the "Holy Spirit"—now descends on the Virgin while the Eagle (Aquila)—an ancient symbol of the Great Father-God—watches over the proceedings.

The birth of the infant sun-god at dawn takes place in the Stable of Augeas (Auriga), as the zodiacal ox (Taurus) and ass (Ursus Major) look on. With the ram (Aries) appearing on the nearby horizon, his mother then lays the newborn sun-god in a feed trough.

It is this simple astronomical event that gives us the Christian "tradition" of the "Three Kings" (belt of Orion) who follow the "Star of Bethlehem" (Sirius) across the sky. The star leads them to the "Virgin Mary" (Virgo), who is "impregnated" by the "Holy Spirit" (Columba), as God (Aquila) governs the event from above.

The Virgin then gives birth to the son-god Ra (Jesus) in a "stable" (Auriga). As farm animals, an ox (Taurus) and an ass (Ursus Major), stand by, Mary (Virgo) lays the divine infant in a "manger," while the "Lamb of God" (Aries) looks on.[198]

20

PRE~CHRISTIAN NATIVITIES
AND THE DEVELOPMENT
OF THE THREE KINGS MOTIF

WITH SUCH ASTRONOMICAL facts at our disposal, it is not surprising to learn then that the entire Christian Nativity itself was presaged by the ancient Egyptians: in the remains of the 3,500 year-old Temple of Amun at Karnak are four beautiful wall-scenes displaying the earliest known depictions of the "Annunciation of the Virgin," the "Immaculate Conception" (or "Descent of the Holy Spirit"), the "Nativity of the Son of God," and the "Adoration of the Divine Child." At this stage in their history the Egyptian Nativity surrounded the great virgin-mother Isis and her heavenly infant the son-god Horus.

In the first panel we find Isis being visited by Thoth (later to become the Judeo-Christian "Angel Gabriel"), who announces that she will be the bearer of the holy son-god.

In the second panel, Isis is impregnated by the ram-headed god Kneph, whose name means "Spirit." Assisting Kneph (whose figure was later used in the development of the Judeo-Christian Holy Spirit), is the cow-headed goddess of dance music, and love, Hathor,[199] who holds the sacred ankh (later to become the Christian cross), the Egyptian symbol of life, to the lips of the now pregnant virgin-mother.

The third panel shows the Nativity itself: as Isis sits on the birthing stool recovering from the delivery, a midwife holds the newborn son-god in her arms.

Finally, in the fourth panel, we see a group of men and deities worshiping Horus, the Divine Child. On one side is Kneph. Directly behind him sit three men offering gifts (later to become the "Three Wise Men" of Christian mythology).

While it is obvious that this 4,000 year-old narrative was taken in its entirety and used in developing the nativity story of Jesus, nevertheless, certain elements of the original legend, as it is found in the New Testament, have been reworked over the centuries in order to conceal its Pagan origins.

The "wise men" of Matthew and Luke were, in fact, something far different than merely sagacious individuals. In the New Testament Greek of the 1st Century, the original word, now replaced with "wise men," was Magus or Magi, a word meaning "the priests of Mithra." More generally speaking, these priests were astrologers, miracle-workers, seers, sorcerers, augers, physicians, and magicians, who worked in Pagan temples devoted to the worship of the savior-sun-god Mithras.

In ancient times, the Magi were among the most respected and sought after members of both Pagan and Jewish society. They and they alone were said to be able to predict one's future, heal a wound, interpret a dream, turn base metal into gold, cast a horoscope, and give propitious dates for marriage, embarking on a journey, or planting crops.

So important were the Magi to the daily life of ancient cultures that they were employed not only by the poorest of families, but also by kings and queens to aid in governmental decision-making.[200] Thus, it is not surprising that the pre-Christian Babylonians, Medes, Persians, and Jews taught that the Magi were the sole prophets capable of predicting the arrival of the Messiah's heraldic star, which would in turn enable identification of the newborn sun/son-god.

Later, during the 1st Century BC, this idea was more fully developed in the nativity story of the Graeco-Roman savior Mithras. According to the popular Pagan legend of the day, the gift-bearing Magi visited the newly born sun-god Mithras in a cave called "the Rock." This occurred on January 6, twelve days after Mithras' birth (on December 25), a day henceforth celebrated in the Mithraic religion as the "Epiphany" (that is, the "Manifestation").

Another Pagan source for both the Star of Bethlehem motif and the Wise Men theme was found by Christian mythographers in the Zoroastrian bible, the *Zend Avesta*. The *Gathas* (or "Hymns") of the *Avesta* are held to be composed by Zoroaster himself, who lived around 600 BC.

One of Zoroaster's many prophecies regarding the "Future Savior" holds great significance for us, for it was written six centuries before the historical birth of Jesus:

> You, my children, shall be the first honored by the manifestation of that divine person who is to appear in the world. A star shall go before you to conduct you to the place of His nativity, and when you shall find Him, present to Him your oblations and sacrifices, for He is indeed your Lord and an everlasting King.[201]

In developing the story of the Wise Men, the later Christian editors of the book of Matthew borrowed from other Pagan sources as well. Both the Roman author Pliny the Elder and the Roman historian Dio Cassius (c. 150-235), for instance, write of another group of Magi who visited a pre-Christian Christ.

This particular small band of astrologers and magicians were led by the head magus Tiridates, a Parthian king who paid a visit of homage to the Pagan Emperor Nero (37-68) near the middle of the 1st Century. Nero, like other Pagan leaders of that era, was well-known as the "Savior of the World," and the "Anointed One, the Eternal Christ."

The visit of the wise men to Nero began, as Dio Cassius writes, when Tiridates

> was driven in the chariot which Nero had sent to him . . . and bending his knee to the earth and lifting his hands, he called him his lord and worshipped him. . . . For he spoke thus: 'I, my lord . . . am thy slave. And I am come to thee as to my God, worshipping thee, even as Mithras. . . .' But Tiridates did not travel back by the way he had come.[202]

Compare this passage with the appended tale of the "Wise Men" as it now stands in the Gospel of Matthew:

> Now when Jesus was born in Bethlehem of Judaea in the days of Herod the king, behold, there came wise men from the east to Jerusalem,
>
> Saying, Where is he that is born King of the Jews? for we have seen his star in the east, and are come to worship him.
>
> When Herod the king had heard these things, he was troubled, and all Jerusalem with him.
>
> And when he had gathered all the chief priests and scribes of the people together, he demanded of them where Christ should be born.
>
> And they said unto him, In Bethlehem of Judaea: for thus it is written by the prophet,
>
> And thou Bethlehem, in the land of Juda, art not the least among the princes of Juda: for out of thee shall come a Governor, that shall rule my people Israel.
>
> Then Herod, when he had privily called the wise men, enquired of them diligently what time the star appeared.
>
> And he sent them to Bethlehem, and said, Go and search diligently for the young child; and when ye have found him, bring me word again, that I may come and worship him also.
>
> When they had heard the king, they departed; and, lo, the star, which they saw in the east, went before them, till it came and stood over where the young child was.
>
> When they saw the star, they rejoiced with exceeding great joy.
>
> And when they were come into the house, they saw the young child with Mary his mother, and fell down, and worshipped him: and when they had opened their treasures, they presented unto him gifts; gold, and frankincense, and myrrh.
>
> And being warned of God in a dream that they should not return to Herod, they departed into their own country another way.[203]

Interestingly, the belief that the Wise Men were kings is not found in the Bible. Rather the notion first appears in the writings of the conservative African Christian, Tertullian (c. 160 - c. 225), who, in the formulation of the Jesuine nativity story, borrowed this Asian Pagan belief and blended it with the Egyptian theme of the Three King-stars of Orion's belt and the Magi of the Roman Mithraic legend.

This was no doubt an effort on the orthodox Father's part to soften the overt Pagan elements of these particular myths. Being raised a Pagan himself, however, Tertullian was very familiar with Pagan mythology in general, and apparently, despite his many apologetic Christian works to the contrary, was not adverse to utilizing various Pagan symbols and concepts in defending orthodox Christianity when necessary.

Thus it was that the original ancient Egyptian legend of Orion's Three Kings and the star Sirius—the Herald of the Sun—became the Graeco-Roman Magi (astrologers or sun-priests), who visited the infant Pagan sun-god Mithras, who in turn became the "Wise Men" who visited the infant Judeo-Christian son-god Jesus.

It was then left only to Origen (c. 185-254), the enigmatic Egyptian Christian theologian, to make the wise men three in number, a "Christian tradition" which also does not appear in the Bible. Allegedly, this number was selected by Origen because of the three gifts (gold, frankincense, and myrrh) given to the infant Jesus, as described in Matthew.[204]

But the mystic Origen, like many other early Church Fathers, was well versed in Pagan religious beliefs and Pagan mythology. Thus, we can be sure that he knew that the New Testament's "three gifts of the Wise Men" were made three to begin with because of their connection with the Pagan celestial religions surrounding Orion and his starry Three Kings.

In the 6th Century Medieval Christians took the three sacred Pagan star-deities, Alnitak, Alnilam, and Mintaka, christianized them, and renamed them, Gaspar, Melchior, and Balthasar, as the biblical scholar Bede (c. 673-735) notes:

> The first was called Melchior. He was an old man, with white hair and a long beard; he offered gold to the Lord as to his King. The second, Gaspar by name, young, beardless, of ruddy hue, offered to Jesus his gift of incense, the homage due to Divinity. The third, of black complexion, with heavy beard, was middle-aged and called Balthasar. The myrrh he held in his hand prefigured the death of the son of Man.[205]

The Mithraic Epiphany, or Twelfth Night, the celebration of the Magi's visit to Mithras' birthplace on January 6 (twelve days after his birth), was christianized by the Western Church, which made it the day on which "the Wise Men visited Jesus' birthplace." This "tradition," however, was not officially adopted by Catholicism until much later, in the year 813.

By way of the mystical Gnostic-Jewish sect the Nazarenes (of whom both Jesus and Saint Paul were said to be members),[206] the Pagan Epiphany entered the dogma of the Eastern Orthodox Church in the 3rd Century, though here, in an effort to rid it of its Judeo-Pagan elements, it was changed to signify the date of Jesus' baptism by John.

This was, no doubt, because January 6 marked the day of the great water festivals of the Greek dying-and-rising god Dionysus, and the Egyptian dying-and-rising god Osiris. On this day, Pagans blessed their rivers and fountains, drinking and immersing themselves in the sacred liquid, later to be used as holy water for sacraments and baptisms.

21

CHRISTIANIZING THE PAGAN CULT OF RELICS

T HE "RELICS," OR skeletons and personal effects of the Three Kings, or Magi, are said to be enshrined at Germany's Cologne Cathedral. But since the Magi were mythological figures—star-symbols of the three-fold nature of humanity (mind/body/spirit)—these particular "relics" can only be the fabrications of well meaning, but overzealous Medieval Churchmen.

Indeed, the idea of worshiping the remains of the dead—called the "Cult of Relics"—is wholly Pagan in nature, dating back to perhaps as far as the Neanderthalian Epoch, 100,000 years ago. Here, archaeologists have found the corpses of Neanderthals intentionally covered (or surrounded) with flowers and red ochre, both sacred symbols of the great Mother-Goddess, the latter of her (menstrual) blood, itself an occult emblem of the universal life force. What we have here is an indication that the Neanderthal people believed in an afterlife and venerated the dead in some manner.[207]

The Pagan cult of relics reached its apex thousands of years later in ancient Egypt, where the mummified bodies of royal elites, common laborers, and even cats, birds, and crocodiles, were held to be sacred. He or she whose holy shroud was violated after death was not eligible for entrance into Heaven, thus the need for great secret tombs buried deep in the Earth, far out in the desert.

In the Graeco-Roman period it was the popular custom to deify humans in an attempt to make them immortal through association with gods and goddesses. This ritual, called the Apotheosis, or the "god-making" ceremony, was gradually adopted by the early Christian Church in Rome, eventually culminating in the development of the ideas of both canonization and the Cult of Saints.

Among the acts of venerating and invoking the saints, the worship of the relics of Christian martyrs, virgins, confessors, and ascetics, was by far the most important. Eventually it was officially ordered that no new church building could be constructed without first being consecrated with holy relics.

By the 2nd Century, the Pagan Cult of Relics had been thoroughly absorbed by Roman Christians, who held their services in the dark dank underground chambers of the catacombs below the cobbled streets of Rome. The superstitious devotion of the masses became so fanatical that eventually authoritarian Church Councils had to step in to restrict it.

Despite this, the Cult of Relics received formal approval by the Western Church at the 2nd Council of Nicaea in 787, though it was not officially adopted by the Western Church until the year 1084, at the Council of Constantinople. So popular was it that the Cult spread like wildfire, particularly during the Crusades, at which time vast amounts of "relics" were carried to Europe from the Holy Land, nearly all of them fake.

Because of the sacred or magic powers they were said to possess, the macabre mementos of exalted religious personages grew in demand. Soon, trafficking in relics became a profitable business, readily seized on by charlatans both inside and outside the Church.

By then, Church authorities had gathered up a massive supply of counterfeit bones, a vital necessity, for every new church now demanded a relic for its communion table; every shop owner wanted them to guard against larceny; knights required them as protection against their enemies; and peasants purchased them (in the form of Jesus' "sweat" and Mary's "milk") to ward off disease and bad luck.

Medieval Church Fathers attempted to counter the accusation that the Cult of Relics and the Cult of Saints were idolatrous in nature by expressing the worship of God alone as *Latria* ("adoration") and the devotion of saints as *Dulia* ("veneration").   But such multifarious theological circumlocutions had little impact.

Today most Protestant sects reject the Cult of Relics altogether, correctly seeing it as a form of ancient Pagan idolatry,[208] while in the Catholic Church it remains a vital aspect of religious worship.

What does the Cult of Relics have to do with Christmas? This is the subject of our next chapter.

22

Festum Nativitatis Christi:
The First Christian Christmas

THE MAIN FOCUS of the Cult of Relics surrounds a form of Pagan sorcery called sympathetic magic. Here, the bones and personal effects of the deceased are thought to bestow beneficent results on those who touch, own, wear, or worship them. It was commonly believed in ancient times that so-called "saints" possessed a divine quality which they had received, by official succession, from Jesus Himself. The intent was to get as "spiritually" close to the Christian Savior as possible.

Yet, a major question continued to plague the early Church Fathers: was Jesus a mythological and symbolic figure (as the Gnostic-Christian Docetists and others claimed), or a historically authentic man (as the anonymous books of Matthew, Mark, Luke, and John maintained)? If He was nothing more than an occult symbol, a "phantasm" as the Gnostic-Christian Basilidians held,[209] not only would the relics of saints become meaningless, but the entire foundation of orthodox Christianity would crumble, and the Church's soon-to-be-realized goal of taking over the Roman Empire would become impossible.

The dilemma came down to this: the majority of the early Christian masses were both converted Pagans and nonliterate. Being essentially steeped in "idolatrous" religious ideas, and uneducated as well, most were wholly incapable of comprehending abstract concepts such as Saint Paul's cosmic ideas of "Christ Consciousness"[210] and "inner rebirth."[211]

For such people, only a literal flesh-and-blood savior, like their beloved Pagan saviors Attis, Dionysus, Horus, Osiris, and Mithras, would suffice.[212] Thus, whether the early Christian Fathers believed that Jesus had been a real historical figure or not (some did not), officially the Church itself would have to treat Jesus as if He were.

Yet, having by now nearly thoroughly paganized the figure of Jesus, the Church was appalled to hear the masses clamoring to celebrate His birthday, just as they had celebrated the birthdays of the pre-Christian Pagan saviors of old.

This latest demand of the Pagan converts created a furor within the Ecclesia (that is, the orthodox mainstream Catholic Church), for the Fathers well knew that the idea of celebrating the personal birthdays of common people, royalty, and divine beings, was clearly a Pagan invention and custom. As Origen himself said:

> In the scriptures, no one is recorded to have kept a feast or held a great banquet on [Jesus'] birthday. It is only sinners [like Pagans] who make great rejoicings over the day in which they were born into this world.[213]

It was such orthodox Christian sentiment that caused the Fathers to at first hesitate in establishing and instigating the celebration of Jesus' birthday. Perhaps, so they thought, it might lead to a resurgence of Paganism within the Church. Thus it was that Origen and others protested vehemently against the Pagan notion of observing Jesus' birthday as if He were a mortal heathen ruler.

Two centuries passed as Jewish-Christians, Pagan-Christians, Gnostic-Christians, and Ecclesiastical-Christians fought over the ramifications of institutionalizing Jesus' birthday.

Adding to the tumult was the question of *when* Jesus had been born. Was His date of birth January 6, as the mystical Nazarene Jewish-Christians claimed, or December 25 as the Pagan-Christians held? And what of the original Christians, the Gnostics, who asserted that, being a deeply arcane symbol, Jesus had not actually been born at all, making His "virgin birth," "crucifixion," and "resurrection" nothing more than spiritual allegories?[214]

The matter was finally settled in the 4th Century when, in the year 313, Constantine the Great passed his Edict of Milan, a legal reform which granted universal religious freedom across the Empire.[215] With the issuing of this decree, there was no longer any reason not to celebrate the birth of Jesus. Indeed, if the orthodox Church Fathers hoped to achieve their goal of world domination, now there was every reason to do so. Thus, as the Liberian Catalogue shows,[216] by the year 336, Roman Christians were already honoring December 25 as the birthday of Jesus, despite the fact that it had not been made official yet.

Eventually, bowing to social, political, and theological pressures, the Church Fathers relented, and in the middle of the 4th Century, not long after the death of Constantine the Great, Pope Julius I (c. 309-352) issued the first mandate ordering that December 25 be honored as Jesus' birthday.

It was not at first called "Christmas," however, and neither did Julius' decree make Jesus' birthday a state holiday. Indeed, on a national level the day remained as it had been under Constantine: the public Pagan holiday, *Dies Natalis Solis Invictus* ("Birthday of the Invincible Sun").

Yet by now, in conjunction with Pope Julius' directive, Christians in many parts of the Empire were celebrating December 25 as Jesus' birthday, using a distinctly Pagan-styled name, *Festum Nativitatis Christi*: the "Festival of the Birth of Christ."

In the manner of all evolving languages, this somewhat cumbersome title was gradually shortened to *Christus Missa* ("Christ's Mass") by Latin Christians sometime in the 5th and 6th Centuries. This abbreviated name reflects the continuing effects of the former glory of Pagan Rome on the Church. For the Roman word *missa* (i.e., "mass") was in turn derived from a form of Pagan communion bread called *mizd*. As we will recall, the *mizd* was central to the Mithraic sacrament: shaped like (or embossed with) a cross, it was believed to contain the actual flesh and blood of the Divine Taurean Bull, slain and sacrificed by the sun/son-god Mithras.

One-hundred-fifty years after Pope Julius I issued his decree, *Christus Missa* at last became an official state holy day under the patronage of Emperor Flavius Justinian (483-565). By the 7th Century, the Christian holiday had spread across the entire European continent. It was during this period that in England the name became *Cristes Mæsse*.

By the 12th Century—in the Middle English of the time—it was modified once again, becoming *Christemasse*. By the late 17th Century, it had acquired its current form in modern English: *Christmas*.

As the holiday diffused over the Indo-European continent, the various peoples who came in contact with it added their own cultural flavor, folklore, customs, symbols, and beliefs, further enlarging what would later be called "Christmas tradition." All of these accretions were of Pagan origins, of course, just as was the very idea of the nativity of the savior Jesus itself. This fact was not lost on the early Christian Fathers.

As late as the 3rd Century, the renowned Church authority Tertullian complained resentfully about those Christians who continued to celebrate the Pagan Winter Solstice festivals under the guise of honoring Jesus' birthday:

> By us, who are strangers to Sabbaths, and new moons, and festivals, once acceptable to God, the *Saturnalia* [Christmas], the feasts of January, the *Brumalia*, and *Matronalia* are now frequented; gifts are carried to and fro, New Year's Day presents are made with din, and sports and banquets are celebrated with uproar; oh, how much more faithful are the heathen to their religion, who take care to adopt no solemnity from the Christians.[217]

23

ANCIENT AND MEDIEVAL PAGAN CONTRIBUTIONS TO CHRISTMAS: SANTA CLAUS

WHILE THE ANCIENT Church Fathers railed mightily against the Pagan elements associated with December 25, the rest of the Western Christian world was busy assimilating more and more Pagan beliefs and practices to Christmas.

By the turn of the 20th Century Christmas was little more than a dazzling array of heathen customs and notions, deeply rooted in the mythologies and astrotheologies of the ancient Indo-European *Zeitgeist*. How these many customs developed, and why they were absorbed into this particular Christian holiday, forms the next part of our exploration into the Pagan origins of Christmas.

Where, for example, did the figures of Santa Claus and Rudolph the red-nosed reindeer come from? What are the true origins of the Yule Log, mistletoe, holly, the evergreen tree, the boar's head, the goose (or turkey), carols, and gift-giving? Why are cards, lights, wreaths, garlands, hearth stockings, nuts, candies, cider, mince pies, plum pudding, processions, feasts, and the pantomime, all now associated so closely with the Christian holy day we call Christmas?

To answer these questions, we need to once again turn to the ancient and Medieval Pagans.

Let us begin with Santa Claus.

By Christian "tradition" the figure of Santa Claus is said to derive from a real man, Nicholas, the Bishop of Myra, Lycia (modern-day Turkey), believed to have died in the year 342.

Yet, curiously, even Christian scholars admit that there is literally no definitive information known about his birth, life, or death. What is more, they freely acknowledge that a myriad of legends and unreliable "facts" were later appended to his "life story." Indeed, what little is known about Nicholas turns out to be a conglomeration of obvious and intentionally invented tales, wholly plagiarized from Pagan mythology.

For example, the so-called "biography" of Nicholas states that he performed countless miracles, such as staying raging storms to save sailors lost at sea, supernaturally doubling a supply of grain so that he could feed his fellow clergymen, and magically raising the dead from a wizard's cauldron. It is even said that after he died his bones excreted a stream of holy oil that could prevent and heal all manner of illnesses.

Other equally fantastic legends of Nicholas abound, such as those suggesting that he demolished Pagan temples with a wave of his hand, and that he could appear in other people's dreams and control their behavior, as he was once said to have done to Emperor Constantine the Great.

In another tale, it is widely rumored that Nicholas brought back to life three children who had been decapitated. It is even asserted, without evidence, that his "relics" were brought to Bari, Italy, in 1087 and that his shrine there became one of the most popular pilgrimage stops in Medieval Europe.

What are we to make of these alleged "facts of history"?

In truth, Nicholas was not a historical person, but rather an invented figure whose legend began in 11th-Century Italy when the orthodox Church Fathers in Rome took over the shrine of the Pagan boon-giving goddess, Pasqua Epiphania, at Bari. It was at this time that a few random bones were gathered together, placed in a specially built church there, and called "the bones of Saint Nicholas."

Indeed, due to the utterly fantastical nature of Nicholas, he can really only be understood as the fictional deified product of the early Catholic Church. Yet why, we must ask, was this figure created to begin with?

The short answer is that Nicholas, like so many other Christian "saints" and deities, was formulated under the pressures of pure political expediency, as we will now explore in more detail.

24

Saint Nicholas
And The King Of The Nixies

IN THEIR ATTEMPT to blend in with the Roman Pagan world, and thereby accrue political power, early Catholic authorities adopted the Pagan ritual of apotheosization ("god-making"), in which historical people and legendary personages were deified in order to give the masses an exemplary figure around which to rally.

The rite, later called "canonization" by Christians, was borrowed chiefly to placate Pagan converts who, along with those from various Jewish sects, comprised the entirety of the membership of the early Church. Those who were apotheosized by the Church were called "saints."[218] According to the modern science of comparative mythology, however, we would now call them "minor deities."

An examination of the apotheosization of Nicholas must begin with a look at the etymological roots of his name, which are not only interesting, but educational, as they give us a clue as to the true origins of Santa Claus himself.

At first glance it would appear that "Nicholas" is merely an English variation of the Greek word *nikolaos*, which means "conqueror for the people." Yet, the word has far more complex origins than this, so we must make a more detailed inquiry if we are to learn the truth about

Santa Claus.

Going back to ancient Greece we find the word *nizein*, which meant "to wash" in water. Over the centuries, as the Indo-European language spread, the early Germanic peoples adapted the word *nizein* to mean an "ocean-demon," calling it a *nihhus*. In Medieval England, the word *nihhus* was modified to *nicor*, meaning "sea-monster."

In more modern times, the Germans rounded off a compound of all of these various words to the word *nix*, which in Germanic folklore is related to a group of traditional characters called Nixies (i.e., water-fairies). The Nix is a male water-sprite, while the Nixy (or Nixie, or Nixe) is a female sprite called a water-nymph or sea-nymph.

Like all minor deities and figures in religious mythology, both the Nix and the Nixy were ruled over by a king. In this case, the King of the Nixies was a Teutonic sea-god called Hold Nickar, a German title-name-phrase meaning the "kindly sea-monster."

Hold Nickar, King of the Nixies, was a Medieval assimilation of the earlier Greek god of the sea, Poseidon, said to live in a palace beneath the Aegean Sea. Poseidon, like his Roman counterpart Neptune, was the protector of sailors, hence his popular nickname, "the Sailor."

When the early mainstream Christian Church, the Catholic Ecclesia, adopted the ritual of apotheosization from the Pagans, they also borrowed the Pagan idea of the "protector-deity." According to this notion, each deity watched over, or governed, various aspects of human nature or life. For example, the Greek goddess Fauna (or Bona Mater) was the governor of fertility and farming, as well as the protector of nature and animals.

In Christianity, the Pagan idea of the protector-governor was borrowed and christianized, becoming the "patron-saint," or "matron-saint." Here, just like earlier Pagan protector-gods and goddesses, each "saint" was assigned the patronship or matronship of a specific, person, place, thing, or act.

In taking over the Roman Empire and its Pagan beliefs, myths, and practices, the Catholic Church found need of a Christian protector of sea-going vessels and sailors, a position once prominently held by the Pagan Amazonian moon-mother-goddess Artemis (or in Latin, Diana). But, as the lunar-deity Diana had already been thoroughly assimilated into the Christian figure of the Virgin Mary, the Fathers turned to the well-known personage of Hold Nickar, the Danish god of the sea and King of the Nixies.

Along the way, various attributes of Poseidon—Hold Nickar's Greek counterpart—were adopted. Chief among these was the title "the Sailor," which was absorbed into Nicholas when Poseidon's temples were eventually taken over and rededicated to the fabricated Christian saint.

In the English language of the Medieval European period, Hold Nickar gradually corrupted to "Old Nick." When he was at last apotheosized, that is, "sainted" (probably sometime in the 10th or 11th Centuries), Old Nick became "Saint Nick," or more formally, "Saint Nicholas." Then, as occurred with so many other so-called "saints," the more scholarly of the Church Fathers designed an elaborate biography for him. Over many centuries "Saint Nick" developed into the patron saint of children, scholars, merchants, and sailors, finally becoming, as we will see, Santa Claus himself.[219]

To this day, in countries like Greece, tradition states that Saint Nicholas' beard and clothes are always soaked with saltwater due to his constant battles with ocean storms in trying to save sinking ships. And many modern Greek ship captains refuse to leave port without an icon of Saint Nicholas on board.

In addition to his associations with Hold Nickar, Saint Nicholas' relationship to the sea and water has other Pagan elements as well.

To begin with, we may assume that Hold Nickar (as has occurred with numerous other male deities) is a masculinization of the worldwide ancient representation of the Female Principle, Goddess, since the Germanic word *hold* (meaning "sweet," "lovely," or "kindly") is a variant of *Holde*, *Hild*, and *Hel*, just a few of the names the Great Mother was once known by.

Another clue that there was an ancient transference and assimilation from female to male here are the many magical "threes" which permeate the "biography" of Saint Nicholas.

There are, for instance, the "three" poverty-stricken girls who Nicholas saves from a life of prostitution by throwing "three" bags of gold into their house on "three" different occasions; there are the "three" imperial officers he saves from a death sentence; and there are the "three" heads of "three" murdered children who he brings back to life.

A preponderance of "three's," such as we find here, suggests not only occult origins, but an almost certain earlier connection with the triple-goddess (the original Trinity),[220] the ancient spiritual representation of birth, life, and death, embodied in the mythic female figures known as the Daughter (the virgin), the Mother (the bride), and the Crone (the wise woman).[221] There is a similar occurrence of "three's" in the "biographies" of other well-known ancient religious figures, such as Saint Paul of Tarsus.[222]

25

WATER, SEA~GODDESSES, AND THE NICOLAITANS

O F MORE INTEREST to us, however, is Saint Nicholas' relationship to Goddess by way of the archetypal symbol water. Water has long been associated with fertility, the parthenogenic "magic" of reproduction, and with Goddess herself, the "Mother of All." Thus, it is logical to assume that Hold Nickar is a transferred male descendent of the Great Mother and her many sea-goddess personifications, all of which long predate the emergence of the Teutonic sea-god.

We have, for instance:

- The Greek sea-goddess Aphrodite (*aphros* is Greek for "foam"), who gave her name to Aphroca, that is, Africa ("the Land of Aphrodite").
- The Canaanite Astarte who, as Athirat, was called "Lady of the Sea."
- The Greek sea-goddess Amphitrite, whose name is sometimes used as a designation for the sea.
- The Greek sea-goddess Doris, the daughter of Oceanus and Tethys, and sister of Amphitrite, whose name is often used to mean the "ocean."
- The Greek Leucothea, the sea-goddess who governs fountains and

brooks.

• The Greek sea-goddess Thetis, the daughter of Doris and stepmother of Achilles.

The Virgin Mary herself was often referred to by Graeco-Roman Christians as Stella Maris; that is, the "Star of the Sea." This name-title, one of the many possessed by the great pre-Christian Mother-Goddess, was first borrowed by the Ecclesiastical Father Jerome (c. 342-420) in the 5th Century, and applied to Mary as part of the process of christianizing the Pagan world. To this day Catholics still regularly and comfortably refer to the Virgin Mary by her Pagan Goddess title: Stella Maris.

Goddess' long associations with water can be seen in the ancient emblem the Vesica Piscis, or "vessel of the fish," an oval or almond-shaped yonic symbol representing the Great Mother's life-bearing pudenda. As such, her primary rituals were performed in temples during the sign of Pisces (February 19 through March 20), and her image was often depicted with fish netting surrounding it.

The Christian Church embraced much of this Pagan symbolism, even using the Vesica Piscis as an artistic framework for portrayals of Jesus and the Virgin Mary.

Other aspects of the almond-shaped female water emblem found their way into Christian myth. For example, the sacred geometric number of the Vesica Piscis is 153, the number of fish caught by Jesus in John's story of the "Miraculous Draught of Fishes."[223]

In sacred gematria (the Greek system of assigning numerical values to words),[224] Mary Magdalene's name features the number 153. Mary Magdalene, another version of Isis as Meri, was, of course, absorbed by Christianity as a member of the Marian triple-goddess, occultly portrayed at the foot of Jesus' cross in the Gospel of the great Christian mystic John.[225]

Every Winter, Italian Christians still intentionally include fish in their traditional Christmas dinner, the *Cenone* ("big dinner"). Most revealing is that early Church calendars used the Vesica Piscis to represent the Feast of Saint Nicholas, a christianization of the old Pagan god Hold Nickar.

It is obvious then that in borrowing from Hold Nickar, his associations with water, goddess-worship, and the sea were also brought along and incorporated into the figure of Saint Nicholas. This move was presaged, however, centuries before when individuals from among the first Christians, the Gnostics, saw in Hold Nickar an apt fertility symbol.

Calling themselves the Nicolaitans or Nicolaites, after the Pagan deity himself, the Graeco-Roman Gnostic-Christian sect petitioned for a return to a more Pagan-oriented religious experience. True to their word, they utilized the cauldron of regeneration in their worship of Nickar, a common ancient Pagan symbol of the great Mother's cosmic womb.

Like certain Hindu and Buddhist sects, as well as countless Greek and Roman religions before them, the Nicolaitans believed that true salvation (self-actualization or spiritual enlightenment) only came by way of frequent and intimate contact with the opposite sex.[226] Subsequently, their wild orgies and bacchanalian feasts brought them denunciation from all sides.[227]

Among those who vociferously condemned the Gnostic-Christian group were the early Jewish-Christians, who made clear their negative feelings towards the Nicolaitans in the highly occultic book of Revelation.[228] As it did with other Gnostic sects, the Catholic Church eventually exterminated the Nicolaitans in the most un-Christian of ways: mercilessly hunted down, they were beaten, imprisoned, tortured, and finally murdered, all under the auspices of the pope and his tyrannical hierarchy.

The suppression and final extinction of the Nicolaitans did little to stem the tide of Pagan assimilation to the figure of Saint Nicholas, however. Indeed, as the centuries advanced and the Christian Cult of Saint Nicholas spread out over Europe, each nation endowed him with the symbols and ideas of their own particular Pagan belief systems.

And so it was that like Mary, Jesus, and a host of other Christian figures, Saint Nicholas gradually absorbed the traits of the various Pagan deities of those countries that he passed through.

26

WODEN, ODIN, AND THOR:
PAGAN GERMANIC INFLUENCES

MUCH OF SAINT Nicholas' figure and legend developed in Medieval Germany, where he was blended with Woden (from which our weekday "Woden's Day," or "Wednesday," derives its name), the god of battle, magic, inspiration, and the dead.

It was from Woden that Saint Nicholas first became associated with December 25, and from whom he assimilated the curious custom of riding across the sky on horseback on Christmas Eve, delivering presents to those "who had been good the preceding year."

Here too we find the origins of the association between the traditional hobby-horse and Christmas.

A town named after Woden (who is also sometimes known as the god Wotan),[229] still survives in England: Woodnesborough, a name meaning "the mound dedicated to the god Woden." Here, every Christmas Eve was celebrated the festival of *Hoodening*, in which a horse's head or skull (real or depicted) was decorated with ribbons and carried from house to house on a pole. The carrier, who "galloped" with the pole held between his legs, was covered in a sheet and was known as "Old Hob." Thus was born the hobby-horse, while the movements the rider performed came to be known as the "Hobby-Horse Dance."[230]

As Germany became christianized, both of these elements were combined in Saint Nicholas due to the popular belief that at the Winter Solstice Woden rode his steed over the roofs of his devotees' homes, giving out blessings to those who were the most faithful.

The Pagan god Woden also gave Saint Nicholas his helpers and toy-makers, the elves. As "god of the dead," Woden was once known as the "Conductor of Souls" or "Elves," as the deceased were called in early Scandinavia.[231] Hence in Saxon mythology Woden was sometimes known as the "Elven King," and was often depicted surrounded by a flurry of elves who accompanied him on his yearly Winter ride to deliver gifts. When the figure of Woden was taken over by Christianity in the development of the Nicholas legend, Woden's elves were also assimilated.

In Nordic countries Woden was known as Odin. Odin played a much larger role in the religious and cultural mythology of the Vikings (and other peoples from the northlands) than Woden did in the folklore of the Germanic tribes to the south. For Odin was not just a minor deity who ruled magic, but, like the Judeo-Christian deity Yahweh or Jehovah, he was the Creator-God himself. It was from Odin, the god who, like Jesus, hung himself on the Tree of Life in order to learn the mysteries of the Universe (thereby becoming enlightened), that Saint Nicholas took on the role of the wise, learned, elderly father figure.

Odin is also the Pagan god from whom Saint Nicholas derived certain aspects of his physical appearance, for the Nordic deity was usually portrayed as a robust male of about fifty years of age, with long curly hair and a flowing beard. Thus, along with being the protector of sailors, Saint Nicholas now became the bearded, long-haired patron saint of scholars.

Hold Nickar, Poseidon, Woden, and Odin were not the only Pagan deities who contributed to the development of the figure of Santa Claus. He also absorbed certain elements from Thor (from which our weekday "Thor's Day," or "Thursday," derives its name), the redheaded Germanic god of thunderstorms and fertility.

As with many other northern European deities, Thor was closely associated with snow, ice, and cold weather. But more importantly, Thor had profound connections with the Pagan Yule, the Norse Winter

Solstice festival honoring the "rebirth" of the Sun in late December.

In Scandinavian countries, Thor, as a lightning-deity, was linked with the fiery Yule Log, particularly if the log was made of the lightning-drawing oak, the god's sacred tree.

When the Yule festival was assimilated into Christmas by the Church Fathers during the Middle Ages, Thor was adopted and applied to the figure of Saint Nicholas as "Father Christmas." Along with Thor came one of his more outstanding aspects: he was said to ride a chariot drawn by bucks (deer) named "Cracker and Gnasher."[232]

27

The Yule Festival, Kriss Kringle, Hearth Spirits, and Fireside Stockings

THE PAGAN NORDIC Yule festival, the time of the great
midwinter fire celebrations, contributed other elements to
Christmas and Santa Claus as well.

In Medieval Europe, Yule Eve, the night of December 24, was
considered a period of great dread and magic, a time when ghosts,
spirits, and demons wandered the Earth in an attempt to prevent the
Sun-child, known as Kriss Kringle (i.e., Chris Kringle) from being born
the following morning. To combat this, propitiatory offerings were left
out that night in order to appease maleficent spirits and to provide
nourishment for the ancestral dead.

More significantly, the Yule Log was placed in the fireplace and lit,
not only to drive away nefarious hearth spirits, but also in an effort to
give additional light to the Sun, aiding it in its struggle to rise into the sky
after its long decline (beginning at the Summer Solstice six months
earlier).

In Provence, France, for example, a child would pour wine over the
Yule Log, after which the grandfather would light it. Prayers for

protection and good health were then said as the wood burst into flames.

In modern Italy, the Yule Log, called the *Ceppo* ("log" or "stump"), is still burned, as wine is sipped and toasts are made for a propitious future. Alongside is the Urn of Fate, a large bowl in which gifts are placed and later distributed to family members. This is none other than a miniaturized variant of the magic cauldron of the old Pagan god Hold Nickar, which is, in turn, a symbol of the supernatural womb of the great Virgin-Mother-Goddess.

To reiterate, such customs were, in effect, indoor versions of the great midsummer bonfires (that is, "blessing fires"), which were lit in the fields during the Summer Solstice. Because this was the period when the days began to shorten and the Sun's light and heat began to wane, the object of the fires was to promote the health and longevity of the Sun and prevent it from "dying."

When Yule was absorbed by the orthodox Christian Church, these various beliefs and customs were passed onto Saint Nicholas, who himself became "Kriss Kringle," the "father of the Yuletide season."

We will add here that the cookies and milk customarily left out for Santa Claus in modern Western homes on Christmas Eve, is a Pagan remnant of the propitiatory meal used to mollify the demons associated with the ancient celebration of Yule.

Of special interest to us is the Pagan hearth spirit who was believed by ancient people to travel down from Heaven to visit humanity. Arriving during the Winter Solstice, he distributed rewards and punishments as he flitted from house to house. In his bright red jacket and conical red cap, this Yuletide fire-deity would fly down the chimney and leave presents for all the members of each family. To prepare for the arrival of the hearth-god, the chimney was swept and cleaned each December (a custom still very much alive in various parts of modern-day Europe).

It was in Medieval Europe that this odd fire-spirit and his annual act of boon-giving were incorporated into the figure of Saint Nicholas.

28

PASQUA EPIPHANIA, MARS, AND SAINT MARTIN: PAGAN ITALIAN CONTRIBUTIONS

W HEN THE CULT of Saint Nicholas passed through Italy in the 10th Century, it assimilated another Pagan deity. This was the gift-dispensing goddess called Pasqua Epiphania ("Passover/ Easter Manifestation"), also known as Befan (the "Grandmother").

According to legend Pasqua Epiphania stuffed the stockings of all good children with presents each year. When this ritual was eventually combined with the solstitial rites of the Yule hearth-spirit, youngsters naturally began hanging their stockings over the fireplace, another Pagan practice gradually infused onto the Saint Nicholas legend.

In Italy the Christian saint absorbed still yet another Pagan divinity. This was the Roman god of war Mars,[233] the deity from which the month of March takes its name, to whom the Martial arts were once devoted, and from whom the word martyr derives. Mars himself originated in ancient Latium as the savior-god Maris, an Etruscan fertility and sacrificial deity.[234]

Like Woden, the Germanic god of war and the dead, the later Romanized version, Mars, was believed to ride across the sky on a white horse of death, an aspect of his yearly ritual in which he ushered in the rebirth of the Spring season.

During the Martinalia festival, Mars was sacrificed in the form of an ox called the "Mart-beast," a ritual symbolizing the renewal of the New Year, which in ancient Rome began on March 1, or in some periods, in late March at or around the Spring Equinox (under the Greek zodiacal sign Aries).

In the process of adopting the Pagan Pantheon, the early Church Fathers utilized the figure of Mars in the creation of the fictional "Saint Martin," or "Martin of Tours," as he is sometimes known. As with Nicholas, a detailed biography was fabricated for Martin, replete with the usual types of miracles so often attributed to invented saints.

In keeping with Mars' image as a battle-deity, Saint Martin was given a militaristic background. Said to have been born to a Pagan army officer around 316, in Sabaria, Pannonia (Hungary), he was converted to Christianity when he had a "vision of Christ" while serving on a military assignment in Amiens, France.

After being discharged for refusing to either fight or bear arms, Saint Martin went on a zealous mission in which he violently annihilated Pagan temples, then ruthlessly converted their former members to the Holy Cross. Possessed with psychic powers and the ability to see visions, he could predict the future as well as perform supernatural feats to save himself from his enemies. Pure Paganism.[235]

In their assimilation of the aggressive Roman deity Mars, the Church Fathers also adopted his Martinalia festival and its accompanying ox-killing ritual. This Pagan Spring celebration was moved to November 11 and renamed "Martinmas," or "Saint Martin's Day."

While the conventional Catholic biography of Martin asserts that he died a natural death on November 8, 399, in Touraine, France, other traditions hold that he was martyred. Indeed, the Pagan sacrificial ritual of Mars was so deeply loved by the populace that the Christian saint who was later developed around him also inevitably came to be associated with the Martinalian oxen rites.

Thus, one ancient legend states that Saint Martin had been killed by "heathens," then "cut up and eaten in the form of an ox," just as had annually occurred with the Mart-beast in ancient Pagan Ireland. The ritual, however, was softened after its adoption by the Church. Henceforth, the entire general populace engaged in the killing of a domestic animal, then sprinkled the threshold of their homes with its blood, all in the name of the "martyr," Saint Martin.[236]

The figure of Saint Martin also has affinities with Mars' northern European counterpart, the Saxon creator-father-god Tiw. Tiw's weekly holy day was called, in Old English, *Tiwesdæg*; or in modern English, "Tuesday," our third day of the week.

As its name suggests, the modern Mardi Gras (French for "Fat Tuesday") is a Christian remnant of Mars' ancient annual celebration, the Martinalia. In modern France the name of the third day of the week still bears the Roman stamp of its earlier Pagan incarnation as *Dies Martis*, or "Mar's Day." In fact, *Mardi* is the French word for Tuesday.

In early northern Germany Tiw was known as *Things*, since a special law-making meeting called *Thing* was held on "Thing-Day," that is, Tuesday. It is from Thing-Day that the German word for Tuesday, *Dienstag*, derives. Accordingly, 3rd-Century Britons referred to the god Tiw as *Mars Thincsus*.

Over the centuries various legendary aspects of Martin naturally came to be confused and combined with Nicholas. For both saints were said to be "destroyers of Pagan temples," both were humanitarians,[237] and both were derived from Pagan deities (Nicholas from Woden, Martin from Mars) who rode through the ancient night skies as savior-gods.

22

THE CHILDREN'S HOLIDAY AND SINTERKLASS: DUTCH CONTRIBUTIONS

THE CULT OF Saint Nicholas finally found its way to the Netherlands in the late Medieval period. The christianized Dutch found this bizarre character and his strangely Christ-like attributes highly appealing.

It so happened that a popular Dutch holiday for children fell on December 6, the same day on which the Church Fathers said Saint Nicholas had been born. It was only natural then that the Woden-like legend of Saint Nicholas riding across snow-clad housetops on a "great white horse" dispensing gifts on the eve of the Winter Solstice, was eventually combined with this children's holiday.

That night, December 5, was then called "Saint Nicholas Eve." Here, the idea of Saint Nicholas giving presents to children was born, and, inevitably, he became the patron saint of children.

It was, in fact, the Dutch who were directly responsible for inaugurating that icon so peculiar to the United States: "Santa Claus." When the Dutch began immigrating to the Americas in large numbers in the 17th and 18th Centuries, it was they who first brought the legend and Cult of Saint Nicholas across the Atlantic from Europe. By now, however, the mythic figure had lost much of his former windswept, rugged Nordic glory, for the Dutch saw Saint Nicholas as lean, tall, and graceful.

His name had changed as well. The English "Saint Nicholas" became, in Dutch, "Sint Nikolass," a name, which over time, was corrupted by English-speaking Americans into "Sint Klass," or, more commonly, "Sinterklass." By the late 19th Century this had corroded further, becoming the well-known "Santa Claus."

Along with this adaptation the Dutch children's holiday of December 6 was transferred to December 25, the "birthday of Jesus," by Americans of British descent. The feast day of Saint Nicholas, however, is still celebrated by the Catholic masses on December 6, while in the Netherlands this day remains a children's holiday and continues to be observed as "Saint Nicholas Day," the time for giving and receiving gifts.

PART THREE

MODERN
CONTRIBUTIONS

30

RUDOLPH THE RED~NOSED REINDEER AND THE SPIRIT OF CHRISTMAS: AMERICAN CONTRIBUTIONS

THE FINAL TOUCHES to the Saint Nicholas/Santa Claus legend were added in the early 19th Century when American author Washington Irving (1783-1859) re-described the Dutch version of Santa Claus as a "bulky man who smoked a pipe and wore baggy pants."

Not long after, in 1822, educator and poet, Clement Clarke Moore (1779-1863), wrote his poem *A Visit From St. Nicholas*. The famous composition, which began, "T'was the night before Christmas," caught the imagination of the German-born, Left-wing U.S. cartoonist Thomas Nast (1840-1902).[238] When Nast illustrated the poem between 1863 and 1886, he portrayed Moore's Saint Nicholas as a kindly, rotund, white-bearded old man—somewhat similar, in fact, to the original Nordic creator-god Odin—an image that has remained popular in the West to this day.[239]

All that was left was to create a marketing gimmick for Santa Claus, one suitable for a 20th-Century capitalistic economy. The contrivance was not long in coming.

In 1939, the legend of Santa Claus absorbed "Rudolph the red-nosed reindeer" from the U.S. store-chain Montgomery Ward. It was here that the ingenious marketing idea of turning Thor's bucks into reindeer was engineered. Cracker and Gnasher became "Dancer" and "Prancer," who, along with a host of other reindeer, were now led by Rudolph, himself guided by the light of his own red nose.

Along with these changes, Thor's chariot was eventually transformed into a sleigh, and the Nordic Santa's home became, naturally, the North Pole.

Having developed over countless millennia from out of a wild assortment of various Pagan deities, the gift-giving patron saint of sailors, scholars, and children was now complete. At last fully christianized, Santa Claus had become an acceptable addition to Christmas across the Western world.

Yet, despite the incredible popularity of the saint and his yearly Winter Solstice Eve ritual, the overtly Pagan background of both Santa Claus and Christmas has proven too much for some.

Just like the early Puritans, there are individual 21st-Century Amish, Mennonites, Jehovah Witnesses, Mormons, and fundamentalist Christians who refuse to celebrate Christmas.[240] At one time, what was once called the Worldwide Church of God, actually publically repudiated the celebration of Christmas, (correctly) calling Santa Claus a "fictional christianization of a Pagan deity," while (incorrectly) associating him, as Old Nick, with Satan.

Even the Catholic Church today admits that Santa Claus is not a Christian figure. Nonetheless, Santa Claus and the celebration of Christmas are heartily embraced by Catholicism.

Santa Claus' European forefather, Saint Nicholas, however, has not fared so well. For, while Santa Claus is an obvious legendary figure, Saint Nicholas is held up as a historical person. Indeed, for centuries the obvious spurious nature of Nicholas and his many supernatural legends have been a vexation to the Church, which has been trying desperately to improve its negative image as a religious organization that disregards authentic history and objective science. And so, in 1969, the Roman Catholic Church officially removed Saint Nicholas from its Calendar of Saints.

In the final analysis, however, it matters little whether Saint Nicholas or Santa Claus are historical figures or not. In all actuality, they are merely symbols of the positive aspects of human nature; human metaphors for the spirit of goodness which resides in each one of us. Since this wonderful spirit deserves a name, Santa Claus is as good as any other.

31

PAGAN ORIGINS
OF THE YULE LOG

L ET US NOW look briefly at a few of the more significant accouterments of Christmas, beginning with the Yule Log, mistletoe, and holly.

As we have seen, Yule began in the lands of the ancient Nordics as a Pagan fire festival celebrating the rebirth of the Sun at the onset of the Winter Solstice. Hence, the Germanic name-title Kriss Kringle (that is, the "Sun-child"), commonly associated with Yule.

Yet, there are more profound implications surrounding Yule and its many connections to Christmas than this simple description may at first suggest. For a deeper understanding, let us turn once again to etymology.

The word Yule derives from *hweol*, the old Anglo-Saxon word for "wheel." The full significance of this derivation is only understood when we learn that the wheel was an ancient universal symbol of the Sun, which was believed to "roll" across the heavens each day.

The wheel has also long been related to the ideas of fate, time, karma, destiny, and fortune. From such notions arose the archetypal Wheel of Fortune, depicted in ancient Roman art as a mandala-like circle surrounding the hub of the Universe. This "hub" was none other than the pudenda of the great goddess of fate, Fortuna, or Lady Luck, as she was later called.

The manipulation of one's destiny became an occult art when the belief emerged that time could be governed through the use of magic and sacred worship as applied directly to wheels and circles. Through a mystical linkage with the cycles of the Sun, ancient kings were sometimes ritually killed at the end of their reign by being tied to a wooden wheel that was set on fire and rolled down a hill. This act was thought to spiritually cleanse the kingdom, making way for the next ruler, who represented the new earthly incarnation of the reborn sun/son-god.

This same idea was utilized by the ancient Britons, though in a less barbaric manner: up until the 19th Century it was customary for people to roll small fiery wheels down hills in order to rid themselves of bad luck.

These notions eventually became connected with both the Midsummer Solstice festival and the Midwinter Solstice festival, since at these two times the Sun, the "Great Cosmic Wheel of Life," seemed to stop rolling through the heavens.[241]

In late June, to prolong the Sun's forward movement, great circular bonfires were lit at the beginning of the European Midsummer celebrations. To this day, in various parts of Europe, wooden wheels are painted with tar, lit on fire, and rolled down a variety of elevations.

During the ancient Winter Solstice in December, however, the situation reversed itself. At this time, all manner of circular movements were banned. People could not ride in their carts (because of the turning wheels), or even make butter (due to the rotation of the paddle). Why? To prevent the Sun from being frightened—in which case it might "roll backward"—delaying the onset of the coming season of longer, warmer days.

But, on Yule Eve (December 24), wooden "fate-wheels" were once again set ablaze and hurled down the hills in order to encourage the Sun in its rebirth the following morning.

As a form of the newborn Sun-deity, Kriss Kringle—later assimilated to the figures of Saint Nicholas and Santa Claus—was actually a symbol of the dying-and-rising savior-sun-king, popular throughout the

Pagan religions of pre-Christian Europe, Africa, Asia, and the Americas.

The word Kriss, of course, is rooted in the old Chaldean word *Chris*, the name of the Chaldees' sun-god, the star which the ancient Jews spelled *heres,* or (without syllables) *hrs.* As we will recall, this word melded into the ancient Greek world as *Christos,* meaning "anointed," where it is found today in English translations of the Bible as "Christ," literally, the sun-god, mystical symbol of spiritual enlightenment. Thus, Kriss Kringle was none other than Chris Kringle; literally, Christ the "sun-child."[242]

An integral aspect of the observance of Yule was the burning of the Yule Log, whose warmth and light was believed to aid the infant sun-god Kriss Kringle in his birth. Today, in various regions of Europe, this ancient belief has translated into the notion that the ashen remains of the Yule Log, or Christbrand ("Sun-torch"), as it is sometimes called, are magical.[243] Indeed, many still believe these ashes have the power to protect homes and barns from lightning and fire, while guarding people and livestock against disease and malevolent spirits.

Just as significant is the Yule Log's ancient association with fertility. As the log has long been regarded as a phallic symbol, it is only natural that the heat which it gives off when burned eventually came to be mystically related to the "heat" generated by the act of procreation. In France, after this holy piece of fertility wood, called the "Noel log," was burned on Christmas Day, its ashes were combined with the dung of livestock to aid them in the birthing process.

This belief lives on today in places like modern Albania, where the ashes of the Yule Log are still sprinkled about the fields in order to make the soil as fertile as possible.

32

Pagan Origins
Of Mistletoe

SUCH ANCIENT PAGAN ideas of fertility also led to the use of both mistletoe, a symbol of the Male Principle, and holly, a symbol of the Female Principle. Both not only remain green throughout the year, but both bear fruit during the Winter season, lending them an aura of eternal vitality, divine fecundity, and supernatural sacrality.

In the Middle Ages mistletoe was believed to possess all manner of miraculous powers, hence its Medieval name, "All-heal." When dried, the leaves of mistletoe turn gold, another trait which provoked the ancient mind to see the plant as possessing magical powers; in this case, the powers of alchemy.

Mistletoe once had mystical associations with another magical plant, the oak. Being a semi-parasitic green shrub, mistletoe often grows on and around the oak tree, and thus seldom touches the ground. Due to this curious trait, mistletoe was thought to be a gift of the deities, since it seemed to magically connect Heaven and Earth.

As a "celestial" plant, mistletoe came to be seen as a symbol of the mystical link between humanity and the Divine, and hence was regarded by the ancients as the most spiritual of all plants. Indeed, one of the names of the Babylonian savior-god Tammuz was the "Mistletoe Branch," aptly revealing mistletoe's early links with savior astrotheology and the concepts of spiritual rebirth and redemption.[244]

Its parasitic life amid oak trees made mistletoe a natural object of worship in the great oak cults of antiquity, which date back to at least the 2nd Millennium BC, where it is found among ancient Pagans[245] and biblical Jews.[246] The intimate connection between these two highly sacred plants can be seen in the belief that mistletoe was the symbolic genitalia of the oak tree. This was no doubt due to the fact that the white berries of the mistletoe were viewed as the sacred drops of semen of the great oak-god himself.

The sacrality of the oak derives from various sources. First, there was the popular notion that its fruits, or "nuts," were mystical symbols of the male testes, the magical orbs which contained the "seeds of life." There was also the ancient belief that fire and lightning-deities, like Thor, Zeus, and Jupiter, made their homes in the oak, a belief that sprang from the fact that this particular tree tends to draw lightning to itself.

In addition, due to its astonishing durability, the oak, like the mistletoe which grows on it, was regarded as "immortal." This, along with its straight majestic form and the hardness of its wood, made the oak a fitting symbol of divine masculinity, strength, heroism, and steadfastness. It was for this reason too that the wreaths worn by the ancient victors of combat and political races were often woven using the foliage of the oak.

At the religious services of the oak cults, particularly popular among the Druids, the supreme oak-deity was worshiped in a series of orgiastic and sacrificial rites. Some 2,000 years ago the ancient Roman author Pliny the Elder described the manner in which the Druids viewed this sacred tree and its mystical companion mistletoe:

> For they believe that whatever grows on these trees is sent from heaven, and is a sign that the tree has been chosen by the gods themselves. The mistletoe is very rarely to be met with; but when it is found, they gather it with solemn ceremony. This they do above all on the sixth day of the moon, from whence they date the beginnings of their months, of their years, and of their thirty years cycle, because by the sixth day the moon has plenty of vigor and has not run half its course.
>
> After due preparations have been made for a sacrifice and a feast under

the tree, they hail it as the universal healer and bring to the spot two white bulls, whose horns have never been bound before. A priest clad in a white robe climbs the tree and with a golden sickle cuts the mistletoe, which is caught in a white cloth. Then they sacrifice the victims, praying that the gods will make their gifts propitious to those to whom they have given it.

They believe that a potion prepared from the mistletoe will make barren animals to bring forth, and that the plant is a remedy against all poisons.[247]

Mistletoe's year round greenery and fertility characteristics made it an ideal icon for the Pagan dying-and-rising saviors of Medieval Europe, who themselves, like the earlier Tammuz, symbolized hope, rebirth, fruitfulness, and eternal life.

Chief among these was the Nordic Pagan savior Balder, son of the creator-god Odin. According to legend, Balder (symbol of the "World-Soul" or messiah archetype) was killed by an arrow made from mistletoe, after which he was expected to return from death to lead his believers in the establishment of a new kingdom of eternal joy and harmony.

Mystically speaking, the death of Balder from the fatal mistletoe arrow represents the germination of new life on the spiritual plane. Or, put another way, the shedding of the savior's blood is meant to cleanse and revitalize the "soul of humanity," hence the ancient custom of killing earthly rulers at the end of their reigns.

This Pagan belief was notably embodied in a particularly gruesome ritual called "the king must die": after being sexually defiled by the chief temple priestess in the New Year fertility ceremony, the king was shot through the heart with an arrow wrapped in mistletoe. He was then dismembered and his body parts were plowed into the fields to revitalize the soil for the Spring planting.

With such ceremonies and myths attached to the mistletoe plant, it is hardly surprising that the Saxon word mistletoe has deeply arcane Indo-European roots, indicating that it was also once directly related to religious sexual rituals. The element *mis* seems to derive from the Sanskrit word *mas*, meaning "messiah"; *el* is, as we have seen, a Semitic word meaning "deity"; while the element *toe* may be a derivation of the Sanskrit word *tal*, meaning a "pit," a universal symbol of the Earth-Goddess' womb.

Such etymological associations would indicate that mistletoe, and its white "semen-drop" berries, were once utilized as symbolic props in sacred ceremonies connected with both the Holy Marriage (Hieros Gamos) of the sun-god and the moon-goddess, and with orgiastic fertility rites. (In mystical Christianity the Hieros Gamos is an inner *spiritual* experience in which the Lower Self becomes one with the Higher Self.)[248] The traditional "kiss beneath the mistletoe" is a remnant of not only the old Pagan redemption ceremonies enacted between the deities and humanity, but also with the orgies once affiliated with the Cult of the Oak.

33

Pagan Origins Of Holly

HOLLY, ANOTHER "TRADITIONAL" Christmas accouterment, was used in these same rituals. Its red berries were regarded as the menstrual blood of Goddess, the sacred fluid of life. The berries of the holly plant, symbols of vitality and rebirth, were used by the Druids and other Pagans in combination with the white berries of mistletoe, symbols of death. As such, both holly and mistletoe became associated with Yule, the Pagan midwinter festival dedicated to the "birth" or "rebirth" of the Sun, which was believed to have "died" six months earlier at the Summer Solstice.

As a perennial plant, holly, like mistletoe and pine trees, remains green throughout the Winter months when the foliage of other vegetation turns color and "dies."[249] Hence its name "holly," a derivation of the Middle English word *holi*, meaning "holy" or "sanctified."

The sacredness of holly can also be seen in its etymological connection with the Old English word *hol*, in modern English, hole. Just as we find in the affiliation of "pit" with mistletoe, the "hole" association with holly indicates to us that holly too was once an aspect of the sacred worship of the yoni of Goddess. Indeed, the hole has long been an archetypal symbol of the vulva, a common feminine motif in the literature, art, and religions of cultures around the world.

Just as significantly, in ancient times holly was once under the matronship of Holle (also known as Hol, Hilde, or Hella), the Teutonic underworld-goddess of Hell, who governed the naming of newborn children (*Hölle* is the German word for "Hell"). It was during Holle's infant initiation rites that a hellish (in German, *höllisch*) scream (in German, *krieschen*) was let loose in order to impress a new soul into the child. This rite was carried over into Christianity as the Hollekriesch baptismal formula in Germany.

The leaves, berries, and particularly the wood of the holly plant, have all been regarded as preventatives against disease, spells, bad magic, and lightning, and also as bringers of good fortune. Not surprisingly, entire forested regions where holly grew were once believed to be the shrines of various divine beings, hence their popular name, the "Holy Wood," or as they would later be called, "Hollywood."[250]

Holly's small size, attractive pointed leaves, colorful berries, and overt sexual symbolism, made it a convenient and popular household decoration. During Yule ancient Pagans hung it, along with its symbolic male counterpart, mistletoe, in their doorways and windows. Naturally, the early Catholic Church saw the use of holly as a "heathen custom" and banned its use as a Christmas decoration.

Nonetheless, like so many other aspects of Christmas, the orthodox Fathers found it impossible to stamp out the practice, and it continues to be an integral facet of the celebration of Jesus' birth among Catholics and Protestants to this day.

34

Ancient Tree Cults And The Savior Osiris: Pagan Origins Of The Christmas Tree

L ET US NOW look briefly at a few of the other Pagan trappings adopted by Christians over the centuries for use in the celebration of Christmas.

One of the more "traditional" Christmas motifs is the Christmas Tree, or Christmas Evergreen. The practice of cutting trees and decorating them in honor of a savior-deity, however, is not original with Christianity. It is, of course, of pre-Christian Pagan origins, as the Old Testament's anti-Christmas tree God, Yahweh, states:

> Thus saith the Lord, Learn not the way of the heathen. . . . For the customs of the people are vain: for one cutteth a tree out of the forest, the work of the hands of the workman, with the ax. They deck it with silver and with gold they fasten it with nails and with hammers, that it move not. [251]

This passage, from the book of Jeremiah, reveals what comparative mythologists have long known: today's "Christmas tree" is actually a remnant of early Pagan tree cults and nature religions. What is more, the religious practice of tree decorating was already widespread in the Middle East by the 6th Century BC, the time in which Jeremiah was composed. The custom, however, arose from even older cultures, dating back to the Bronze Age.

Many thousands of years before the rise of Christianity, it was the custom not only to worship trees, but to sacrifice specially selected men, women, and children on trees in order to appease a particular tree-deity.

By the advent of the Graeco-Roman period, the tree and its mystical symbol, the World Tree, had been stylized, producing the form of the simple (Latin) cross so well-known today. Rather than having to travel to the sacred grove, the Holy Wood, this portable cross now enabled sacrifices and religious services to be carried out at the convenience of the worshipers.

Thus began the great period of the immolation of saviors on tree-crosses, in which many an innocent victim, or scapegoat, was crucified for the sins of the community. The religious myths of this phase are permeated with legends of savior-gods—such as the Phrygian Attis, the Greek Prometheus, the Nordic Odin, the Hindu Chrishna, and the Judeo-Christian Jesus—who were said to have been crucified on trees.[252] Hence in death, all sacrificed saviors wore the foliage crown of the honored tree-deity.[253]

What caused the ancients to hold trees in such sacred esteem?

The worship of trees stems from the early agrarian cultures of prehistory, which saw in trees the embodiment of the great, all nourishing Mother-Goddess. For trees offered protection from wild animals, cold, rain, wind, and Sun, supplied kindling for cooking fires, and pitch and rubber for sealing baskets and pottery. They furnished wood for the building of homes, shrines, and temples, and for the construction of weapons, canoes, and carts. Their foliage was used for making beds and pillows, and their branches harbored various high-protein prey items, such as insects, birds, and small mammals, much sought after by early hunters.

The tree itself supplied nourishment in the form of sap (for sweetening), water (for sustenance), leaves (for teas), and sundry fruits such as apples, bananas, walnuts, olives, oranges, avocados, coconuts, and berries.

In addition, trees, with their aromatic splendor and physical beauty, fulfilled the aesthetic sense and, by acting as trail markers, helped define the landscape of a particular region, as well as the territorial parameters of a tribe or people.

Lastly, with their thick, spreading ground roots, contoured trunks, outstretched branches, and leafy crowns, trees possess the vague shape of a human being. From time immemorial these characteristics have made trees the ideal symbol of the all-nurturing Mother-Goddess who "gave birth to the Universe and all sentient beings."

It was natural that the primitive mother-tree motif eventually gave way to the more complex Tree of Life concept, and the accompanying belief that the sacred World Tree contained the very life force of the Cosmos itself. Its roots descended to the bowels of the Earth, the place of demons and the Underworld, while its branches touched the sky, the place of beneficent deities and Heaven.

The Tree of Life figures predominately in the sacred literature and legends of ancient peoples, though it is best known to Westerners through its appearances in the myths and writings of the early biblical Jews.[254] Most notable is the role of the Pagan Tree of Life in the Hebrew Creation legend as found in the book of Genesis.[255]

Identical images of Goddess standing next to the Tree of Life appeared not only all across the Near East, but over the entire Aegean world. In many of these Pagan portrayals the Tree is shown surrounded by a fructifying fountain of water, a symbol of Goddess' life-giving love.

Christianity, too, eventually adopted the imagery of the "archaic and universally disseminated symbol," the World Tree, from the Pagans and Jews in the early centuries of the Christian Era. As other religions had done before them, the storytellers and myth-makers of the Church imposed their own values and agendas on the Pagan idea of the Cosmic Tree. Jesus' cross itself was now said to have been made of the wood of the Genesaic Tree of Good and Evil. Such crass literalizations were designed for the non-literate orthodox masses.

On a mystical level Christianity's assimilation of the Tree of Life concept still retained its overt Paganistic elements, all derived from the once reviled religions of pre-Christian "heathens." The Church could ill afford to disregard such a powerful sacred symbol of salvation, renewal, regeneration, resurrection, fertility, and immortality, as the Pagans' World Tree.

When the practice of sacrificing humans on trees began to lose its grisly appeal, small effigies were hung on trees in their place. Among the trees held to be most appropriate for this ritual were the evergreens, which, like the laurel, mistletoe, and holly, retained their vibrant color and vigor throughout the year. Hence, as a tree possessing the "seeds of immortality," the sacred evergreen soon became the center of great fertility cults and sacrificial rituals.

In pre-Christian Phrygia, for example, there were priests known as the Dendrophori ("tree-bearers"), who served under the savior-god Attis, said to have been born on December 25 to the virgin-mother Nana. Once a year, on the Spring Equinox, March 22, one of the priests' most important functions was to carefully choose and cut an evergreen from the Sacred Grove and carry it to Attis' temple. Here, they would decorate it in preparation for his great sacrificial rite, one in which he was to be nailed to the tree for the salvation of humanity.

Three days later, on March 25, after a harrowing journey to the Underworld, Attis would rise from the dead as the "Resurrected Son," whereupon his followers would partake of his body in the form of bread.

In ancient Egypt, deities themselves were said to have been born of trees. Osiris, for example, was birthed under a kesbet tree, Re or Ra came from a sycamore tree, Horus sprang from an acacia, and Wepwawet came from a tamarisk tree. It was here, in fact, in Egypt, that the Christmas tree, as it is known today, was derived.

As in other early cultures, the Egyptians identified young trees with the newborn sun-god, one of the many reasons trees played an important role in their religious myths. The origins of this connection are to be found in the 4,000 year-old legend of the great Egyptian savior-god Osiris.

According to Osirian mythology, the great deity was cut into thirteen pieces (one for each of the thirteen 28-day lunar months)[256] and locked in a coffer by his jealous brother, Set (who became the biblical Seth),[257] then cast adrift on the Nile River. Osiris' grieving widow, the great mother-goddess Isis, was beside herself, for not only had she lost her husband, but she had just given birth to his son, the divine child and savior Horus.

As time passed, Osiris' coffer floated down the Nile and out into the Mediterranean Sea, where it at last came to rest on the Phoenician coast. As it lay in the sand a tree grew up around it, eventually completely enclosing the chest in its writhing branches.

One day a rich man happened by. Appreciating the tree's beauty, he had it cut down and carved into a pillar, which he then had placed in his palace at Byblus (present-day Jubayl, Lebanon).

When Isis came to the city in search of her husband's body, she sensed his presence in the tree and split it open. Osiris' body parts spilled out. A joyous Isis gave the pillar to the King of Byblus as a gift, who later set it up in Isis' own temple. Here, the sacred tree-pillar was venerated by the people for many generations.

Soon, however, the magic pillar began to take root and grow. Isis, aware now of the sacred powers of the sprouting tree, brought the various pieces of Osiris' body to its base on the holy day of the Sun's rebirth, December 25, and breathed into his mouth. The magic ritual succeeded: the body of Osiris was reformed and he was brought back from the dead—though much to Isis' chagrin, her husband's penis had been eaten by a fish named Abtu.

It was from this period, the dawn of the Cult of Osiris, that among Near Eastern religions, trees came to be intimately connected with both the Pagan Winter Solstice festival and the rebirth of the sun-god, or son-god, as he was also called.

Yet, the pine tree of the Osirian myth was venerated for something far more important than merely as a sacred tree. The stump-pillar and the tree which grew from it were regarded as magic phallic symbols, closely linked to the Egyptian savior, whose missing reproductive member was revitalized each December 25 in the decoration and worship of the evergreen.

One of the images used in these rituals was a fish. Not just any fish, but one already mentioned: Abtu ("Abyss"), who also went by the title "The Fish of Isis." Here, in occultic form, we have the fulfillment of the sacred sexual union (Hieros Gamos) between the Earth-Mother-Goddess (Isis) and the Sky-Father-God (Osiris). For the "abyss," like the "hole," has long been a symbol of the female sexual orifice, as has been the fish (for obvious reasons). The pine tree, with its conical phallic shape, made up the other half of the holy ritual, completing the cosmic pairing of the Divine Feminine and the Divine Masculine.

Thus, it was on December 25 that in honor of the resurrection of Osiris, his followers cut down an evergreen and hollowed it out. From the woody refuse they formed a sculpture of the corpse of Osiris, then "buried" it back in the hollowed-out center of the tree. This icon was maintained for the following year, after which it was carried to the sacred Egyptian town of Denderah (related to the ancient Greek word *dendron*, "tree") to be burned in the Sacred Hall of Osiris.

In fact, many ancient Egyptian cities, such as Mendes, Philae, Abydos, and Busiris, possessed a tomb of Osiris (in reality, a symbol of Isis' womb or vulva). Commonly, not far from the sarcophagus, followers planted a tree, a symbol that the great Father-God had been resurrected into eternity.

Here then, in the pre-Christian Pagan myth of the Egyptian savior Osiris, as well as in his immortal phallic pine tree, we have the roots of the modern Christmas tree.

There were many more additions and developments to come, however.

35

DEVELOPMENT OF THE CHRISTMAS TREE IN THE MEDIEVAL PERIOD

FROM ANCIENT EGYPT the Cult of Osiris and the accompanying practice of venerating evergreens on December 25 was carried into the Graeco-Roman world during the 1st Century BC. The Pagan Romans took quickly to evergreen worship. Every year on the Winter Solstice a fir was cut from the local sacred pine grove and placed in the Temple, where it was decorated with small effigies, figures, and fetishes. These symbolized the many sacrificial deities, sun/son-gods, and resurrected saviors of the Roman Pantheon.

The Romans also hung toys and trinkets on the Winter Solstice evergreen, while those of the Druidic religion tied apples decorated with gold to its branches. To many early Pagan sun-worshipers the little balls and apples which were draped on the solstice fir pine were representations of the male testes, the female breasts, and other erotic "fruits of love," while the gilded shining apples symbolized the golden halo of the savior-sun-god—as we have observed, an occult emblem of the Crown Chakra (spiritual enlightenment). One of these sun-gods was Apollo ("manly" beauty), whose masculine name has distant affinities with the solaristic word apple, or *apol*, as it was spelled in Old Europe.[258]

At the top of their evergreen trees the ancients placed images of the virgin-mother-goddess Virgo, a hopeful reminder of the warm days of Spring that lie ahead, and of the coming "resurrection" of her savior-son. Depicted in ancient art with angel-like wings, Virgo's name also means "sprig" or "sprout," references to her in her form as a Spring-goddess who survives the "death" of the Winter Solstice and is "reborn," like Jesus, at the Spring Equinox (Easter/Passover). The traditional "angel" placed on top of the modern Christmas tree is the modern Christian descendant of this ancient Pagan custom.[259]

These practices were carried from the Graeco-Roman world into Medieval Europe where the Scandinavians, Germans, and others added their own peculiar beliefs and rituals to the evergreen traditions of Yule.

It was here, according to Christian legend, that the German Reformationist leader Martin Luther (1483-1546) became the first to decorate the December tannenbaum (German for "fir tree") with lighted candles. Allegedly these were meant to represent the stars which shone over Bethlehem on the night of Jesus' birth.

Another legend, however, offers a more realistic view of how Luther came to be "the first man ever to decorate a Christmas tree."

One Winter's night, while walking home through a pine grove, he looked up and glimpsed a wondrous image: the twinkling of stars dancing about in the boughs of the evergreens above. He was so moved that he decided there and then to try and recreate the delightful sight in his home. This story has a ring of truth to it lacking in the traditional version.

Still, we can hardly expect that Luther, a fervent anti-Catholic, would have celebrated the Christian version of Christmas, a wholly Catholic creation. For the same reason it is impossible to accept that he would have invented a practice so closely associated with Catholicism and its overtly Pagan customs.

Indeed, as we will shortly discover, the tradition of trimming the tree with lights derives from a far earlier era when Pagan Romans decorated their sacred evergreens with gold, silver, fruits, effigies, small globes, and phallic candles, in honor of the "Mother-goddess of Light," Juno Lucina.

The legend of Luther and the "first lighted Christmas tree" is further weakened by historical records themselves. These reveal that while

Germans were celebrating Christmas with indoor fir trees as early as 1605, it was not until the year 1737 that the first use of candles on such trees was chronicled (again, in Germany).

It was not until the middle of the 19th Century that the "Christmas tree," as it was now called in central Christian Europe, found its way from Germany to English-speaking countries.

This was due to the efforts of Prince Albert (1819-1861), who brought the custom, a product of ancient Pagan tree worship, from his native Germany to England when he married the queen of Great Britain, Victoria (1819-1901), in 1840.[260] His placing of a pine tree in Windsor Castle for the first time made quite a stir, and set an international trend that would carry far and wide.

With Thomas Edison's (1847-1931) invention of the incandescent, carbon-filament light bulb in 1879,[261] it was only a matter of time before these small glittering lights replaced candles on Christmas trees. By 1895 the White House in Washington, D.C. was trimming its trees with electric lights.

With these developments, the evergreen tree, a truly archaic and universal symbol of hope and eternal life, has remained an intrinsic aspect of the Western Christian holy day, Christmas, ever since.

36

GREETINGS, PLUM PUDDING, THE CHRISTMAS WREATH, AND MINCE PIE

A **MYRIAD OF OTHER** Christmas customs have come down to us as "traditions" of this Christian holiday. Yet again, on closer examination we find that these so-called "conventional" accouterments all derive from pre-Christian sources.

The traditional greeting "Merry Christmas," for example, is actually a remnant of the days when December 25 was celebrated in ancient Rome as the Brumalia, the final day of the orgiastic Saturnalia festival, held from December 17 to December 24. The great quantities of alcohol that were consumed, and the wanton debauchery that took place during this Winter Solstice celebration indeed made it a "merry" Pagan holy day.

We also have the traditional plum pudding, long associated with Christmas and Christianity. Yet, with its round, reddish, flaming shape, there can be little doubt that it began long ago as a Pagan Sun symbol.

The Christmas wreath and the Christmas garland are also said to be of Christian origin. Indeed, tradition holds that the custom of the Christmas wreath derives from the fact that Christ's crown of thorns was made of holly.

Actually, as noted earlier, the "crown of thorns" motif is itself (as is the use of holly) of pre-Christian Pagan origins: to the Pagan mystics of Graeco-Roman times, the crown was a symbol of the final achievement of spiritual enlightenment, long associated with solar theology and solar symbology. As their circular shapes suggest, both wreaths and garlands were once regarded as Sun symbols, symbols that entered mainstream Christianity very early on. [262]

Both have even earlier Pagan roots as vulva symbols of the great Mother-Goddess: during both fertility rites and Sacred Marriage ceremonies (the Hieros Gamos), a garland or wreath was placed over the top of the temple pillar (the phallic "Rock") symbolizing the mating of the Earth Mother with the Heavenly Father. [263]

The mince pie, now an accepted Christmas dessert, was once condemned by the early Church since it was then well-known to be a derivation of the consecration cakes used in the Winter Solstice sacraments of the early Pagans. This is why, as late as the 18th Century, the Christmas-loathing New England Puritans forbade the making of this popular treat.

The problem surrounded the fact that in earlier Pagan times, consecration cakes, the forerunners of the mince pie, were made in casings that were shaped like coffins. This idea was borrowed from the ancient Egyptian custom of baking coffin-shaped pastries of Osiris, which were eaten by banquet goers during Winter Solstice festivities.

Despite the overt "heathen roots" of the mince pie, the inherent love of Pagan religion and ritual proved too powerful even for the orthodox Christian Church. Today, the eating of mince pies at Christmas time remains as popular among both Catholics and Protestants as it once was in Pagan Rome.

37

DRINKS, NUTS, BOAR'S HEAD, AND GIFT-GIVING

THE HOT CIDER or mead drink consumed at the Christmas dinner too has deep roots connected with Paganism's Birthday of the Sun. Cider is made from the apple, long a holy symbol of Goddess; for when horizontally cut, the core of the apple reveals a five-pointed star—the sacred pentacle—itself a Pagan symbol of the human form and of the Life Force, both gifts of the Great Mother.[264] Thus it is that cider is one of the "nectars of the gods," appropriately imbibed on December 25, the day of the sun-god's rebirth.

Eggnog, originally only used by the English upper class (eggs and milk were once rare and expensive), is a relative newcomer to the world of traditional Christmas drinks. But its many associations with the pre-Christian religions of the archetypal dying-and-rising sun-god make it a natural fit.

The egg is not only a universal symbol of fertility (physical and spiritual), but it is also an emblem of the *prima materia*, "original matter." Thus the "World Egg" appears in numerous ancient creation myths, for from it hatched the earth and all living creatures. The World Egg is a macrocosm of the hen's egg, which became the Easter Egg, a symbol of the Spring-Goddess Eostre, who rules the period when the Sun-God emerges from the grave to begin the Pagan New Year (Spring Equinox).

This makes the egg the ultimate Christian symbol of resurrection: the egg white symbolizing purity and perfection (Jesus), the egg yolk symbolizing the golden sun (Christ).   Thus the Cosmic Egg commemorates the rebirth of the sun-god/son-god who "dies" at the Summer Equinox (Midsummer), "visits" the dark Underworld at the Autumnal Equinox (Halloween), begins to "rise" from Hell at the Winter Solstice (Christmas), and is "born again" on March 21, the first day of the astrological sign Aries (Easter).

Nuts, now a conventional Christmas food, began in earlier times as staples of Pagan orgies and feasts. Nuts are steeped in Pagan symbolism, much of it surrounding sexuality and fecundity. Such beliefs certainly arose from the astonishing potency of the small hard-shelled fruit which enables them to produce trees such as the enormous, nearly indestructible oak.

Nuts also possess visual sexual symbolism. Walnuts, for instance, resemble the human testes and so were widely regarded as a male potency talisman—hence the slang word "nuts," still in use to this day, to describe these two male reproductive glands.

Almonds, with their vulva-like oval shape, were believed to carry the efficacious magic of Goddess and all feminine powers (hence, the Vesica Piscis), and so were used as a female fertility amulet.

Over time the nut, which was both a consumable and a seed, naturally came to be viewed as an aphrodisiac. Few foods then were more fitting for the December 25 Yule festival—which featured Pagan orgies in honor of the rebirth of the Sun's life force—than nuts.

The boar's head, a staple of Christmas dinners around the world for centuries, comes down to us as an aspect of early Pagan solar theology. From ancient Egypt and Scandinavia, to ancient Rome and Britain, the wild boar, with his "round head and golden bristles," was considered a mystical Sun symbol.

The wild pig appeared in the myths of the early Saxons and Greeks, and was annually sacrificed at the Winter Solstice festival all across the Indo-European world. This was chiefly to placate the sun-god, who, according to one of the more common myths, died from a wound inflicted by a boar's tusk.

The custom of gift-giving on Christmas arose in part, as we have seen, from various Pagan sources such as the Saxon-Frankish savior-god Woden and the Italian boon-giving goddess Pasqua Epiphania. The practice is, in fact, of great antiquity, having originally begun with the early Romans, who exchanged good-luck presents with one another during the Winter Solstice festival.

The 4th-Century Greek writer, Libanius, describes the gift-giving frenzy that accompanied the Pagan Saturnalia and Brumalia festivities:

> The impulse to spend seizes everyone. He who through the whole year has taken pleasure in saving . . . becomes suddenly extravagant. . . . A stream of presents pours itself out on all sides.

The Christmas tradition of wrapping gifts in boxes is linked to both the sacred pine tree and the Winter Solstice. In ancient times a "Christmas box" was itself a gift, for the word box comes from the Greek word *pyxos*, meaning both a box tree (a type of evergreen) and a receptacle or container (into which a present is placed). The Bible records the practice among the Hebrews as early as 700 BC, when Isaiah says:

> I will set in the desert the fir tree, and the pine, and the box tree together.[265]

Boxing Day, celebrated the first weekday after Christmas, is still observed across the United Kingdom, Canada, and Australia (among other nations). Here, boxes containing various items such as candies, fruits, and nuts (as we have seen, all rooted in ancient Paganistic Winter Solstice customs), are given to those in the service industry, including mail carriers, doormen, and porters.

38

LIGHTS, CANDLES, THE
TURKEY, AND THE GOOSE

THE CUSTOM OF lighting lights and burning candles at Christmas has its roots in the Hellenistic period, when midwinter fires were lit to encourage the rising, or rebirth, of the sun-god on December 25. Later, when this practice was brought indoors, small lamps and candles became a natural replacement for the huge outdoor bonfires.

By the 4th Century, under Constantine the Great, Pagans celebrating *Dies Natalis Sol Invictus* and the Grecian Helia on December 25, were already cutting pine boughs on which to hang lights in honor of the annual return of Sol or Helios.

Of special significance was the Yule Candle, as it was called in the early Medieval period. Lit at midnight on the night of December 24, it was hoped that it would burn into the following morning, thereby bringing good luck to the household.

Candles themselves have a long history as Pagan phallic symbols and were once connected with the penis-like lightning bolts of the great male thunder-gods, such as Thor, Summanus, Jupiter, and Zeus. According to traditional Pagan belief, the womb of the Mother-Earth was fertilized by the thunder-deities when their reproductive organs (i.e., lightning) struck the ground.

In addition, in the pre-Christian Roman Empire, candles were a vital aspect of the veneration of Juno Lucina, the "Mother of Light." This matron of the Sun, the Moon, and the stars was also believed to "light" the eyes of newborn creatures, thereby giving them sight.

The candle worship of this light-goddess at the annual Winter Solstice festival was later adopted by Christianity: the Pagan Lucina became "Saint Lucy," and her celebratory candles were transferred to Christmas and the Christmas tree, where, as solar symbols, they continue to play an important role to this day.

The Christmas turkey or goose has been handed down to Christianity from ancient Pagan religions dating back at least 4,000 years. Like all birds in general, the goose was universally seen as a symbol of the heavens, and hence as an emissary from the unseen spirit world of the deities. Its traits as a faithful monogamous mate, a vigilant parent, and a fertile reproducer of offspring, made it an ideal religious symbol among Pagans around the ancient world, from China to Africa, from Ireland to Mesopotamia.

The Greeks, for example, saw the goose as the sacred bird of the love-goddess Aphrodite; in India it was the holy bird of the father-god Brahma (who later became "Abraham" in Judeo-Christian mythology); to the Romans it was the bird of both Juno, the "Queen of Heaven," and of Cupid, the god of love; and in Egypt the goose was dedicated to Seb, the foster father of the savior-son Horus.

We have seen that the figure of Joseph, the foster father of Jesus, was patterned on, among other mythic characters, the Egyptian Seb, and so we should not wonder that the Christmas goose of modern day Christianity ultimately derives from the ancient Egyptians.

According to Egyptian mythology, the goose hatched forth from the World Egg and so came to be associated with the immortal Osiris, himself a savior-son-god who arose each December on the Winter Solstice. Indeed, in ancient Egypt the word *sa* meant both "goose" and "son," a dual reference to the goose's readiness to sacrifice itself to a predator or hunter in order to save its offspring.

Each year in late December the families of ancient Egypt would sacrifice and eat a goose (or "son") in honor of the son-god Osiris and his rebirth on the annual solstitial holiday. The custom passed down into the early centuries of the Christian Era, when Pagans, converting to Christianity, brought the practice with them into the orthodox Roman Church.

Catholic Christianity adopted the Pagan convention, certainly aware of its Pagan "sacrificial son" motif and its relationship to the Egyptian Seb's later Jewish imitation, Joseph. When the custom was brought to the Americas with the English colonists in the 17th Century, the plenitude of the wild turkey made it a natural replacement for the European Christmas goose.

32

Carols, Pantomime, Candies, Pastries, Fruits, Gift-Giving, and Christmas Cards

TODAY'S JOYOUS CHRISTMAS carolers, robust holiday dinners, and Christmas Day parades with their ostentatious floats, colorful costumes, and boisterous music, also began as accouterments of the Pagan Yuletide solar festivals of antiquity. On the first day of the Winter Solstice, sacred hymns were sung, holy meals were taken, and a large procession of gayly clad worshipers carried the image of the sun-god through the city to the temple.

The modern Christmas pantomime, or Mumming Play, began in the ancient Pagan world of the Graeco-Romans as the *Pantomimus*. This theatrical form, with its sublime death and resurrection solar theme and soaring vocal accompaniment, was derived from even earlier Egyptian theatrical plays and was immensely popular across the ancient world from China to Israel.

In 16th-Century Italy this "play without words" developed into the *Commedia dell'arte*, a form of Italian comedy whose stock plots and characters were obtained from Pagan Egypt and Rome. "Harlequin," for instance, is a derivation of the Egyptian savior-son-god, Har or Horus;

"Columbine" is a remnant of the Great Mother figure in her zodiacal dove form, Columba; "Pantaloon" comes from the Egyptian Atum, or Ra, the sun-god-father; and the modern clown "Set" began in the earliest ancient Egyptian mime plays as the demonic Egyptian god of the Underworld, Seth.

When the pantomime was eventually incorporated into British Christian "tradition," it became known as the Christmas Panto. Though this knowledge has been largely lost today, Britons at the time were well aware that its text, songs, and comical themes derived from far earlier Pagan tales dating all the way back to ancient Egypt.

The eating of candies, fruits, and pastries at Christmas time has its origins in the Sun festivals of Pagan Rome. Unlike the toys, appliances, clothing, electronics, and other items that are customarily given on our modern Christmas day, these were, in fact, the primary gifts exchanged among families and friends during the ancient December celebration which honored the rebirth of the Sun. When Christianity officially adopted the Roman Winter Solstice festival in the 4th Century, it also assimilated the Pagan custom of eating sweets.

Finally, we have the practice of giving and receiving Christmas cards, yet another "Christian tradition" with its origins in the solar religions of Paganism. The custom began as part of the early Roman celebration of the New Year, traditionally held during the Ides (middle) of March.[266] In the northern regions of the Empire the New Year was observed during Yule in December due to the Winter Solstice.

As it remains to this day, ancient New Year's celebrations surrounded a carnival-like atmosphere of drinking, gluttony, parties, and sexual freedom. For such "sins" a mock king was sacrificed, allowing the populace to "turn over a new leaf" on the first day of the New Year. This "new leaf" was honored by the exchanging of actual leaves or pieces of paper wishing the recipient good fortune in the coming year. As this was primarily a secular holiday, these "cards" were often decorated with scenes of nature and animals.

During the late Medieval period this Pagan New Year custom was gradually assimilated by the Catholic Church as part of the celebration of "Christ's Mass." Over time the cards took on a distinctly religious look, in this case, Christian, though the nature scenes of the earlier Pagan cards remained popular motifs.

By the 19th Century they were printed commercially: the earliest-known printed Christmas card was made in 1843 for an Englishman by the name of Sir Henry Cole. The first known use of the term "Christmas card" came shortly thereafter, in 1883, though doubtlessly, the term was used orally long before.

From that time forward Christmas cards have been an integral aspect of the celebration of Christmas all over the world. It was precisely during this period, the late 19th Century, that the celebration of Christmas itself began to first take hold in the United States.

We will now look at how it was first received in the "New World."[267]

40

CHRISTMAS IN
THE MODERN WORLD

WITH THE ARRIVAL of the Vikings on the shores of North America in the 10th Century, the way was opened up for the inevitable European conquest of the Americas. By the 16th Century, Spanish explorers began to establish permanent settlements in the Caribbean and what is now Florida, while the 17th Century brought the colonization (in 1607) of what would later become Virginia. This was followed thirteen years later (in 1620) by the landing of the English Pilgrims in New England.[268]

We might assume that with the arrival of both Catholic Spaniards and Protestant Britons on American soil, that Christmas too would quickly become a national holiday. Quite the contrary. In fact, in 1659 the leaders of the Massachusetts Bay Colony forbade the celebrations of Jesus' birth in any manner, even passing a law against it. The decree said, in part, that anyone

> who is found observing, by abstinence from labor, feasting, or any other way, any such days as Christmas day, shall pay for every such offense with five shillings.[269]

Despite the fact that the statute was overturned in 1684, in 1685 famed Massachusetts judge Samuel Sewall happily observed that as of yet, no one was celebrating Christmas.[270] Indeed, the official observance of Christmas in North America continued to go almost wholly unnoticed until the middle of the 19th Century. Why?

The Christian Fathers of the early Puritan colonies viewed Christmas not only as a sacrilegious Catholic import for which there was no biblical injunction, but also as a holiday steeped in Pagan traditions dating back many thousands of years. This sentiment has continued on in certain Christian sects to this very day. As noted, at one time, every Winter the fundamentalist Worldwide Church of God sent out an anti-Christmas pamphlet preaching against the "immorality" of celebrating the birth of Jesus.

In *The Plain Truth About Christmas*, for instance, Church authorities correctly assert that Jesus was not born on December 25, that the Twelve Apostles never once celebrated Christ's birthday, that the Bible contains no command to recognize it, and that above all, the celebration of birthdays is a Pagan not a Christian custom. If God had wanted humanity to honor Jesus' birth, the pamphlet goes on to say, He would have provided us with the Savior's precise birth date *and* instructions on how to celebrate it. This He clearly did not do. Why? Because Christmas is an invention of man, not God. Even worse for many Christians, it is a *Pagan* human invention.[271]

These same anti-Christmas sentiments held true for most Americans from the 17th Century until the 19th Century. The New York *Tribune*, for example, carried not a single Christmas ad in its pages in 1841, and as late as 1847 there was not a single college in New England that observed Christmas.

After the horrors of America's War for Southern Independence (1861-1865) began to recede,[272] clever retailers sought to boost their profits by offering special "Christmas sales" during the Winter months. The idea caught on and by 1870 December had turned into the most profitable month of the year for U.S. merchants.

Today Christmas is more an industry than a religious holiday; a multi-billion dollar-a-year commercial enterprise without which most businesses could not survive, so closely linked is it with many of the world's major economies. Indeed, Christmas sales account for at least one-half of most stores' entire yearly earnings.

Acknowledging this, many Christians themselves (ignorant of the merry-making Pagan holidays from which this particular celebration derives) lament the fact that Christmas is no longer a purely religious holiday, one connected to the birth of Jesus. Rather, now it is solely about shopping, Santa Claus, Christmas trees, and gift-giving. It is no longer even called the "Christmas season," they complain. It is now merely the "holiday season."

A few recent attempts have been made for a return to a less overtly materialistic, more spiritual celebration using such battle cries as, "let's keep 'Christ' in Christmas." Yet such statements seem strangely paradoxical when viewed in the objective light of modern comparative religious studies. For, as we have seen, there was no *Christian* Christ in the original Christmas to begin with.

There were plenty of Pagan Christs, however: hundreds of pre-Christian sun-gods, savior-gods, and son-gods, nearly all born of virgin mothers around the Winter Solstice in late December.

Indeed, if we were to use history as a guide, December 25 would today be known, not as "Christmas," but as "Sunmas," that is, *Sun's Mass*; or as the ancient Romans accurately called it, *Dies Solis Natilis Invicti*: "Birthday of the Invincible Sun."

In the 6,000 years that December 25 has been utilized as a day of religious festivals and worship, only for a fraction of that time has it been thought of as a purely "Christian" holiday, and this itself was a recent development, beginning only late in the 19th Century.

It is a rather curious fact that Christmas is celebrated at all by the 900 million Protestants of the world. After all, "Christ's Mass" is an invention of the Roman Catholic Church, the Christian sect which Martin Luther and other "herectics" *protested* against in 1529, inaugurating the great Protestant Reformation.

The worldwide population of Catholics, now numbering 1.2 billion, would seem to be the only Christians who should properly be celebrating this holiday, the Catholic Church's obvious Pagan structure, look, feel, tone, belief system, architecture, literature, language, clothing, orders, and myths serving as living proof.

Yet, aside from this curious situation, Christmas is not to be considered the sole property of the Catholic Church. At best we can say that, with the assistance of the Pagan converts of the early Church, Catholicism developed the specific "Christian" notion of what Christmas is today.

However, even this, the modern image of Christmas is ultimately of Pagan origins, much of it of which dates back to the ancient Egyptians living around 3000 BC. Along the way, December 25 became the "birthday" of thousands of gods, goddesses, saviors, messiahs, nature-deities, and even historic Pagan rulers. Christianity is only the latest of the world's religions to absorb this magical day, making it appear as a "Christian tradition."

41

Modern Variations On The Pagan Christmas Theme

ALL OVER THE world, far older cultures continue to practice the ancient rites associated with the Winter Solstice, the birth of the Sun/Son by his virgin-mother (a goddess associated with water, the Moon, and fertility), the arrival of the New Year, and the period we call the months of November, December, and January (formerly the ninth, tenth, and eleventh months of the Pagan calender).[273]

In Japan celebrations honoring the New Year, called *Ganjitsu*, begin in November and run through January 7. Gifts are exchanged, pine boughs and bamboo stalks (called *Kadomatsu*) are placed around doors, fireworks are displayed, temple bells toll, and the city streets overflow with parades and fairs.

In Thailand the New Year, called *Loy Krathong* ("Floating Lotus Cups") is held in mid-November. This Asian holiday began in ancient times as the period in which the goddess Mae Khogkja (the "Mother of the Water") was venerated in the hopes that her life-giving spirit would purify and renew the hearts of the people. Again, we find a Pagan carnival-like atmosphere prevailing as the towns and villages fill with fairs, street vendors, storytellers, actors, dancers, and musicians.

In Russia the Winter months herald the arrival of both the New Year and D'yed Moroz ("Grandfather Frost"). As it is for their American counterparts, this is a time of merriment for the Russian people who, in the great Pagan tradition, hold parties, march in parades, and exchange gifts with one another. Wearing a long dark blue coat trimmed with white fur, carrying a staff, and sporting a white beard, D'yed Moroz and his Pagan-based companion, Snegurochka (the "Snow Maiden"), are said to deliver presents to all Russian families by sleigh on New Year's Eve, January 1.

In modern Sweden and Finland Christmas falls on December 13. This holiday, honoring the mythical Saint Lucia, derives from the Pagan holy day known as the "Festival of Lights," and its reigning goddess, Juno Lucina (the "Mother of Light"), who gave humans both physical eyesight and spiritual inner sight (via the Third Eye, that is, intuition), the latter mentioned numerous times by Jesus and Saint Paul.[274]

In Denmark Paganism masquerades behind a facade of a myriad of "Christmas traditions." A group of elves, called Julenisse, are placated with puddings (solar symbols), while the most popular elf, known as Nisse, is carefully catered to in order to prevent his mischievous jokes from getting out of hand.

During Christmas celebrations Danes serve red wine (symbolic of the great Goddess' life-giving menstrual blood), along with a special rice pudding in which a "magic almond" is hidden. As we will recall, the almond, artistically known as the Vesica Piscis, has long been a symbol of Goddess' Sacred Yoni. Christmas trees (symbols of the phallus) are decorated and carols are sung (a remnant of the "merry" tunes delivered during Pagan Winter Solstice revelries).

In Italy it is not Santa Claus who delivers presents during Winter celebrations, but the Pagan witch La Befana, whose name in Italian means "The Epiphany." Traveling across Italy on her broom, she drops gifts down the chimneys of "good girls and boys" on January 6, on the Feast of the Epiphany—originally the date of the great Pagan water festivals devoted to such savior-gods as Dionysus and Osiris (just two of the pre-Christian models who provided elements for the Paganized Jesus).

In modern Greece the Christmas meal includes *Christopsomo*, or "Christ bread," a vestige of the ancient Pagan sacramental meal of holy bread, eaten during the Epiphany, the sacred mass of the sun-god

Mithras. Greek hearth fires are kept burning throughout the entire Twelve Days of Christmas (in accord with the twelve astrological star-signs) in order to encourage the rebirth of the Sun, and offerings are made to the Naiads, or water-spirits, the Grecian equivalent of the Germanic water-sprites known as Nixies, presided over by the Teutonic sea-god called Hold Nickar, later known as Saint Nicholas, then Santa Claus.

In the Netherlands it is not Christmas but *Sinterklaas Avond* ("Saint Nicholas Eve") which is eagerly awaited. This night, which falls on December 5, signals the arrival of Sinter Klass and his cohort Zwarte Piet ("Black Pete"), who, amid the usual festivities of parades, parties, and feasting, disperse gifts to Dutch families.

Sinter Klass is, as we have discussed, merely the Dutch version of the midwinter solar-god Kriss Kringle (the "sun-child"), who was, in turn, modeled on the Pagan sea-god Hold Nickar. And as the accompanying celebratory accouterments of *Sinterklaas Avond* fittingly illustrate, the entire Dutch holiday is little more than a christianized Roman Saturnalia, a Greek Helia, a Norse Yule, and a Graeco-Roman *Dies Natalis Solis Invictus*.

Modern-day Switzerland celebrates Christmas with the coming of *Christkindli*, the "Christ child," who arrives bearing gifts on his reindeer-drawn sleigh. December 6 marks the start of the *Chlausjagen* (the "Claus hunt") festival, or Feast of Saint Nicholas. In the weeks before the Winter Solstice, processions are held, bells are rung (to scare off evil spirits), pine trees are decorated, tree candles are lit, and carols are sung. The wife of Father Christmas is named Lucy, another Christian personification of the old Pagan goddess Juno Lucina, the "Mother of Light." Large homemade doughnuts are baked by the Swiss at Christmas. Called *ringli*, these are eaten warm right from the oven, ideal miniature symbols of the Sun.

In France the feast of *Reveillon* is held at midnight on Christmas Eve in preparation for the arrival of Pere Noel ("Father Christmas") the next day. The Yule Log is burned from Christmas Eve until New Year's Day, again, as we have seen, an ancient Pagan custom of encouraging the newborn sun-god. In earlier times this log was then later used as a plow wedge, believed to bestow fertility on the soil and good luck to the family.

Reveillon, of course, is but an Indo-European remnant of pre-Christian Pagan feasts in honor of the Winter Solstice. Noel, the French word for Christmas, derives from the French phrase *les bonnes nouvelles*, meaning "the good news"—the return ("resurrection") of the Sun ("Son") indeed being good news.

Paganism continues to live on in Ireland's Christmas customs as well. The Irish place lighted candles in their windows, allegedly for Joseph and Mary as they look for shelter. In truth, these derive from far earlier Pagan Winter Solstice festivities in which candles were lit in honor of the light-goddess Lucina, Lucia, or Lucy (from which we get the word lucid).

Irish Christmas candles, male phallic symbols, are red (symbolic of Goddess' life-giving menstrual blood), and are decorated with sprigs of holly, an old Pagan symbol of the Divine Feminine. Three puddings are made, three being the holy number of the great Celtic triple-goddess (known across the Emerald Isle as the Morrigan), and food is left out overnight after the Christmas meal. The Irish say this is to symbolize "hospitality." But, this tradition has its roots in the ancient Pagan custom of leaving propitiatory offerings out overnight in order to mollify evil spirits and to provide nourishment for the ancestral dead.

During the celebration of Christmas in Mexico, Pagan practices abound. One of the more popular of these is the breaking of the piñata (or pignatta, meaning "clay pot"), a colorful but hollow paper-mache figure filled with sweet treats. The piñata, usually designed in the shape of a bull, is an obvious derivation of the ancient Pagan custom of sacrificing bulls.

In ancient Rome this ceremony was known as the *Taurobolium*. Here, a bull's throat would be slit over metal grates, after which the fresh blood would drip down onto human devotees sitting in a pit below—the belief being that the sacrificial red liquid, the "life force," would cleanse (that is, regenerate) the soul of the sinner.

Piñatas have other Pagan associations, such as the far earlier images of various Pagan Underworld demon-gods who were often portrayed as bull-headed monsters. In modern christianized Mexico this creature now personifies the Christian demon-deity Satan (also a Pagan figure, in this case derived from the ancient Egyptian serpent-god Sata), or the Devil (derived from the ancient Indo-European mother-goddess known as Devi), who entices one to do evil. Thus, if a blindfolded individual (a symbol of faith) can break the piñata with a stick (a symbol of virtue), she or he receives "God's reward" (symbolized by the candies packed inside).

In Spain Christmas-New Year's festivities culminate on January 6, called Three Kings' Day, after the legend of the "Three Wise Men." This folktale is based on the ancient Pagan Cult of Orion whose "belt" was composed of three stars, or "kings." As usual, the ancient Pagan customs of gift-giving, merrymaking, and parties are practiced.

One of the more notable of these customs is the Spanish parade known as a *cabalgata* ("cavalcade"), or more fully, *la Cabalgata de los Reyes Magos* ("the Cavalcade of the Royal Astrologers," that is, the Three Kings). The *cabalgatas* derive from an earlier Pagan Spanish tradition in which the townspeople marched through the city on the eve of the Epiphany. As they went, they carried torches, banged on pots, blew horns, and yelled.

Today this event is erroneously seen as an effort to help the Three Wise Men locate a particular city by sound. Actually, this is merely a remnant of the ancient Pagan Twelfth Night custom (held, like the Three Kings' Day festival on which it was patterned, on January 6) in which the town's paraders hit pans, screamed, and rang bells, attempts to scare away stray spirits and demons.

All of these various cultural celebrations are but modern versions of the ancient Pagan midwinter festivals which honored the bringing in of the Fall harvests and the lengthening of daylight beginning on the Winter Solstice.

Not surprisingly, new variations on this ancient theme continue to emerge in contemporary cultures. Kwanzaa, an African-American holiday that begins on December 26 and ends on January 1, is just one example of this universal drive to seek physical and spiritual renewal in the Winter months.

Founded by Dr. Maulana Karenga in 1966, it is claimed that this is not a religious holiday. Nonetheless, like all other Winter celebrations, it is clearly based (knowingly or unknowingly) on archetypal religious rites, best epitomized in the ancient Pagan rituals surrounding autumnal and midwinter commemorations. Indeed, the word "Kwanzaa" is Kiswahili (an East African language) for "The First Fruits of the Harvest."

With such Pagan agrarian associations, it is not surprising that in Kwanzaa special emphasis is placed on the Nguzo Saba (the "Seven Principles"),[275] its symbol, the Mishumaa Saba ("Seven Candles"), and the Menorah-like, seven-branched candelabrum, the Kinara. For the number seven has a long Pagan tradition of arcane symbolism and sacrality associated with spiritual enlightenment through physical union.[276]

Innumerable seven-fold philosophies predate not only the invention of Kwanzaa, but the rise of Christianity and Judaism as well. Such Pagan antecedents include the "Seven Pillars of Wisdom" of Aphrodite and Artemis, in which initiates seeking the attainment of all seven "pillars" (secret sacred knowledge) were required to pass through a series of harsh and lengthy physical and spiritual trials. This belief system was, in turn, founded on an even earlier religion called the Cult of the Seven Mothers (or Sisters), astronomically represented, according to ancient Indo-European mythology, in the seven-star system, the Pleiades.

Even the colors of the seven Kwanzaan candles—three are green, three are red, and one is black—are of Pagan origins: green is the archetypal color of the Earth, and of immortality, hope, tranquility, revitalization, and the Feminine Principle; red is the archetypal color of love, sex, energy, war, and the Masculine Principle; and black is the archetypal female color of fertility, mystery, and spiritual rebirth.

During the celebration of Kwanzaa, a number of other Pagan practices take place: on each of the seven nights (between December 31 and January 1), for example, the family recites one of the Seven Principles while lighting a new candle. Accompanying this ritual, a libation known as tambiko is consumed from the unity cup, itself an ancient Pagan chalice symbol of family and of the womb of the great Mother-Goddess.

Finally, on December 31, a celebratory feast called the Kwanzaa Karuma is held, and the ancient Pagan practice of exchanging gifts follows.

42

In Summary

WHAT HAVE WE learned on our journey to uncover the origins and evolution of Christmas?

This holiday is but one of countless variations on a Pagan theme that dates back many thousands of years to the dawn of prehistory. While we acknowledge both the historical Jesus and his divinity, at the same time it is patently obvious that much of His biography is the syncretic result of the assimilation of hundreds of pre-Christian Pagan solar-saviors and sun-deities, along with their accompanying legends and myths.

Unlike modern Christians, early Christians readily understood and accepted this fact, which is why they unhesitatingly portrayed Him in their artwork with a flaming golden halo, blazing white robes, and a glowing self-luminescence, with brilliant beams of light shooting out in all directions. To them it was apparent that the mythical Jesus at least (that is, the Cosmic Christ), was none other than a Christian Helios or Apollo, Pagan sun-gods each widely known as "the Good Shepherd" and the "Light of the World."

Santa Claus has a similar story. Nothing can disguise his origins as a Pagan solar-deity: with his bright red suit, radiating whiskers, and long tendriled hair, he rises up and down the smokey chimney as flames roar around him, every aspect of him revealing that he is none other than the christianized Nordic sun-god Odin, an archetypal figure himself ultimately founded on the solar-deities of prehistory.

And so, here Christmas remains to this day, a Pagan wolf in Christian sheep's clothing.

Yet, it is its Pagan foundations which make Christmas a truly universal holy day. Indeed, it is for this very reason that the figures, themes, trappings, myths, ceremonies, beliefs, customs, and practices of Christmas should be completely inoffensive to non-Christians. For every known people, society, culture, nationality, religion, and race has observed the birth of the Sun under one name or another, each December—Christianity being merely the latest member of this worldwide group. Even the ancient humanistic, atheistic Greeks celebrated the Winter Solstice and the new rising of the solar-god, just as some modern non-believing scientists do today.

Thus, in the end—when it comes to Christmas—it matters little whether we count ourselves Christian, Gnostic, Pagan, Buddhist, atheist, henotheist, Zoroastrian, humanist, Jew, pantheist, Hindu, agnostic, rationalist, Deist, positivist, animist, freethinker, monist, secularist, skeptic, existentialist, nihilist, stoicist, hedonist, sophist, determinist, subjectivist, empiricist, metaphysicist, absolutist, relativist, solipsist, universalist, atomist, primitivist, phenomenologist, mechanist, materialist, or futilitarian.

As etymology alone shows, Kriss Kringle and Christ are identical. For both their names derive from the same source: the ancient Egyptian word *krs* or *karast* (mystically meaning the "immortal soul"), which passed into Babylonia as the Chaldean word for the Sun, *crs* or *chris*, the archetypal symbol of God in man (theosis). Truly, the Christ is "the true Light which lighteth every man that cometh into the world," as the Bible's great mystic John declared.[277]

According to no less an authority than Saint Paul, the founder of Christianity itself, the Great God of the Pagans and the Great God of the Christians are indeed one and the same, as he noted in his famed sermon to the Athenians on Mars' Hill nearly 2,000 years ago.[278]

And so Christmas has always truly been and will always truly remain, whatever name one chooses to call it, the Birthday of the Sun.

The End

I am the light of the world

Christ

(John 8:12)

NOTES

1. For a detailed discussion of the Tetramorph, see Seabrook, SBD, s.v. "Tetramorph (Christian)."

2. Matthew 22:32.

3. See e.g., Matthew 5:1-48; 6:1-34; 7:1-29; 10:5-42; 11:25-30; 15:10-11; 16:25; 18:3; 22:29-30; Mark 3:31-35; 10:13-31; Luke 6:20-38; 8:19-21; 11:9-13; 12:15, 22-34; 14:26; 17:21; 20:34-38; 21:17.

4. Matthew 13:10-17; Mark 4:10-12; 11:33; John 8:23.

5. Matthew 7:12.

6. Luke 11:9-13.

7. The Christian belief in reincarnation was common throughout the 1st Century, as Jesus' own words and teachings reveal. Tragically, the doctrine was condemned and banned at the Council of Constantinople in the year 538 by Emperor Justinian I, after which overt references to it were removed from the Bible. Despite the Catholic Church's efforts, traces of the teaching of reincarnation remain throughout the New Testament. Examples include: Matthew 3:1-2; 11:11-15; 14:1-2; 16:13-14; 17:10-13; Mark 6:14-15; 7:1-13 ; 8:27-28; 9:11-13; 12:38-40 ; Luke 1:13-17; 9:7-8, 18-19; John 1:19-21, 25; 3:3-13; 8:56-58; 9:1-3; 14:1-3, 12; Romans 9:10-14; Hebrews 2:2-3; Revelation 3:12. The Israelites (early Jews) also embraced reincarnation. Old Testament examples include: Deuteronomy 31:2; Jeremiah 1:5-6; Proverbs 8:22-31; Obad 1:15; Malachi 4:5. For more on reincarnation and Christianity, see Seabrook, SBD, s.v. "reincarnation."

8. Matthew 6:22; 13:16; Luke 12:34.

9. Matthew 11:15; 13:16; Mark 4:9, 23; 7:16.

10. John 3:3-7.

11. Matthew 4:4; Luke 12:23; John 4:32.

12. John 10:33-35. See also Genesis 3:22; Psalms 82:6; Isaiah 41:23.

13. Luke 3:6.

14. John 14:20; 17:21.

15. Jesus often intentionally broke Jewish religious laws in order to illustrate both their uselessness in relation to spiritual growth and His disdain for organized mainstream religion. See e.g., Matthew 6:5; 8:22; 12:1-15; 23:13-33; 24:5, 23-28; Mark 1:35; 2:16, 18, 23-28; 7:2-8; John 4:22-24.

16. Luke 5:37-38.

17. Matthew 5:43-44; Mark 12:29-34; Luke 6:27-38; John 13:34-35; 15:12-13. For more on the many spiritual laws taught by Jesus, see Seabrook, SBD, s.v. "Jesus."

18. The four canonical Gospels are well-known to have been written anonymously decades after Jesus' death (Luke was written over 150 years later), then redacted numerous times by still many others—not what objective scientists would normally consider trustworthy historical material. As a number of scholars have pointed out, there is not even enough *genuine* information on the historical Jesus to write a one paragraph biography on him. For more on the historicity of Jesus, see Seabrook, SBD, passim.

19. 2 Corinthians 5:7.

20. From the *Book of Q*, Matthew 7:7.

21. Seabrook, SBD, s.v. "Christianity."

22. Seabrook, SBD, s.v. "Christianity."

23. Seabrook, SBD, s.v. "Christianity."

24. Claims for other far older Venus images exist, such as the Venus of Berekhat Ram, Israel, believed by some to be carved by *Homo erectus* some 230,000 years ago. Whether authentic or not, it is clear that worship of the great Virgin-Mother-Earth-Goddess predates the worship of the great Father-Sky-God ("Heavenly Father") by many tens of thousands of years. For artistic portrayals of male deities do not begin to appear in the archaeological record until about 6000 BC. The Virgin-Mother-Goddess then was the original Supreme Being, the primordial "God."

25. Archaeologists first gave the name "Venus" to these particular figurines because they assumed that they were somehow connected to love and sex (ruled by the Roman goddess Venus), and even "prehistoric pornography." However, it is patently clear that Cro-Magnons' female images had nothing to do with either love or sex. They were fertility or fecundity symbols, embedded in artistic portrayals of the first known Supreme Being: the Creatrix of the World, the great Virgin-Mother-Goddess.

26. Here we find the origin of the holiness and magicality surrounding the number thirteen, later to be absorbed by Christianity in the story of Jesus and His Twelve Disciples. For more on biblical numerology, see Seabrook, SBD, s.v. "numbers."

27. For more on the origins and evolution of Goddess-worship, see my books, *Britannia Rules*; *The Goddess Dictionary of Words and Phrases*; and *The Book of Kelle*.

28. An example is the tradition among many men to tattoo the word "Mother" (not "Father") on their arm.

29. Lacking a paternal instinct, the average man must be taught by society how to be a husband and a father. The awful results of failing to socialize young men for marriage and parenthood can be seen all around us.

30. Many of us will be familiar with these archetypes due to their common usage in the traditional deck of cards, in Tarot cards, in astrology (the Zodiac), children's fairy tales, and in ancient fables and myths, both secular and religious.

31. See 18.3.3 and 20:9.

32. For one thing, the writing styles of these two passages are jarringly different than those that precede and succeed them. For another, the statements regarding Jesus do not fit in with the rest of the text, but instead, stand out for their peculiarity. Josephus then, a Jew born in Jerusalem shortly after Jesus' death, never once mentions Christ in all of his many detailed writings. Why?

33. de Volney, p. 118. We will note here that, according to de Volney, at one time Asians universally referred to Christ not as Jesus, but as Buddha.

34. Mysteriously, Saint Paul (like Saint James, Saint Peter, and Saint John) never quotes Jesus, which is strange since Christians have long considered Christ the greatest teacher the Western world has ever known. Even more odd, Paul neglects to make any reference to Jesus' miracles, His Ascension, the Twelve Apostles, or the empty tomb, as anyone familiar with Paul's *genuine* letters can attest. Note: the authentic letters of Paul are as follows: 1 Thessalonians (written about the year 52, this is the earliest known piece of orthodox Christian literature), Romans, 1 Corinthians, 2 Corinthians, and Galatians. Many religious scholars consider the rest of Saint Paul's so-called "letters" to be late forgeries in his name, as they do not match his thought or the writing style of the time period (mid 1st Century). Some go even further, discounting *all* of the Pauline letters as *pseudographia* ("false writings"). For more on Paul, see Seabrook, SBD, s.v. "Paul."

35. Matthew 5:39; Luke 6:29.

36. Some modern groups maintain that not only did Jesus marry, but He was also a polygamist whose many wives included Mary, Elizabeth, and Martha. Foremost among the promoters of this view have been the Masons, allegedly the Nazis, and the pseudo-Christian denomination called the Mormons, also known as The Church of Jesus Christ of Latter-Day Saints, or LDS. (I refer to Mormonism as a false Christian faith because it is not Bible-based.) For proof, supporters of this theory offer John's story of the "marriage at Cana," which they assert was Jesus' own wedding. See John 2:1-2. See the following footnote. For more on this topic, see Seabrook, SBD, s.v. "Cana wedding."

37. Did Jesus marry and bear at least one child? According to the Knights Templar, as well as several ancient and Medieval legends, He did. This belief states that Jesus secretly married Mary Magdalene (whom the Gospel of Philip hints He often kissed on the mouth), and that they had a child named Sarah (Hebrew for "princess"). After Jesus' crucifixion and ascension, Mary and Sarah escaped, taking a boat across the Mediterranean Sea to France, where Mary died and Sarah married into French royalty. One of Sarah's descendants was Princess Basina of the Thuringians (Germany). In the early part of the 5th Century, Basina married King Clodion, one of the long-haired kings of France. The couple then bore a son named Merovee, or Merovech, who grew up to become King of the Franks. Thus began the Merovingian dynasty, Jesus' alleged bloodline, from which thousands today descend. (I myself am a descendant: King Merovee is my 49th great-grandfather.) The claim that mortals descend from deities is not unique to Christianity. The family of Julius Caesar (the *Gens Julia*), for example, maintained that they were descendants of both the god Aeneas and the goddess Venus, while the early Pagan English kings claimed descent through Brutus, a descendant of the goddess Aphrodite. For more on this topic, see Seabrook, SBD, s.v. "Son of Man."

38. Luke 3:23.

39. Matthew 14:25-33.

40. 1 Corinthians 15:35-38.

41. Matthew 20:19; 28:6-7; Mark 10:34; 16:6; Luke 18:33; 1 Corinthians 15:4.

42. Malachi 4:2; Matthew 17:2; John 1:1-10.

43. Luke 2:11; John 4:42; Acts 5:31; 13:23; 2 Timothy 1:10; Titus 3:6; 2 Peter 1:11; 1 John 4:14.

44. Matthew 11:19; 21:12-13; Mark 2:15-16; John 14:6.

45. Matthew 5:44.

46. According to this view, because Jesus preached that there is no marriage in the Afterlife (that is, no sex or reproduction; see Matthew 22:29-30), He found it necessary to set an example for His followers by remaining unmarried and asexual throughout His earthly incarnation. Indeed, it is Jesus' bachelor status and life of celibacy, as portrayed in the four canonical Gospels, that were the basis for the development of clerical celibacy in the Catholic Church.

47. Genesis 1:29; Proverbs 15:17; Exodus 20:13; Luke 18:20. Adding weight to the opinion that Jesus was a vegetarian was Eusebius who, in his *Ecclesiastical History*, states that Jesus' brother James was raised a vegetarian (Book 2, Chapter 23). Additionally, in his book *The Proof of the Gospel*, Eusebius notes that the Twelve Apostles were both vegetarians and teetotalers (Book 3, Chapter 5). *The Essene Gospel of Peace* also states unequivocally that Jesus was a vegetarian. Jesus was not without His followers in this regard. Other early Christian vegetarians of note included: Basil the Great, Jerome, Tertullian, Clement of Alexandria, Arnobius, Origen, and John Chrysostom. John the Baptist appears to have been a vegetarian of some type, as well (see e.g., Matthew 3:4). For more on this topic, see Seabrook, SBD, s.v. "Essenes"; s.v. "Gospel of the Kingdom of God"; s.v. "Pythagoras."

48. Contrary to mainstream orthodox teaching, the Gnostics were the original Christians, and the Gnostic Church was the original Christian Church. Though there were dozens, perhaps hundreds of different Gnostic cults, groups, sects, and denominations, Gnosticism was unified under at least one great principle: a belief in the *Gnosis*, Greek for "knowledge." The *Gnosis* was not intellectual *outer* knowledge learned from books, preachers, priests, and teachers (tuition), as found in orthodox Christianity, but spiritual *inner* knowledge that can only be gleaned from a one-on-one personal relationship with the Divine (in-tuition). For more on this topic, see Seabrook, SBD, s.v. "Gnosis"; s.v. "Gnosticism."

49. Remnants of Saint Paul's Docetist beliefs can still be seen scattered throughout the New Testament, for example, 2 Corinthians 5:16. Paul never claimed to have met, seen, or encountered the human Jesus. Only the invisible presence of the Gnostics' Cosmic Christ, or "phantasm," which appeared to him one day while he was traveling on the road to Damascus. See Acts 9:1-8. For more on this topic, see Seabrook, SBD, s.v. "Paul."

50. John 19:2; 1 Corinthians 9:25; 2 Timothy 4:8; 1 Peter 5:4.

51. James 1:12; Revelation 2:10.

52. The true authorship of the four canonical Gospels is not known with any certainty, despite the imposing names "Matthew," "Mark," "Luke," and "John" superficially affixed to their title pages. For not one original manuscript of any of the four Gospels has ever been found. As we will see, it was not until the end of the 2nd Century that these names were invented by the Church Father Irenaeus to tie in with the Four Compass-gods of Pagan astrology. As these four names were not attached to the four canonical Gospels until after the year 180 then, it is obvious that these four books were originally compiled anonymously. For example, neither Bishop Papias or Bishop Marcion of Sinope (an early Gnostic-Christian leader) were aware of the Gospel of John when they were both writing around 140. The New Testament books as a whole were not accepted as canonical (by the Catholic Church) until the 4th Century, over 300 years after Jesus died. For more on this topic, see Seabrook, SBD, *passim*.

53. Wace and Schaff, Vol. 1, pp. 172-173.

54. Concerning the *Book of Q*, it is customary to divide individuals into two schools of thought. *Conservative* or *fundamentalist Christians* reject the theory, believing that every statement in the Bible is the inerrant Word of God. *Liberal Christians* believe that the Bible was written piecemeal, that it is a "layer cake" of a wide variety of ideas compiled over three or four centuries. I myself feel that this categorization is not altogether accurate, for one can be a liberal Christian and still accept the Bible as the Word of God, and one can be a fundamentalist Christian and still question certain aspects of the Bible. Either way, since it is impossible to read the New Testament without noticing its glaring inconsistencies, contradictions, and errors, not to mention its overt copying of pre-Christian myths and motifs, I maintain that those who take the entire Bible literally, with every word being inspired by God, are operating out of faith, while those who see the Bible as a brilliant if sometimes faulty work of human hands, are operating from their intellects. Thus, I would categorize the two groups as the faith-based school and the intellect-based school, rather than as conservatives and liberals. For more on this topic, see Seabrook, SBD, s.v. "Gospel of Q."

55. See Luke 1:1-4. Even Saint Paul wrote (or dictated) his own Gospel. See e.g., Romans 2:16; 16:25; 2 Timothy 2:8. See Seabrook, SBD, s.v. "Paul."

56. Matthew 11:25. The form of Christianity preached by most Christian faiths, denominations, sects, branches, offshoots, and cults today is so complex—to the point of being literally indecipherable, that we can be sure it has little to do with the original, pure Christianity taught by Jesus. For more on this topic, see Seabrook, SBD, s.v. "Christianity"; s.v. "Gospel."

57. Matthew 5:44.

58. Matthew 5:7.

59. Matthew 7:1-2; Luke 6:37.

60. Matthew 5:3, 5.

61. Matthew 5:6, 8.

62. Matthew 5:9.

63. Luke 6:34-35.

64. Matthew 6:34; Luke 12:6-7.

65. Forman, pp. 153-154.

66. Matthew 15:4.

67. Luke 14:26.

68. See Matthew 1:1-16 and Luke 3:23-38.

69. Matthew 1:1-16.

70. Luke 1:26-35.

71. See Luke 2:5, 16, 41; 3:23.

72. Romans 1:3-4.

73. Matthew 1:16.

74. Luke 3:23.

75. Mark 1:9.

76. John 1:35-36.

77. Adding more suspicion to the already existing confusion here, neither the Epistles or the book of Revelation mention the Virgin Birth. Instead, Saint Paul says that Jesus was "made of the seed of David according to the flesh" (Romans 1:3); that is, Jesus was a normal man born of two human parents. For more on this topic, see Seabrook, SBD, s.v. "Son of Man"; s.v. "Son of God"; s.v. "virgin birth."

78. Matthew 1:25, for example, is a repetition of 1:21, while Matthew 1:18, 20, contradict 1:23, 25.

79. Matthew 2:1.

80. Luke 1:26; 2:39; 4:16.

81. Like Adonis, Jesus was also said to have visited Hell after His resurrection in order to preach to the dead. See e.g., 1 Peter 3:19; 4:6. The four canonical Gospels, along with Paul, neglect to mention this particular legend. Thus, the tale of Jesus journeying down to the Underworld must be regarded as a Pagan myth, one borrowed from the pre-Christian stories of other ancient gods said to have descended into Hell. These would include: Balder, Osiris, Hercules, Chrishna, Hermes, Rhampsinitus, Dionysus, and Orpheus, among many others.

82. Matthew 26:34; Luke 22:60; John 13:38.

83. Mark 14:30.

84. Matthew 28:1-6.

85. Mark 16:1-8.

86. Luke 23:55-56; 24:1-10.

87. John 20:11-12.

88. Matthew 27:33.

89. Mark 15:22.

90. John 19:17.

91. Luke 23:33.

92. See e.g., Matthew 10:2-4; Mark 3:16-19; Luke 6:14-16; Acts 1:13.

93. Matthew 28:1-20; Luke 24:1-53.

94. John 20:1-31; 21:1-25.

95. Mark 16:1-20.

96. Acts 1:1-3.

97. For more on this topic, see Seabrook, SBD, s.v. "Jesus."

98. From the very beginning of the Faith some 2,000 years ago, good and well-meaning Christians have questioned the so-called "inerrancy" of the Bible. For more on this topic, see Seabrook, SBD, s.v. "Gospel."

99. Matthew 18:3.

100. See e.g., Genesis 6:1-4.

101. Confusingly, Luke addresses his Gospel to Theophilus, the Bishop of Antioch (Luke 1:3). The problem is that Theophilus did not become bishop until 169. If accurate, then the Gospel of Luke could not have been written before that year, much later than the year 105 usually accorded its inception.

102. H. A. Washington, Vol. 7, p. 139.

103. This list represents but a fraction of the thousands of actual syncretic adoptions that have occurred between Christianity and Paganism.

104. Bede, pp. 88-89.

105. See e.g., Matthew 9:30; 16:20; Mark 10:17-18; Luke 5:12-14; 22:66-70; John 5:31; 6:26; 8:50, 54.

106. See e.g., Matthew 17:14-20; Mark 9:23; 11:23.

107. See e.g., Matthew 9:20-22; Mark 5:34; 10:52; Luke 8:48-50; 17:19.

108. See e.g., Matthew 9:27-30. For more on Jesus and the power of self-healing, see Seabrook, JATLOA.

109. Luke 8:50.

110. Mark 6:1-6.

111. See e.g., Matthew 8:1-4; Mark 7:31-36; Luke 5:12-14; 8:49-56.

112. Luke 5:15-16.

113. See e.g., Matthew 16:13-20; Mark 8:27-30; 9:2-9; Luke 9:18-21.

114. See e.g., Matthew 16:13; Mark 8:38; Luke 22:48; John 12:34-36. For more on this topic, see Seabrook, SBD, s.v. "Son of Man."

115. Jesus founded no church, detested organized religion, and espoused a simplistic childlike doctrine designed only to help humanity grow spiritually and live happier healthier lives. Today, however, a complex, labyrinthian, paganized religion with tens of thousands of denominations has been built up around Him, something He never intended and which He actually fought against right up to His crucifixion. Already by the 3rd Century, educated and intelligent men like Pliny the Younger were referring to the new overly elaborate faith called Christianity as "an odious superstition." For more on this topic, see Seabrook, SBD, s.v. "Christianity."

116. Colossians 3:11.

117. John 10:34.

118. John 1:9.

119. Genesis 1:27.

120. Remnants of this ancient Christian view can still be found in the Bible. See e.g., Matthew 13:55; Mark 6:3.

121. We will note here that there were hundreds of female sun-goddesses among prehistoric and ancient religions as well, many of them predating the rise of the idea of the male sun-god.

122. Frazer, TGB (3rd edition), Vol. 1, p. 3.

123. Exodus 34:20.

124. John 1:29, 36.

125. The Americas too have a long history of offering human sacrifices in order to appease the gods and goddesses. The Native-American Aztecs, for example, were enthusiastic practitioners of ritual murder, as were the Pawnee, who continued the custom right up into the early 1800s.

126. See e.g., Leviticus 16:8, 10, 26.

127. Micah 6:7.

128. Genesis 22:1-19.

129. 2 Chronicles 33:1-6.

130. 2 Kings 16:1-3; 2 Chronicles 28:1-3.

131. 2 Kings 3:27.

132. 1 Kings 16:34.

133. 2 Samuel 21:9.

134. 2 Kings 17:9-17.

135. John 3:3.

136. See John 1:29, 36.

137. We will note here that in the Southern Hemisphere, the Winter Solstice falls at the opposite time of year, namely on June 20 or June 21 (depending on the calendar). However, Christians living in that hemisphere, such as Australian Christians, do not observe Christmas at their Winter Solstice (in Summer). Rather they do so at the same time most Christian nations in the Northern Hemisphere do, on December 25.

138. See Amos 5:26.

139. For biblical examples of the Pagan "three days" motif, see Hosea 6:2; Matthew 16:21; 17:23; 20:19; Mark 9:31; Luke 9:22; 18:33; 24:7; 24:46; John 2:19.

140. Mithraism was officially banned by the Catholic Church in the year 376.

141. Despite the violent prohibition against it by the Catholic Church, Mithraism survived into the Middle Ages as the Gnostic-Christian "heresy" known as Manichaeism.

142. Nolloth, p. 123.

143. Jesus' Twelve Apostles and their associated astrological star-signs are as follows: James, Aries the Ram; Andrew, Taurus the Bull; Thomas, Gemini the Twins; Nathaniel, Cancer the Crab; Judas, Leo the Lion; James the Just, Virgo the Virgin; Jude, Libra the Scales; John, Scorpio the Scorpion; Philip, Sagittarius the Archer;

Simon, Capricorn the Goat; Matthew, Aquarius the Water Bearer; and Peter, Pisces the Two Fishes. The Twelve Days of Christmas were patterned on these ancient Pagan-Christian connections, beginning with James (Aries) on December 26, ending with Peter (Pisces) on January 6. For more on this topic, see Seabrook, SBD, s.v. "Apostles"; s.v. "Twelve."

144. Ahriman's name derives from the Iranian term *Angra Mainya,* meaning "destructive thought."

145. 1 Corinthians 10:4. We will note here that Saint Paul's view that Jesus was the Rock upon which the Church was built was aggressively opposed by other Christians, among them the unknown authors of the book of Matthew, who maintained that Saint Peter, not Jesus, was the cornerstone of Christianity. See e.g., Matthew 16:17-19. The Catholic Church itself agreed with "Saint Matthew" not Saint Paul, for in the end, it built the Vatican not over any sacred sites connected with Jesus, but over the alleged burial site of Saint Peter, a christianized version of the Mithraic Pagan city-god Petra (the "Rock"). This explains why the papal throne, called Saint Peter's Chair, is nearly identical with the ancient Throne of Mithras, complete with decorative astrological signs and Pagan solar symbols.

146. John 14:26.

147. Malachi 4:2.

148. John 8:12; 9:5. See also John 1:1-10.

149. Luke 3:23. The original Hebrew word here, *Heli,* means "ascending," an occult reference to the rising Sun; that is, the resurrecting Son.

150. Matthew 17:1-2.

151. Mark 16:2, 6.

152. Matthew 13:43.

153. The etymological association between the words Sun and son are aptly shown in the German word for Sun: *sonne.*

154. Frazer, TGB (3rd edition), Vol. 1, pp. 304-305.

155. Charles II, the "Merry Monarch," forty-ninth king of England, is my 4th cousin.

156. Seabrook, SBD, s.v. "Osiris." Osiris is a Latinization of the Egyptian word *Usir,* "mighty" or "powerful."

157. See e.g., 1 Samuel 10:1; 1 Kings 1:39.

158. The eleven Jesuses of the Bible are: (1) Joshua, head of the Israelites, successor of Moses: Exodus 17:9; (2) Joshua, a son of Jehozadak or Josedech: Hagar 1:1; (3) Jehu, son of Nimshi: 1 Kings 19:16; (4) Joshua, governor of Jerusalem under King Josiah: 2 Kings 23:8; (5) Joshua, a resident of Beth-Shemesh: 1 Samuel 6:18; (6) Jeshua, a high priest: Ezra 2:2; (7) Jesus the Christ: Matthew 1:16; (8) Jesus Barabbas: Matthew 27:17; (9) Jose, one of Jesus' ancestors: Luke 3:29; (10) Joshua (Jesus), the son of Nun: Acts 7:45; Hebrews 4:8; (11) Jesus Justus, a Jewish-Christian: Colossians 4:11.

159. John 10:30.

160. The Greek savior-god Adonis and the Babylonian savior-god Tammuz were identical. As even a casual reading of ancient Greek and Babylonian mythology will reveal, much of the legendary material found in Jesus' biography was originally borrowed from these two Pagan deities.

161. See e.g., Genesis 37:9; Deuteronomy 4:19; 17:13; 33:14; Joshua 10:12-13.

162. Isaiah 3:17-18.

163. While there are numerous legends surrounding Lady Godiva, she was in fact a real person who lived from about 980 to 1067. The wife of Leofric III, Earl of Mercia, England, Lady Godiva is my 31st great-grandmother.

164. We use the phrase "Christ motif" here, not as an insult to Christianity, but in a factual and historical sense, as there were countless numbers of Christs in the Pagan religions that existed before the Christian Era. For those who have "eyes to see" and "ears to hear" (see e.g., Deuteronomy 29:4; Ezekiel 12:2; Matthew 13:15-16; Ephesians 1:18), this can only aid us in better understanding and appreciating the Christian Christ.

165. One of the better known examples of Old Testament plagiarism is the Judeo-Christian Flood Myth found in Genesis 6-9. In creating it, ancient Hebrew scribes and storytellers borrowed heavily from a number of traditional neighboring Pagan flood myths, all in existence long before the writing of the Old Testament, or even the appearance of the Hebrews. Among the flood myths used were those of the ancient Egyptians, Sumerians, Assyrians, East Indians, Persians, and Chaldeans. The flood legend Old Testament writers relied on most intensely, however, was the Babylonians' *The Epic of Gilgamesh*.

166. See Genesis 32:28. The full etymology of the word Israel, or Is-Ra-El, is as follows: "Is" comes from the name of Egyptian virgin-mother-moon-goddess, Isis. "Ra" comes from the name of Ra, the Egyptian father-sun-god (from whom we get the word "ray"). "El" is the Semitic word for "deity" or "god" (El is also the name of both a Canaanite god and a Phoenician bull-god). Thus, Is-Ra-El began as either a primitive Pagan female-male deity (i.e., "the God Is-Ra"), or perhaps a Pagan triple-deity symbolizing the Sacred Family, comprised of the Female Principle (Isis), the Male Principle (Ra), and their Divine Child (El). Note that the plural of El is Elohim, meaning a multitude of gods and goddesses, while the feminine singular of Elohim is Eloah ("Goddess"). Elohim is a common word in the Old Testament, as the early Jews (Hebrews) were polytheistic, worshiping a pantheon of Semitic deities. See e.g., Exodus 15:11; 22:28; Deuteronomy 31:16; Joshua 24:14-15; Judges 2:12; 10:6, 14; 2 Chronicles 25:15, 20; Psalms 82:1; 86:8; 138:1; Daniel 5:4, 11, 14, 23.

167. See Matthew 2:15.

168. See Ruth 1:20.

169. That the Queen of Heaven Isis and Ashtaroth, or Ashtoreth, as she was also known, were the same, is acknowledged throughout the Old Testament. See e.g., 1 Kings 11:5, 33; 2 Kings 23:13; Jeremiah 44:15-19; 24-25.

170. See Revelation 12:1.

171. The worship of Isis was once so popular that her cult spread all across Europe, even to England, where there was a thriving Isisian Temple in what is now Southwark, London.

172. For more on the many connections between Krishna and Jesus, see Seabrook, SBD, s.v. "Krishna."

173. See Matthew 2:13-15.

174. Incredibly, Sirius B was not discovered by modern scientists until 1844. Yet the Dogons' knowledge of the star—assuming their claim is true—is thousands of years old, dating back to pre-dynastic Egypt (prior to 3200 BC).

175. Contrary to ancient Roman mythology, Mormons (LDS) teach that Lucifer (i.e., Satan or the Devil) and Jesus are brothers, both the children (like all of us) of God the Father and Goddess the Mother. For more on this interesting topic, see the Website: www.bible-truth.org/jesusbro.htm. Also see the Mormons' own *The Pearl of Great Price*: Abraham 3:27-28; Moses 4:1-4; as well as the following official Mormon Web

page: www.lds.org/library/display/0,4945,11-1-13-6,00.html. For more on the official Mormon view, see in particular, Ludlow, s.v. "Devils"; "Mother in Heaven."

176. Along with Mark Twain, Walt Whitman, Ralph Waldo Emerson, and many others, I believe that the man called William Shakespeare was not the true author of the brilliant works attributed to him. In my opinion the best guess currently for the real "Shakespeare" was my cousin the 17th Earl of Oxford, Edward de Vere (my 6th great-grandfather was the 3rd Earl of Oxford). Other possible candidates for "Shakespeare" include Christopher Marlowe, Francis Bacon, and Fulke Greville.

177. Shakespeare, *Julius Caesar*, II, ii.30.

178. For more on the many connections between Buddha and Jesus, see Seabrook, SBD, s.v. "Buddha."

179. Matthew 2:1-2.

180. Numbers 24:17.

181. Malachi 4:2.

182. Revelations 22:16. For more on the Pagan antecedents of the Star of Bethlehem and the Nativity of Jesus, see Seabrook, SBD, s.v. "Star of Bethlehem."

183. Augeas was the mythic king of Elis, a member of the Argonauts, and the owner of the stables.

184. In Pagan numerology, 10 equals 1 (by adding 1 and 0), the sacred number of God, the Alpha and Omega, the beginning and end of all things. December was truly the "beginning" of the sun-son-god's life due to his birth (or annual rebirth) at the Winter Solstice. See Revelation 1:8; 22:13.

185. Matthew 2:11.

186. Luke 2:7.

187. See *The Infancy Gospel of James* (*Protevangelium Jacobi*), 14:11-14. In ancient times, caves were sometimes used as stables (as they still are in various parts of the world today). Thus, the meaning of "cave" and "stable," as it was utilized in early religious literature, was often interchangeable. We will also note that not only were many Pagan deities born in caves, many were worshiped in them as well. Among these were: Mithras, Poseidon, Cybele, Hercules, Apollo, and Demeter.

188. Matthew 2:1.

189. Most of the elements of the Nativity of Jesus were borrowed from Paganism and added to the books of Matthew and Luke by Christian mythographers in the 4th Century, during the great rewriting of the Bible under Emperor Constantine the Great. Some 1,000 years later, the Catholic Church was still benefitting from this great conspiratorial coverup, as Pope Leo X noted: "It was well known how profitable this fable of Christ has been to us." That this event truly took place is clear from the many overt discrepancies and careless handling of the texts that appear throughout the New Testament. For example, as we have seen, Joseph is given two different fathers (see Matthew 1:16 and Luke 3:23), while various passages in the Matthaean version repeat and contradict one another. Matthew 1:25, for instance, is a repetition of Matthew 1:21; while Matthew 1:18 contradicts Matthew 1:23, and Matthew 1:20 contradicts Matthew 1:25. The Nativity story is completely absent from the books of Mark and John, which is altogether shocking if the earth-shattering events recorded in Matthew and Luke are true. In the case of Mark, the earliest of the canonical Gospels, this is no doubt because the Jesuine birth legend had not been fully developed at the time of its composition. This theory is supported by the fact that Saint Paul's *genuine* letters, written long before the four canonical Gospels, also neglect to make any mention of the details of Jesus' birth, or even of His miracles or the Twelve Apostles. In the case of John—written in Ephesus sometime in the 2nd Century—one can only conclude that he did not have access to the Jesuine nativity material by then in general circulation. For more on this topic, see Seabrook, SBD, s.v. "Gospel."

190. That is, moving at about 186,000 miles a second, it would take light about 4.2 years to travel from Proxima Centauri to Earth.

191. Contrary to popular opinion, the early Hebrews were intensely involved in astrology (see e.g., Genesis 1:14; 2 Kings 23:5), particularly the more mystically-oriented Jewish sects. They called the Zodiac, after the Chaldeans, *Galgal Hammazaloth*: the "Circle of Signs" (in Mesopotamia the Zodiac was called, *Hadronitho Demalusche*: the "Circle of Signs"). For an example of the four compass-gods of the early Hebrews, see Ezekiel 1:10 (compare with Revelation 4:6-7, the four compass-gods of the later Hebrews, c. early 2nd Century). Astrology is still very much alive among some mystical Jewish groups (e.g., Kabbalah) and Christian groups (e.g., the Gnostics). For more on this topic, see Seabrook, SBD, s.v. "astrology."

192. While the celestial religion of astrology originated in ancient Mesopotamia, the version of astrology that has come down to us today is far different than the systems used in Babylonia and Egypt 5,000 years ago. Modern day astrology is chiefly an amalgamation of ancient Grecian astrology (from 500 BC), and various revisions developed during the Medieval period. Refinements continue to this day. Uranus, Neptune, and Pluto, for example, seem to have been unknown to the ancients and were added to astrology (as they were discovered) in the 18th, 19th, and 20th Centuries respectively. And recently (in 2006), Pluto was demoted by astronomers from planet status to dwarf planet (or minor planet) status, and renamed asteroid number 134340. How, or if, this will affect modern astrology remains to be seen.

193. We will note here that the Latin word *Orion* is a derivation of the Latin words *oriens*, meaning "rising Sun," and *orior*, meaning "to be born," or "to rise."

194. These three celestial objects took on profound divine significance in nearly all ancient cultures, from Africa and South America to Asia and Europe.

195. Aquila derives its name from the mythological eagle sent to take Ganymedes to Olympus.

196. During the formation of the mythological aspects of Jesus' life story, this name was applied to John the Baptist as the "Herald of the Son of God." See e.g., Matthew 3:1-3. For more on this topic, see Seabrook, SBD, s.v. "John the Baptist."

197. It was around the solar cult of Ra (sometimes confused with, and thus also variously known as, Amon, Amon-Ra, and later Aton) that the world's first known monotheistic religion began (there were, no doubt, earlier Pagan monotheistic belief systems; however, Egypt's is the first recorded). This occurred under the reign of the Pharaoh Akhenaten (Amenhotep IV), who ruled from 1375 to 1358 BC. Amon means "Hidden"; Aton means "Sun disk." Though the monotheistic religion of the sun-god was later rejected and discarded by Egyptians after Akhenaten's death, the idea of worshiping a single sun/son-deity was eagerly adopted by the then polytheistic Israelites (Exodus 20:3). As proof of this appropriation, see Psalm 104 for an almost exact copy of Akhenaten's monotheistic poem to the sun-god, "Hymn of the Aton." From Judaism, where God was called *shemesh tsddhakah*, "the Sun of Righteousness" (Malachi 4:2), the idea of monotheism passed into mainstream Christianity through 1st Century Jewish-Gnostic sects, like the Essenes, who were by then referring to God as *ben tsddhakah*, "the Son of Righteousness." Yet, to this day, despite Christianity's professed "monotheism," the Church continues to steadfastly cling to the polytheism of the Old Religion, as the yearly celebration of Christmas and the worship of the great sun/son-god aptly attest. For examples of references to the

Judeo-Christian Pantheon of gods, goddesses, spirits, demons, beasts, monsters, dragons, devils, and angels, see e.g., Matthew 4:6, 11; 8:16, 31; 9:34; 12:24, 28; 13:41, 49; 16:27; 24:31; 25:31, 41; 26:53; Mark 1:13, 34; 3:22; 5:9, 12; 8:38; 13:27; 16:9; Luke 4:41; 8:2, 27, 30, 33; 9:1; 10:17; 11:15; 12:9; John 1:51; 10:34-35; Acts 19:27-28; 34-35; 1 Corinthians 6:3; 8:5; Hebrews 1:6-7; 12:22; 1 Peter 3:22; Jude 1:6; James 2:19; Revelation 5:11; 7:1; 8:2; 12:7; 16:4; 21:12. For more on this topic, see Seabrook, SBD, s.v. "gods and goddesses."

198. For more on the connection between pre-Christian nativities and Jesus, see Seabrook, SBD, s.v. "Nativity."

199. According to ancient Egyptian mythology, Hathor (whose name means "house of Horus") aided the newborn sun-god up to the heavens atop her horns. As such, she came to be regarded as "the solar eye."

200. See e.g., Exodus 7:11; Daniel 2:2.

201. Robert Taylor, "The Star of Bethlehem," *The Comet*, Vol. 1 (New York, NY, 1832-1833), p. 58.

202. Soltau, pp. 73, 75.

203. Matthew 2:1-12.

204. Matthew 2:11.

205. Fouard, Vol. 1, p. 67.

206. See Matthew 2:23; Acts 24: 1-5. For more on the Gnostic background of Jesus, see Seabrook, SBD, s.v. "Gnosticism."

207. The Neanderthals' use of red ochre in their burials probably signifies an attempt to imbue the dead with the Great Mother's life force, enabling them to continue living on the Other Side. Flowers sprinkled across Neanderthalian corpses no doubt represented love, as they still do—as any modern funeral director will attest.

208. A curious historical footnote: the chief patron of Martin Luther (1483-1546), the leading anti-Catholic and Protestant reformer, was Frederick the Wise of Saxony (1482-1556), who maintained an enormous collection of valuable relics.

209. Basilides, a 2nd-Century Gnostic-Christian teacher and leader from Alexandria, Egypt, taught that Jesus' physical body was an illusion, a "phantasm," as he referred to it. Such Gnostics believed that matter is temporary and thus illusionary. It was for this reason that Basilides maintained that Jesus did not die on the cross, for Divine Energy cannot die. Rather, Jesus substituted a man named Simon of Cyrene, who was forced to carry the cross, after which he was crucified instead of Jesus. While this view is rejected by mainstream Christians today, remnants of the original story can still be found in the canonical Gospels. See e.g., Matthew 27:27-35. To add further confusion, and interest, to this theory, the man Pilate wished to crucify instead of Jesus the Christ was also named Jesus, in this case, Jesus Barabbas. Some hold that the former was switched with the latter at the last minute, which means that Jesus still "died on the cross"—just not the one Christianity teaches. For vestiges of this ancient legend, see e.g., Matthew 27:15-26. For more on this topic, see Seabrook, SBD, s.v. "Crucifixion."

210. See e.g., 1 Corinthians 2:16; Philippians 2:5.

211. See e.g., 2 Corinthians 5:16-17; Colossians 1:26-27.

212. Many of the ancients did not grasp that these Pagan saviors themselves were not historical personages, and that they were merely metaphors representing deeply mystical spiritual truths. For more on this topic, see Seabrook, SBD, s.v. "gods and goddesses."

213. Herbermann, Pace, Pallen, Shahan, and Wynne, Vol. 10, s.v. "Natal Day."

214. This belief was strongest among the Gnostic sect known as the Docetists. Saint Paul, who the Bible portrays as holding a confusing number of contradictory views (no doubt because his biblical biography, like that of Jesus, has been reworked countless times by subsequent authors and mythographers), espoused various elements of Docetism, such as the belief that Jesus was not a flesh and blood human being. See e.g., 2 Corinthians 5:16. Like other Christian mystics and Gnostics, Paul also held that the stories of the Old Testament were not literal, true-life events, but rather were spiritual allegories, meant to hide ancient occult knowledge and wisdom from the uninitiated. See e.g., Galatians 4:21-24. As such, those Christians who take the Bible literally, according to Paul, are committing a grave sin. As the saint himself asserted: "The letter killeth, but the spirit giveth life" (2 Corinthians 3:6). The "uninitiated" Paul refers to were those who were not part of his cult (1 Corinthians 1:10-12; 4:6, 16), and those who did not follow his Gospel (Romans 2:16; 16:25; 2 Titus 2:8). He taught, like other early Christian mystics (most importantly the Gnostics) what he himself called "the hidden wisdom" (1 Corinthians 2:7). What was this "hidden wisdom," in Greek, literally the "*Mistikos Sophia*"? From the name itself, it was certainly related to the mysteries of the Sacred Feminine, for Sophia was the great Greek wisdom-goddess (known as Sapientia in Rome, and as Shekina in mystical Judaism), worshiped widely across the Roman world. What we know for sure is that Saint Paul's Gnostic initiation cult had three levels of spiritual attainment. These were, starting from the lowest: 3) the Beginners or the Somatics ("Bodies"); 2) the Progressing or the Psychics ("Souls"); and 1), the highest level, the Perfect or the Pneumatics ("Spirituals"). Saint Paul makes reference to this last group in his first letter to the Corinthians: "Howbeit we speak wisdom [Sophia] among them that are perfect; yet not the wisdom [Sophia] of this world, nor of the princes of this world, that come to nought: But we speak the wisdom [Sophia] of God in a mystery, even the hidden wisdom [Mistikos Sophia], which God ordained before the world unto our glory" (1 Corinthians 2:6). The Perfect or Pneumatics believed that they did not need the healing salvation of Jesus's death because through their Gnostic schooling they had already found the inner Kingdom of God mentioned by Jesus (Luke 17:21); that is, the occult Parousia or mystical inner Second Coming. Thus, they considered themselves spiritual royalty, spiritual "kings," far above and beyond the uninitiated. The New Testament portrays Saint Paul chastising the Perfect for holding this "arrogant" belief (see e.g., 1 Corinthians 4:8), but this seems to be a late interpolation by Catholic priests. For more on Paul, see Seabrook, SBD, s.v. "Paul."

215. "The Edict of Milan" was, in truth, not an edict, nor was it issued in Milan. It was a policy agreed on by both Constantine the Great and Licinius after a meeting in Milan.

216. The Liberian Catalogue (or Philocalian Calendar) was composed in the 4th Century by an unknown writer referred to as "The Chronographer of 354." The Catalogue, a record of Roman Bishops beginning with Saint Peter (r. 31-64) and ending with Pope Liberius (r. 352-366), is but one document of a larger almanac composed by the mysterious author.

217. Tille, p. 86. Note: These words were penned by Tertullian in the year 230.

218. The word "saint" is a Middle English word derived from the Late Latin word *sanctus*, meaning "sacred." It should be noted that early Christianity took this title-name from the pre-Christian Jews, who, in turn, borrowed it from various Graeco-Roman Pagan sects who called themselves, in Greek, *Hagios*; that is, "The Sacred Ones." In the New Testament, the Jewish sect known as the mystical Nazarenes (later mislabeled "Christians"), called themselves "The Saints" (see e.g., Acts 9:13; 26:10; Romans 15:25; Revelation 15:3), or "The Elect" (see e.g., Mark 13:22; Colossians 3:12). In the Old Testament, early Jews also referred to themselves as

"The Saints" (see e.g., Psalms 148:14), or in Hebrew, *Chaciyd*, or *Qadowsh*. This is the same as the Jewish title-phrase (translated into English), "The Chosen" (see e.g., 2 Samuel 6:1; Psalms 78:31; Luke 23:35), or "The Holy Ones" (see e.g., Daniel 4:17).

219. To this day, the term "Old Nick" is still used on occasion as one of the many names for the Christian demon-god the Devil. The confusion is a carry-over from the Medieval period when *Hold Nickar* was still widely known as a "fearsome sea-monster."

220. Nearly all pre-Christian religions possessed one or more a trinities. In ancient Rome, for example, the major trinity was made up of the god Jupiter and the goddesses Juno and Minerva. One of the minor Greek trinities was the Triple Graces, comprised of the three goddesses Aglaia (splendor), Thalia (abundance), and Euphrosyne (jollity). All trinities, male, female, or mixed, descend from the original, prehistoric, all-female trinity, later known as the Triple-Goddess. For more on this topic, see Seabrook, SBD, s.v. "Trinity."

221. Naturally, the Pagan triple-goddess—each of the three individual females often known as Meri—shows up in Christian mythology. See e.g., John 19:25.

222. For examples of some of the magical "threes" that appear in Saint Paul's "biography," see Acts 9:9; 17:2; 19:8; 20:3, 9, 31; 23:23; 15:1; 27:19; 28:7, 11-12, 15, 17; 1 Corinthians 13:13; 14:27, 29; 2 Corinthians 12:2; 12:14; 13:1; Galatians 1:18.

223. John 21:1-11.

224. The word gematria probably derives from, or has associations with, the words *geo* ("earth") and *matri* ("mother"); thus meaning "earth-mother," that is, the great Virgin-Earth-Mother-Goddess.

225. John 19:25.

226. In the ancient Graeco-Roman world the practice of seeking nirvana or spiritual enlightenment through sex was known as Horasis, while to the Old Testament Jews it was called Yada, meaning to "know" (see e.g., Genesis 4:1). Horasis was often achieved through the use of temple prostitutes (a practice called sacred or religious prostitution). To this day the custom remains an element of the religious philosophy known as Tantric Yoga, where the Divine Feminine is honored through the worship of the great Hindu mother-goddess Shakti. Strangely, in the book of Acts 2:17, the anonymous author predicts that in the "last days" God will "pour out" Horasis on faithful young Christian men (the word "visions" here is a purposeful mistranslation of the original word *horasis*, that is, the attainment of Christ Consciousness or spiritual enlightenment through ecstatic sex). Horasis or Yada, though practiced among the early Israelites, was later sternly condemned by Hebrew authorities (see e.g., Leviticus 19:29; 20:5; 21:9; Deuteronomy 32:18). Israel, no doubt, absorbed the tradition from surrounding peoples, such as the Canaanites and Mesopotamians, who practiced religious prostitution in their worship of the goddesses Anath and Belit-ili respectively. Note: Belit-ili was later absorbed into Jewish mythology as Lilith, becoming both Adam's first wife and the dreaded night-hag of Isaiah 34:19, where, demonized, she appears as a "screech owl." For more on sacred prostitution, see Seabrook, AT.

227. Saint Paul castigated some of his followers at Corinth for indulging in similar practices. See e.g., 1 Corinthians 6:9-20.

228. See e.g., Revelation 2:6, 14-15.

229. The god Woden/Wotan also gave his name to the Kentish family surname Wooten or Wootton.

230. A relative of the word *hob* is the Welsh word *hap*, meaning "fortune."

231. The Middle English word "elf" derives from the Old Norse word *alfr*, which in turn derives from the Latin word *albus*, meaning "white." This name-word was originally an allusion to the pale color often associated with apparitions, ghosts, and phantoms. More importantly, however, *albas* referred to the pale white color of the European moon-goddess Europa, who gave her name to that continent. *Albas* has other associations with the Moon, the Mother-Goddess, goddess-worship, and Pagan Europe. Among the first inhabitants of England, for example, was a Celtic people known as the Albiones, who arrived on the island sometime after 600 BC. They took their name from the great Celtic mother-moon-goddess Albion, whose name means "White Face" or "White Moon." So central was she to the Albiones ("followers of Albion") that they named both themselves and their territory after her. To this day, Albion has the honor of being England's first known name. For more on this topic, see Seabrook, BR.

232. The idea of deities being carried about in deer-drawn carriages was not uncommon in ancient myth. The moon-goddess Diana, as another example, was said to ride in a chariot pulled by bucks.

233. In ancient Greece, Mars was called Ares, now spelled Aries.

234. Mars and Maris, of course, both derive, like most ancient male deities, from an earlier female prototype; in this case, the prehistoric goddess Mar or Mari, who would become the virgin-mother Isis-Meri in Egypt, the virgin-mother Myrrha in Greece, and the Virgin Mary in Christianity.

235. Whether Saint Martin was a historical personage or not must be left to the reader. What is clear, however, is that his biography is made up almost solely of standard Pagan mythological motifs, themes, and legends. For many Christians, this fact alone calls into question the reality of his existence.

236. In England, the tradition of slaughtering livestock on Saint Martin's Day continued into modern times.

237. Nicholas was said to have given his material riches (inherited from his wealthy parents) to the poor, while Martin, a pacifist of sorts, was said to have founded a religious center in Touraine, and, as Bishop of Tours, opposed the ill treatment of heretics.

238. Nast was a Republican, which was the Liberal party in the mid 1800s. The Democrats of that period formed the Conservative Party. For more on this topic, see Seabrook, ALWALJDWAC.

239. Nast is also well-known for two other creations: the elephant and donkey symbols of the Republican and Democratic parties. Note: here in the South, traditional Southerners will always remember Nast, not as a great Civil War artist, but as a pro-North partisan Liberal who used his artwork to unfairly smear Dixie and the Conservative party, then known as the Democrats (now known as the Republicans). For more on the truth about America's so-called "Civil War," see Seabrook, LW; Seabrook, AL; Seabrook, EYWTATCWIW; Seabrook, AWAITBLA, etc.

240. Many of these individuals also do not observe Easter, Halloween, or personal birthdays, all being Pagan, not Christian, festivals and customs.

241. Actually, this is an illusion, caused by the Earth shifting on its axis.

242. Kriss is a variation of the Old High German word *Krist*, meaning "Christ," which means the "Sun." Kringle is a dialectal variation of the German word *kindl*, which is a diminutive of the German word *kind*, meaning "child." Thus, Kriss Kringle means "sun-child."

243. "Brand" is a Middle English word meaning both "torch" and "sword." It almost certainly derives from the Old English word *bærnan*, "to burn."

244. Ancient Hebrew (Jewish) women continued to worship the Pagan savior-god Tammuz even after his cult was banned. See e.g., Ezekiel 8:14. The Jewish obsession with this Babylonian "Only Begotten Son" (known to the Romans as Adonis) survives in the name of the fourth month of the Jewish calendar: Tammuz.

245. See e.g., Ezekiel 6:13.

246. See e.g., 1 Chronicles 10:12.

247. Frazer, TGB (2ⁿᵈ edition), Vol. 3, p. 327.

248. For more on this topic, see Seabrook, SBD, s.v. "Cana Wedding"; "Cross"; "Oil"; "Sacrament"; "Dove"; "Paul"; "Reincarnation"; "Washing the Feet."

249. Nearly all wild vegetation is perennial; that is, it lives year-round, no matter what the weather or climate. At the same time, however, most of these same plants do not remain green during the winter months. Instead, they either drop their foliage completely, or it turns color, often gold, yellow, red, or brown. To the ancient mind, such plants seemed to "die" and be "reborn" the following Spring. In reality, as we now know, they merely go dormant during the cold season in order to conserve energy. Little wonder that the few plants which remain green 365 days a year, like holly, mistletoe, and pine trees, were accorded sacred, magical, or divine status thousands of years ago.

250. We will note here that despite the fact that it is now considered the "Babylon of North America," the modern-day city of Hollywood, California, has sacred origins, as its holy name suggests. First settled in 1888 by a temperance society under one Horace Wilcox, Hollywood was originally planned as a Christian Eden of chastity and virtue. Only non-drinkers were allowed to live in the utopian community, and until the 1920s, when the film industry moved in, there were no crimes and hence no jails.

251. Jeremiah 10:2-4.

252. The allegory of saviors being sacrificed on trees was still exceedingly popular in the 1ˢᵗ and 2ⁿᵈ Centuries, and hence was used, not surprisingly, in the development of the mythological, occultic, and theological elements of Jesus' life story. See e.g., Acts 5:30; 10:39; 13:29; Galatians 3:13; 1 Peter 2:24. But being hanged in a tree as a ritual form of death was no mere myth. Many historical figures actually met their demise in just this fashion. One of these was a man named Jesus ben Pandira who, on Passover Eve around the year 100 BC, was put to death and hung in a tree. The Bible itself records the custom, and there can be no question that many perished in this exact manner in the years prior to the emergence of Christianity. See e.g., Joshua 8:29; 10:26; 2 Samuel 21:9; Esther 2:23. Such events, such as the crucifixion of Jesus ben Pandira, certainly contributed to the biographical details of Jesus Christ's death as formulated by 1ˢᵗ-, 2ⁿᵈ-, and 3ʳᵈ-Century mythographers. For more on this topic, see Seabrook, SBD, s.v. "Crucifixion."

253. Like his Pagan counterparts, Jesus too wore the tree crown at the time of His sacrifice to the triple-goddess variously known as Mar, Mer, Meri, Mari, Marina, Mariam, or Mary. For a biblical example of the Christian triple-goddess, see the "three Marys" of John 19:25. For examples of Jesus' tree crown, see Matthew 27:29; Mark 15:17; John 19:2.

254. See e.g., Proverbs 3:18; 11:30; 13:12; 15:4; Revelation 2:7; 22:2, 14.

255. See Genesis 2:9; 3:22, 24.

206 CHRISTMAS BEFORE CHRISTIANITY

256. In the pre-patriarchal world, known as the Matriarchate, time was calculated by the Moon not the Sun. Since the Moon's monthly twenty-eight-day phase matched the twenty-eight-day menstrual cycle of women, the Moon took on immense feminine sacrality, particularly in its "horned" phase as the crescent Moon. Additionally, the number thirteen became holy because it was associated with the great Pagan Mother-Goddess and her Twelve Priestesses, the latter who were often portrayed as star-goddesses. Thus, using the annual transit of the Sun (365 days) as a foundation, the matriarchal calendar developed into a thirteen-month year, each month with twenty-eight days. This Pagan imagery was later adopted by Christianity (see Revelation 12:1). Many modern peoples, such as the Jews and Chinese, continue to use the ancient lunar calendar in one manner or another. Christians too continue to rely on the old Pagan lunar calendar, in this case, to annually calculate the date of Easter Sunday (Passover to Jews), itself a Pagan holiday dedicated to, as its name indicates, the Saxon Spring-goddess Eostre (from whence we also derive the word estrus). Our modern word Monday is a paganistic vestige of the time when the Western world honored the Moon on the second day of the week: Monday derives from Moon-day, which comes from the Old English word *monandæg*, the "Moon's Day."

257. Genesis 4:25.

258. My copy of *The Oxford English Dictionary* maintains that the etymology of the word apple is unknown (s.v. "apple"). However, it is probable that Apollo was named after the apple or the apple was named after him. For more on this topic, see R. Graves, TWG, pp. 256-257.

259. Known by the ancient Egyptians as the great mother-goddess Isis, mother of the savior-sun-god Horus, the Roman Virgo was, of course, another one of the many models for the Judeo-Christian Virgin Mary.

260. As a neo-Victorian I am proud to be a cousin of Queen Victoria, the English ruler who gave her name to the Victorian period.

261. Actually, Edison only improved on lightbulb designs that had been created by others before him.

262. See e.g., 1 Corinthians 9:25; James 1:12; 1 Peter 5:4; Revelation 2:10.

263. For examples of early Jewish megalithic pillar worship, see Genesis 28:22; Jeremiah 2:26-28; Deuteronomy 32:4, 15, 18; 34:31, 37.

264. As noted here, the pentacle or pentagram is decidedly not a Satanic (death) symbol, as mainstream Christianity has long taught. It is the opposite. It is an ancient life symbol, one belonging to female religion, best known today as Wicca (Witchcraft), a loving, positive nature religion that does not believe in Satan or the Devil. The pentacle was demonized, like Wicca itself, by the Church in order to suppress its use. However, this attempt, like all others that have tried to demolish Paganism and its emblems, failed. The life-affirming symbolism behind the pentagram was perfectly captured in the late 1400s by a brilliant Christian mystic and initiate of female religion. I am referring here to Leonardo da Vinci and his magnificent drawing, "Vitruvian Man."

265. Isaiah 41:19.

266. Under the Pagans' Julian Calendar, the ancient Roman New Year began on or near the Spring Equinox under the zodiacal sign Aries (ruler of the month of March), as the names of the months November (the Latin word for "ninth month") and December (the Latin word for "tenth month") reveal. At the time, January was the eleventh month, while February was the twelfth, and thus final, month of the Roman year. As proof, to this day Pisces (which rules the month of February) is both the twelfth and the last sign in the Zodiac. Modern Pagans, as well as some Christians, continue to celebrate the New Year on the first of every March (or, in some cases, near the end of March on the Spring Equinox), just as it was originally observed under the Pagan Julian Calendar. Why do Westerners today observe the New Year on January 1 then? In 1582, in yet another vain attempt to blot out all vestiges of Paganism, the Catholic Church usurped and replaced the Julian Calendar with the Gregorian Calendar (named after Pope Gregory XIII). In the process, unintuitively, January became the first month, and January 1 became the new first day of the New Year. To many, however, Spring (i.e, March) still naturally "feels" like the beginning of the New Year, not Winter (i.e., January). I am among them.

267. I place the term New World in quotes because it was only a "new world" to the newly arriving Europeans—a concession to Native Americans, millions of whose ancestors had been inhabiting North America for at least the previous 40,000 years.

268. Contrary to popular belief, and the claims of Northerners (mainly New Englanders), the (European) history of the United States began in the South (Jamestown, Virginia), not in the North (Plymouth, Massachusetts).

269. *The Living Church*, Vol. 46, No. 10, January 6, 1912 (Milwaukee, WI) p. 350.

270. Judge Sewall despised Paganism and its holy days (such as Christmas) so intensely that he presided over the 1692 witch trials in Salem, Massachusetts, at which time some twenty innocent people were hanged or "pressed to death." I say "innocent" because the charge was "consorting with the Devil." Yet there is no Devil in the Wiccan belief system: only a Father-God and a Mother-Goddess, and an assortment of largely beneficent nature-deities. True witches do not believe in the Devil.

271. In April 2009, the name of the Worldwide Church of God was changed to Grace Communion International. Along with this transformation, the Church's old ban on Christmas was lifted. New teachings now encourage members to celebrate Christmas, though "as a religious holiday, not a commercialized one."

272. This conflict is incorrectly known in the North and by New South scallywags as the "Civil War." For more on this topic, see my many books on Lincoln's War.

273. The original European Pagan New Year began, of course, on the first day of Spring—the Spring Equinox, the beginning of the astrological period ruled by Aries (March-April). It ended on the last day of the astrological period ruled by Pisces, which marks the end of Winter (February-March).

274. See e.g., Jesus' references to the Third Eye (and the Third Ear, "inner hearing" as opposed to outer physical hearing) in Matthew 13:15-16; Mark 8:18; Luke 10:23; 12:34. Saint Paul refers to inner sight as "the eyes of your understanding being enlightened" in Ephesians 1:18. The Third Eye is also esoterically alluded to in the Old Testament in Job 42:5 and Psalms 18:28. For more on these topics, see Seabrook, SBD, s.v. "Third Ear"; s.v. "Third Eye."

275. The Seven Principles of Kwanzaa are: (1) unity; (2) self-determination; (3) collective work and responsibility; (4) cooperative economics; (5) purpose; (6) creativity; and (7) faith.

276. According to sacred numerology, the male number three added to the female number four equals seven, the number of the Hieros Gamos ("Sacred Union"), occultly speaking, spiritual enlightenment. Seven's connection with the Virgin-Mother-Goddess and the Female Principle began long ago, tens of thousands of years before the rise of patriarchal (that is, male- or father-based) religion. For example, the Venus of Willendorf (Austria), which is some 25,000 years old, has seven concentric horizontal circles drawn on her head. The occult number seven appears hundreds of times throughout the Bible, as sacred numerology was widely practiced among ancient Jews and Christians. See e.g., Genesis 2:2-3; 7:4; 8:4, 10, 12; Exodus 12:15; 13:6; Leviticus 23:8; Numbers 29:32; Deuteronomy 16:8; 28:7; Joshua 6:4, 6, 8, 15; 18:2, 5, 6, Judges 14:15; 1 Samuel 6:1; 2 Samuel 21:6; 1 Kings 18:43, 44; 2 Kings 5:10; 1 Chronicles 27:10; 2 Chronicles 7:8; Nehemiah 7:72; Esther 1:10; Job 2:13; Psalms 119:164; Proverbs 9:1; Isaiah 11:15; Jeremiah 34:14; Ezekiel 3:16; Daniel 4:16; Amos 5:8; Micah 5:5; Zechariah 4:10; Matthew 12:45; 15:36; 22:25; Mark 8: 5-6; Luke 8:2; Acts 6:3; Hebrews 11:30; Revelation 1:4, 12, 20; 3:1; 5:1, 6; 8:1-2; 10:3, 7; 12:3; 15:1, 7; 17:9; 21:9. For more on this topic, see Seabrook, SBD, s.v. "numbers."

277. John 1:9.

278. Acts 17. As an example, the Jewish father-god Yahweh was rightly seen by many in the ancient world as indistinguishable from the Thracian-Phrygian father-god Sabazios, the Greek father-god Zeus, and the Roman father-god Jupiter. Thus, all four of these non-Christian deities are the same as the "God" of the Christians' New Testament, commonly referred to as Jehovah—a word itself revealingly created from the name of the Pagan savior-god Adonis. For more on this topic, see Seabrook, SBD, s.v. "Jehovah."

BIBLIOGRAPHY

Abanes, Richard. *One Nation Under Gods: A History of the Mormon Church*. New York, NY: Four Walls Eight Windows, 2002.

——. *Becoming Gods: A Closer Look at 21ˢᵗ-Century Mormonism*. Eugene, OR: Harvest House, 2004.

Adler, Margot. *Drawing Down the Moon*. Boston, MA: Beacon Press, 1981.

Akerley, Ben Edward. *The X-rated Bible*. Austin, TX: American Atheist Press, 1989.

Albright, William Powell. *Yahweh and the Gods of Canaan*. New York, NY: Doubleday, 1968.

Allen, Paula Gunn. *The Sacred Hoop: Recovering the Feminine in American Indian Traditions*. Boston, MA: Beacon Press, 1986.

Allison, Dale C., Jr. *Resurrecting Jesus: The Earliest Christian Tradition and Its Interpreters*. New York, NY: T and T Clark, 2005.

Ames, Winthrop (ed.). *What Shall We Name the Baby?* 1941. New York, NY: Pocket Books, 1974 ed.

Andrews, George C. *Extra-Terrestrials Among Us*. 1986. St. Paul, MN: Llewellyn, 1993 ed.

Andrews, Ted. *The Occult Christ: Angelic Mysteries, Seasonal Rituals, and the Divine Feminine*. St. Paul, MN: Llewellyn, 1993.

Angus, Samuel. *The Mystery-Religions and Christianity: A Study of the Religious Background of Early Christianity*. 1925. New York, NY: Citadel Press, 1966 ed.

Ardrey, Robert. *African Genesis*. 1961. New York, NY: Dell, 1972 ed.

——. *The Territorial Imperative*. 1966. New York, NY: Delta, 1968 ed.

Armstrong, Karen. *A History of God: The 4000-Year Quest of Judaism, Christianity and Islam*. New York, NY: Knopf, 1993.

Aron, Robert. *Jesus of Nazareth: The Hidden Years*. New York, NY: William Morrow and Co., 1962.

Arterburn, Stephen, and Jack Felton. *Toxic Faith: Understanding and Overcoming Religious Addiction.* Nashville, TN: Oliver-Nelson Books, 1991.

Ashe, Geoffrey. *The Virgin: Mary's Cult and the Re-emergence of the Goddess.* 1976. London, UK: Arkana, 1988 ed.

——. *Dawn Behind the Dawn: A Search for the Earthly Paradise.* New York, NY: Henry Holt, 1992.

Asherman, Allan. *The Star Trek Compendium.* New York, NY: Pocket Books, 1989.

Asimov, Isaac. *A Short History of Biology.* Garden City, NY: Natural History Press, 1964.

Astrov, Margot (ed.). *The Winged Serpent: An Anthology of American Indian Poetry.* 1946. Greenwich, CT: Fawcett, 1973 ed.

Atkins, Gaius Glenn, and Charles Samuel Braden. *Procession of the Gods.* 1930. New York, NY: Harper and Brothers Publishers, 1936 ed.

Attwater, Donald. *The Penguin Dictionary of Saints.* 1965. Harmondsworth, UK: Penguin, 1983 ed.

Augstein, Rudolf. *Jesus Son of Man.* New York, NY: Urizen, 1977.

Augustine. *De haeresibus ad Quodvultdeum 46* ("Synopsis of the Entire System"). 5th Century.

——. *Confessions* (R.S. Pine-Coffin, trans.). Circa 400. Harmondsworth, UK: Penguin, 1961.

Avalon, Arthur. *Shakti and Shakta.* New York, NY: Dover, 1978.

Ayto, John. *Dictionary of Word Origins.* New York, NY: Arcade, 1990.

Bachofen, Johann Jakob. *Myth, Religion and Mother Right.* Princeton, NJ: Princeton University Press, 1967.

Baigent, Michael. *The Jesus Papers: Exposing the Greatest Cover-Up in History.* San Francisco, CA: HarperSanFrancisco, 2006.

Baigent, Michael, and Richard Leigh. *The Dead Sea Scrolls Deception.* 1991. New York, NY: Touchstone, 1993 ed.

Baigent, Michael, Richard Leigh, and Henry Lincoln. *Holy Blood, Holy Grail.* 1982. New York, NY: Dell, 1983 ed.

——. *The Messianic Legacy.* New York, NY: Dell, 1986.

Bailey, Sandra Buzbee. *Big Book of Baby Names.* Tucson, AZ: HP Books, 1982.

Barbet, Pierre. *A Doctor at Calvary: The Passion of Our Lord Jesus Christ as Described by a Surgeon.* New York, NY: P. J. Kennedy and Sons, 1953.

Baring, Anne, and Jules Cashford. *The Myth of the Goddess: Evolution of an Image.* 1991. Harmondsworth, UK: Arkana, 1993 ed.

Baring-Gould, Sabine. *Curious Myths of the Middle Ages.* New York, NY: University Books, 1967.

Barnouw, Victor. *An Introduction to Anthropology: Physical Anthropology and Archaeology*. Homewood, IL: Dorsey Press, 1971.

Barnstone, Willis (ed.). *The Other Bible: Ancient Esoteric Texts*. New York, NY: Harper and Row, 1984.

Baroja, Julio Caro. *The World of Witches*. Chicago, IL: University of Chicago Press, 1965.

Barrett, Charles Kingsley (ed.). *The New Testament Background: Writings From Ancient Greece and the Roman Empire That Illuminate Christian Origins*. New York, NY: Harper and Row, 1961.

Bauvel, Robert, and Adrian Gilbert. *The Orion Mystery: Unlocking the Secrets of the Pyramids*. New York, NY: Three Rivers Press, 1995.

Bayley, Harold. *Archaic England: An Essay in Deciphering Prehistory From Megalithic Monuments, Earthworks, Customs, Coins, Place-names, and Faerie Superstitions*. London, UK: Chapman and Hall, 1920.

Bede, Saint. *Ecclesiastical History of the English Nation*. L. Gidley, trans. (Originally written in the year 731.) Oxford, UK: James Parker and Co., 1870 ed.

Begg, Ean. *The Cult of the Black Virgin*. Harmondsworth, UK: Arkana, 1985.

Bell, Robert E. *Women of Classical Mythology: A Biographical Dictionary*. 1991. Oxford, UK: Oxford University Press, 1993 ed.

Ben-Abba, Dov. *Hebrew-English, English-Hebrew Dictionary*. Nazareth, Israel: Massada-Press, 1977.

Bennett, Jonathan. *Rationality*. 1964. London, UK: Routledge and Kegan Paul Ltd., 1971 ed.

Besant, Annie. *Esoteric Christianity or the Lesser Mysteries*. London, UK: Theosophical Publishing Society, 1905.

Best, Robert M. *Noah's Ark and the Ziusudra Epic: Sumerian Origins of the Flood Myth*. Fort Myers, FL: Enlil Press, 1999.

Bhagavad Gita (Juan Mascaró, trans.). c. 500 BC. Harmondsworth, UK: Penguin, 1962.

Bhaktivedanta, A. C. (Swami Prabhupāda). *The Science of Self Realization*. 1977. Los Angeles, CA: Bhaktivedanta Book Trust, 1983 ed.

Bharati, Agehananda. *The Tantric Tradition*. New York, NY: Samuel Weiser, 1975.

Biedermann, Hans. *Dictionary of Symbolism: Cultural Icons and the Meanings Behind Them* (James Hulbert, trans.). 1989. New York, NY: Facts On File, 1992 ed.

Bierlein, John Francis. *Parallel Myths*. New York, NY: Ballantine Wellspring, 1994.

Binder, Pearl. *Magic Symbols of the World*. London, UK: Hamlyn, 1972.

Black, Matthew. *The Scrolls and Christian Origins: Studies in the Jewish Background of the New Testament*. New York, NY: Charles Scribner's Sons, 1961.

Bly, Robert. *Iron John: A Book About Men*. 1990. New York, NY: Vintage Books, 1992 ed.

Boardman, John, Jasper Griffin, and Oswyn Murray (eds.). *The Roman World*. 1986. Oxford, UK: Oxford University Press, 1988 ed.

Boates, Karen Scott (ed.). *The Goddess Within*. Philadelphia, PA: Running Press, 1990.

Bock, Janet. *The Jesus Mystery*. 1980. San Ramon, CA: Aura, 1995 ed.

Bostwick, Arthur Elmore (ed.). *Doubleday's Encyclopedia*. 1931. New York, NY: Doubleday, Doran, and Co., 1939 ed.

Bouquet, Alan Coates. *Comparative Religion: A Survey and Comparison of the Great Religions of the World*. London, UK: Penguin, 1942.

Bowden, John. *Archaeology and the Bible*. Austin, TX: American Atheist Press, 1982.

Branston, Brian. *Gods of the North*. London, UK: Thames and Hudson, 1955.

Bratton, Fred Gladstone. *Myths and Legends of the Ancient Near East: Great Stories of the Sumero-Akkadian, Egyptian, Ugaritic-Canaanite, and Hittite Cultures*. New York, NY: Thomas Y. Crowell, 1970.

Breasted, James Henry. *Ancient Records of Egypt* (five vols.). Chicago: IL: University of Chicago Press, 1906.

Brewster, Harold Pomeroy. *Saints and Festivals of the Christian Church*. New York, NY: Frederick A. Stokes, 1904.

Bridgwater, William (ed.). *The Columbia-Viking Desk Encyclopedia*. 1953. New York, NY: Viking Press, 1968 ed.

Brier, Bob, and Jean-Pierre Houdin. *The Secret of the Great Pyramid: How One Man's Obsession Led to the Solution of Ancient Egypt's Greatest Mystery*. New York, NY: HarperCollins, 2008.

Briffault, Robert Stephen. *The Mothers: The Matriarchal Theory of Social Origins*. 1927. New York, NY: Macmillan, 1931 (single volume, abridged) ed.

Briggs, Katherine. *The Vanishing People: Fairy Lore and Legends*. New York, NY: Pantheon, 1978.

Brinkley, Dannion, and Kathryn Brinkley. *Secrets of the Light: Lessons From Heaven*. New York, NY: HarperOne, 2008.

Bronowski, J. *Science and Human Values*. 1956. New York, NY: Harper Colophon, 1965 ed.

Brownrigg, Ronald. *Who's Who in the New Testament*. 1971. New York, NY: Oxford University Press, 1993 ed.

Bucke, Richard Maurice. *Cosmic Consciousness: A Study in the Evolution of the Human Mind.* 1901. New York, NY: Dutton, 1969 ed.

Budapest, Zsuzsanna Emese. *The Holy Book of Women's Mysteries* (Part 1). 1979. Oakland, CA: Susan B. Anthony Coven No. 1, 1982 ed.

——. *The Holy Book of Women's Mysteries* (Part 2). Oakland, CA: Susan B. Anthony Coven No. 1, 1980.

Budge, Ernest Alfred Wallis. *Egyptian Magic.* London, UK: Kegan, Paul, Trench, Trübner, and Co., 1901.

——. *Osiris and the Egyptian Resurrection.* Vol. 1. London, UK: Philip Lee Warner, 1911.

——. *Amulets and Talismans.* 1930. New York, NY: Citadel, 1992 ed.

Bulfinch, Thomas. *Bulfinch's Mythology: The Age of Fable, the Age of Chivalry, Legends of Charlemagne* (one vol.). New York, NY: Thomas Y. Crowell, 1913.

Bullough, Vern L., and Bonnie Bullough. *The Subordinate Sex: A History of Attitudes Toward Women.* 1973. Baltimore, MD: Penguin, 1974 ed.

——. *Women and Prostitution: A Social History.* 1978. Buffalo, NY: Prometheus, 1987 ed.

Burke, James. *Connections.* Boston, MA: Little, Brown and Co., 1978.

Burn, A. R. *The Pelican History of Greece.* 1965. Harmondsworth, UK: Penguin, 1968 ed.

Burne, Jerome (ed.). *Chronicle of the World.* Mount Kisco, NY: Ecam, 1989.

Burr, William Henry. *Self-Contradictions of the Bible.* 1860. Amherst, NY: Prometheus, 1987 ed.

Burrell, Sidney A. *Handbook of Western Civilization: Beginnings to 1700* (Vol. 1). 1965. New York, NY: John Wiley and Sons, 1972 ed.

Burtt, Edwin A (ed.). *The Teachings of the Compassionate Buddha.* New York, NY: Mentor, 1955.

Butler, Bill. *Dictionary of the Tarot.* New York, NY: Schocken, 1975.

Butler, Trent C. (gen. ed.). *Holman Bible Dictionary.* Nashville, TN: Holman Bible Publishers, 1991.

Caesar, Gaius Julius. *The Conquest of Gaul* [*Gallic War*] (S. A. Handford, trans.). 51 BC. Harmondsworth, UK: Penguin, 1951, 1988 ed.

Calasso, Roberto. *The Marriage of Cadmus and Harmony* (Tim Parks, trans.). New York, NY: Alfred A. Knopf, 1993.

Calvocoressi, Peter. *Who's Who in the Bible.* 1987. Harmondsworth, UK: Penguin, 1990 ed.

Campanelli, Pauline. *Ancient Ways: Reclaiming Pagan Traditions.* 1991. St. Paul, MN: Llewellyn, 1992 ed.

Campbell, Joseph. *The Hero With a Thousand Faces*. 1949. Princeton, NJ: Princeton University Press, 1973 ed.

——. *The Masks of the Gods: Primitive Mythology*. Vol. 1. 1959. Harmondsworth, UK: Arkana, 1991 ed.

——. *The Masks of the Gods: Oriental Mythology*. Vol. 2. 1962. Harmondsworth, UK: Arkana, 1991 ed.

——. *The Masks of the Gods: Occidental Mythology*. Vol. 3. 1964. Harmondsworth, UK: Arkana, 1991 ed.

——. *The Masks of the Gods: Creative Mythology*. Vol. 4. 1968. Harmondsworth, UK: Arkana, 1991 ed.

——. *Myths to Live By*. New York, NY: Bantam, 1972.

——. *The Power of Myth* (with Bill Moyers). New York, NY: Doubleday, 1988.

——. *Transformations of Myth Through Time*. New York, NY: Harper and Row, 1990.

Campbell, Reginald John. *The Life of Christ*. New York, NY: D. Appleton and Co., 1921.

Camphausen, Rufus C. *The Encyclopedia of Erotic Wisdom*. Rochester, VT: Inner Traditions International, 1991.

Cannon, Dolores. *Jesus and the Essenes*. Huntsville, AR: Ozark Mountain Publishers, 1999.

Cantor, Norman F. *Inventing the Middle Ages*. New York, NY: William Morrow and Co., 1991.

Capra, Fritjof. *The Tao of Physics: An Exploration of the Parallels Bewteen Modern Physics and Eastern Mysticism*. 1975. Boston, MA: Shambala Publications, Inc., 1991 ed.

Carlyon, Richard. *A Guide to the Gods: An Essential Guide to World Mythology*. New York, NY: Quill, 1981.

Carpenter, Edward. *Pagan and Christian Creeds: Their Origin and Meaning*: New York, NY: Blue Ribbon, 1920.

Carpenter, Joseph Estlin. *The First Three Gospels: Their Origin and Relations*. London, UK: Philip Green, 1906.

——. *The Historical Jesus and the Theological Christ*. Boston, MA: American Unitarian Association, 1912.

Carson, Anne. *Goddesses and Wise Women: The Literature of Feminist Spirituality, An Annotated Bibliography* (1980-1992). Freedom, CA: Crossing Press, 1992.

Carter, Jesse Benedict. *The Religious Life of Ancient Rome: A Study in the Development of Religious Consciousness, From the Foundation of the City Until the Death of Gregory the Great*. Boston, MA: Houghton Mifflin, 1911.

Case, Shirley Jackson. *The Historicity of Jesus*. Chicago, IL: University of Chicago Press, 1912.

Cassius, Dio. *The Roman History: The Reign of Augustus* (Ian Scott-Kilvert, trans.). C. 214-226. Harmondsworth, UK: Penguin, 1988 ed.

Cavendish, Richard. *A History of Magic*. 1987. Harmondsworth, UK: Arkana, 1990 ed.

Cerminara, Gina. *Many Mansions*. 1950. New York, NY: Signet, 1967 ed.

Chaisson, Eric. *Cosmic Dawn*. New York, NY: Berkeley Books, 1984 ed.

Chamberlin, Eric Russell. *The Bad Popes*. New York, NY: Dial Press, 1969.

Chetwynd, Tom. *Dictionary of Sacred Myth* ("Language of the Unconscious," Vol. 3). London, UK: Aquarian Press, 1986.

Christian, C. W. *Friedrich Schleiermacher*. Peabody, MA: Christian Book Distributors, n.d.

Christie-Murray, David. *A History of Heresy*. Oxford, UK: Oxford University Press, 1976.

Chronicle of the World. Mount Kisco, NY: Ecam Publications, 1989.

Church History in the Fulness of Times. Church Educational System (eds.). Salt Lake City, UT: The Church of Jesus Christ of Latter-Day Saints, 1989.

Cirlot, J. E. *A Dictionary of Symbols*. 1962. New York, NY: Philosophical Library, 1983 ed.

Clark, Jerome. *Unexplained! 347 Strange Sightings, Incredible Occurrences, and Puzzling Physical Phenomena*. Detroit, MI: Visible Ink Press, 1993.

Clark, W. E. Le Gros. *History of the Primates*. 1949. Chicago, IL: University of Chicago Press, 1968 ed.

——. *The Antecedents of Man*. 1959. New York, NY: Quadrangle Books, 1978 ed.

Clemen, Carl. *Primitive Christianity and Its Non-Jewish Sources*. Edinburgh, Scotland: T and T Clark, 1912.

Coates, James. *In Mormon Circles: Gentiles, Jack Mormons, and Latter-Day Saints*. 1990. Reading, MA: Addison-Wesley, 1992 ed.

Cohen, Daniel. *The Encyclopedia of the Strange*. New York, NY: Avon Books, 1985.

Cohen, Edmund. *The Mind of the Bible-Believer*. 1986. Buffalo, NY: Prometheus, 1988 ed.

Collins, Joseph B. *Christian Mysticism in the Elizabethan Age*. New York, NY: Octagon, 1971.

Collins, Sheila D. *A Different Heaven and Earth: A Feminist Perspective on Religion*. Valley Forge, PA: Judson Press, 1974.

Comay, Joan. *Who's Who in the Old Testament (Together with the Apocrypha)*.

1971. New York, NY: Oxford University Press, 1993 ed.

Compton's Pictured Encyclopedia. 1922. Chicago, IL: F. E. Compton and Co, 1957 ed.

Comte, Auguste. *Catéchisme Positiviste*. 1852.

Condon, R. J. *Our Pagan Christmas*. Austin, TX: American Atheist Press, 1989.

Confucius. *Analects*. 6th Century BC.

Conway, J. D. *What the Church Teaches*. New York, NY: Harper and Brothers, 1962.

Cotterell, Arthur. *A Dictionary of World Mythology*. 1979. New York, NY: Oxford University Press, 1990 ed.

——. *The Macmillan Illustrated Encyclopedia of Myths and Legends*. New York, NY: Macmillan, 1989.

Cover, Lois Brauer. *Anthropology For Our Times*. New York, NY: Oxford Book Co., 1971.

Cramer, Raymond L. *The Psychology of Jesus and Mental Health*. 1959. Grand Rapids, MI: Zondervan Publishing House, 1972 ed.

Cross, Frank L., and Elizabeth A. Livingstone. *The Oxford Dictionary of the Christian Church*. 1957. London, UK: Oxford University Press, 1974 ed.

Crossley-Holland, Kevin. *The Norse Myths*. New York, NY: Pantheon, 1980.

Cumont, Franz Valéry Marie. *The Mysteries of Mithra*. New York, NY: Dover, 1956.

——. *Oriental Religions in Roman Paganism*. New York, NY: Dover, 1956.

——. *Astrology and Religion Among the Greeks and Romans*. New York, NY: Dover, 1960.

Dalley, Stephanie (trans.). *Myths From Mesopotamia: Creation, the Flood, Gilgamesh, and Others*. 1989. Oxford, UK: Oxford University Press, 2008 ed.

Daly, Mary. *Beyond God the Father: Toward a Philosophy of Women's Liberation*. Boston, MA: Beacon Press, 1973.

——. *Gyn/ecology: The Metaethics of Radical Feminism*. Boston, MA: Beacon Press, 1978.

Dante, Alighieri. *Inferno* (Thomas G. Bergin, trans.). New York, NY: Appleton-Century, 1948.

Dart, John. *The Jesus of Heresy and History: The Discovery and Meaning of the Nag Hammadi Gnostic Library*. New York, NY: Harper Collins, 1988.

Dasgupta, Amitava, with Lochlainn Seabrook. *Autobiography of a Non-Yogi: A Scientist's Journey From Hinduism to Christianity*. Spring Hill, TN: Sea Raven Press, 2015.

Davidson, Gustav. *A Dictionary of Angels*. 1967. New York, NY: The Free Press, 1971 ed.

Davidson, Hilda Roderick Ellis. *Gods and Myths of Northern Europe*. 1964. London, UK: Penguin, 1990 ed.

——. *Pagan Scandinavia*. New York, NY: Frederick A. Praeger, 1967.

——. *Gods and Myths of the Viking Age*. New York, NY: Bell, 1981.

——. *Myths and Symbols in Pagan Europe: Early Scandinavian and Celtic Religions*. Syracuse, NY: Syracuse University Press, 1988.

Davies, A. Powell. *The Meaning of the Dead Sea Scrolls*. New York, NY: Mentor, 1956.

Davis, John J. *Biblical Numerology: A Basic Study of the Use of Numbers in the Bible*. 1968. Grand Rapids, MI: Baker Book House, 1988 ed.

Dawkins, Richard. *The Selfish Gene*. 1976. New York, NY: Oxford University Press, 1978 ed.

——. *The Blind Watchmaker*. New York, NY: W. W. Norton, 1987.

Day, Michael H. *Fossil Man*. New York, NY: Bantam Books, 1971 ed.

De Chardin, Pierre Teilhard. *The Phenomenon of Man* (Bernard Wall, trans.). 1955. New York, NY: Harper and Row, 1965 ed.

Decker, Ed, and Dave Hunt. *The God Makers: A Shocking Exposé of What the Mormon Church Really Believes*. Eugene, OR: Harvest House, 1984.

Decker, Ed, and Caryl Matrisciana. *The God Makers II: Startling New Revelations About Modern-Day Mormonism*. Eugene, OR: Harvest House, 1993.

Delaney, John J. *Pockey Dictionary of Saints*. 1980. New York, NY: Image, 1983 (abridged) ed.

Delehaye, Hippolyte. *The Legends of the Saints: An Introduction to Hagiography*. New York, NY: Fordham University Press, 1962.

Dellow, E. L. *Methods of Science*. New York, NY: Universe Books, 1970.

Dennis, Rabbi Geoffrey W. *The Encyclopedia of Jewish Myth, Magic and Mysticism*. Woodbury, MN: Llewellyn, 2007.

Derk, Francis H. *A Pocket Guide to the Names of Christ*. 1969. Minneapolis, MN: Bethany House, 1976 ed.

De Rosa, Peter. *Vicars of Christ: The Dark Side of the Papacy*. New York, NY: Crown, 1988.

Desroches-Noblecourt, Christiane. *Tutankhamen*. Boston, MA: New York Graphic Society, 1963.

de Volney, Constantin François. *The Ruins, or, A Survey of the Revolutions of Empires*. 1791. London, UK: James Watson, 1857 ed.

de Voragine, Jacobus. *The Golden Legend, or Lives of the Saints* (seven vols.). C. 1260. London, UK: J. M. Dent and Co., 1900 ed.

Didron, M. *Christian Iconography; or, The History of Christian Art in the Middle Ages* (two vols.). London, UK: Henry G. Bohn, 1851.

Dione, R. L. *Is God Supernatural?: The 4,000-Year Misunderstanding.* New York, NY: Bantam, 1976.

Dixon, Dougal. *After Man: A Zoology of the Future.* New York, NY: St. Martin's Press, 1981.

Doane, Thomas William. *Bible Myths and Their Parallels in Other Religions.* New York, NY: University Books, 1971.

Donahue, Phil. *The Human Animal.* New York, NY: Fireside, 1985.

Donaldson, E. Talbot (trans.). *Beowulf.* New York, NY: W. W. Norton and Co., 1966.

Dorward, David. *Scottish Surnames: A Guide to the Family Names of Scotland* Glasgow, Scotland: HarperCollins, 1995.

Douglas, Stephen. *The Redhead Dynasty.* Corona del Mar, CA: NewStyle Communications, 1987.

Dowley, Tim (ed.). *The History of Christianity.* 1977. Oxford, UK: Lion Publishing, 1990 ed.

Dowling, Levi. *The Aquarian Gospel of Jesus the Christ: The Philosophical and Practical Basis of the Religion of the Aquarian Age of the World and of the Church Universal.* Los Angeles, CA: Royal Publishing Co., 1909.

Downing, Christine. *The Goddess: Mythological Images of the Feminine.* New York, NY: Crossroads Publishing, 1984.

Doyle, Arthur Conan. *The Coming of the Fairies.* 1921. New York, NY: Samuel Weiser Inc., 1975 ed.

Drake, Stillman. *Discoveries and Opinions of Galileo.* Garden City, NY: Anchor, 1957.

Drews, Arthur. *The Christ Myth.* Amherst, NY: Prometheus, 1998.

Dumézil, Georges. *Archaic Roman Religion* (two vols.). Chicago, IL: University of Chicago Press, 1970.

Dundes, Alan (ed.). *The Flood Myth.* Berkeley, CA: University of California Press, 1988.

———. *Holy Writ As Oral Lit: The Bible As Folklore.* Lanham, MD: Rowman and Littlefield, 1999.

Dunner, Joseph (ed.) *Handbook of World History: Concepts and Issues.* New York, NY: Philosophical Library, 1967.

Durant, Will. *The Story of Civilization: Volume 1—Our Oriental Heritage.* 1935. New York, NY: Simon and Schuster, 1954 ed.

Dyer, Thomas F. T. *British Popular Customs, Present and Past: Illustrating the Social and Domestic Manners of the People.* London, UK: George Bell and

Sons, 1900.

Eban, Abba. *Heritage: Civilization and the Jews*. New York, NY: Summit, 1984.

Egyptian Book of the Dead, The (E. A. Wallis Budge, trans.). 1895. New York, NY: Dover Publications, 1967 ed.

Ehrman, Bart D. *The Orthodox Corruption of Scripture: The Effect of Early Christological Controversies on the Text of the New Testament*. Oxford, UK: Oxford University Press, 1993.

——. *Lost Scriptures: Books That Did Not Make It Into the New Testament*. Oxford, UK: Oxford University Press, 2003.

——. *Lost Christianities: The Battles for Scripture and the Faiths We Never Knew*. Oxford, UK: Oxford University Press, 2003.

——. *Misquoting Jesus: The Story Behind Who Changed the Bible and Why*. New York, NY: HarperCollins, 2005.

——. *Jesus, Interrupted: Revealing the Hidden Contradictions in the Bible*. New York, NY: HarperCollins, 2009.

Eimerl, Sarel, and Irven DeVore. *The Primates*. New York, NY: Time-Life, 1965.

Einhorn, Lena. *The Jesus Mystery: Astonishing Clues to the True Identities of Jesus and Paul*. Guilford, CT: Lyons Press, 2007.

Einstein, Albert. *The World as I See It*. 1932. Secaucus, NJ: Citadel Press, n. d.

Eisenman, Robert, and Michael Wise. *The Dead Sea Scrolls Uncovered*. Shaftesbury, Dorset, UK: Element Books, 1992.

Eisler, Riane. *The Chalice and the Blade: Our History, Our Future*. New York, NY: Perennial, 1987.

Elder, Dorothy. *From Metaphysical to Mystical: A Study of the Way*. Denver, CO: Doriel Publishing Co., 1992.

Eliade, Mircea. *Images and Symbols: Studies in Religious Symbolism*. 1952. Princeton, NJ: Princeton University Press, 1991 ed.

——. *The Sacred and the Profane: The Nature of Religion* (Willard R. Trask, trans.). 1957. San Diego, CA: Harvest, 1959 ed.

——. *From Primitives to Zen*. 1967. New York, NY: Harper and Row, 1977 ed.

——. *A History of Religious Ideas*. Vol. 1 (*From the Stone Age to the Eleusinian Mysteries*). Chicago, IL: University of Chicago Press, 1978.

——. *A History of Religious Ideas*. Vol. 2 (*From Gautama Buddha to the Triumph of Christianity*). Chicago, IL: University of Chicago Press, 1982.

——. *A History of Religious Ideas*. Vol. 3 (*From Muhammad to the Age Reforms*). Chicago, IL: University of Chicago Press, 1985.

Ellis, Albert. *The Case Against Religion: A Psychotherapist's View*. Austin, TX: American Atheist Press, n.d.

Ellis, Peter Berresford. *A Dictionary of Irish Mythology*. 1987. Oxford, UK: Oxford University Press, 1992 ed.

Eliot, Alexander. *The Universal Myths: Heroes, Gods, Tricksters, and Others*. New York, NY: Meridian, 1976.

Elliot, Neil. *Sensuality in Scandinavia*. New York, NY: Weybright and Talley, 1970.

Emerson, Ralph Waldo. *Essays of Ralph Waldo Emerson*. Garden City, NY: Famous Classic Library, 1941.

Encyclopedia Britannica: A New Survey of Universal Knowledge. 1768. Chicago, IL/London, UK: Encyclopedia Britannica, 1955 ed.

Enslin, Morton Scott. *Christian Beginnings*. New York, NY: Harper and Brothers, 1938.

———. *The Literature of the Christian Movement*. New York, NY: Harper and Brothers, 1938.

Erasmus, Desiderius. *Praise of Folly* (Betty Radice, trans.). 1509. Harmondsworth, UK: Penguin, 1971 (1987 ed.).

Erdman, David V. *The Selected Poetry of William Blake*. New York, NY: Signet, 1976.

Erman, Adolf. *The Literature of the Ancient Egyptians*. New York, NY: Benjamin Blom, 1971.

Eusebius (of Caesarea). *The Proof of the Gospel*. New York, NY: Macmillan, 1920 ed.

———. *The Ecclesiastical History of Eusebius Pamphilus*. New York, NY: Stanford and Swords, 1850 ed.

Evans, Bergen. *Dictionary of Mythology*. 1970. New York, NY: Laurel, 1991 ed.

Evans, Elizabeth Edson. *The Christ Myth: A Study*. New York, NY: Truth Seeker Co., 1900.

Farmer, David Hugh. *The Oxford Dictionary of Saints*. 1978. Oxford, UK: Oxford University Press, 1992 ed.

Farrell, Deborah, and Carole Presser (eds.). *The Herder Symbol Dictionary: Symbols from Art, Archaeology, Mythology, Literature, and Religion* (Boris Matthews, trans.). 1978. Wilmette, IL: Chiron, 1990 ed.

Farren, David. *Sex and Magic: How to Use Spells, Potions, and Magic to Improve and Enhance Your Sexual Life*. 1975. New York, NY: Barnes and Noble, 1976 ed.

Feather, Robert. *The Secret Initiation of Jesus at Qumran: The Essene Mysteries of*

John the Baptist. Rochester, VT: Bear and Co., 2005.

Feder, Kenneth L. *Frauds, Myths, and Mysteries: Science and Pseudoscience in Archaeology*. Mountain View, CA: Mayfield Publishing Co., 1990.

Fell, Barry. *America B.C.* 1976. New York, NY: Pocket Books, 1989 ed.

Ferguson, George. *Signs and Symbols in Christian Art*. 1954. London, UK: Oxford University Press, 1975 ed.

Feuerstein, Georg. *Sacred Sexuality: Living the Vision of the Erotic Spirit*. 1992. New York, NY: Tarcher, 1993 ed.

Fideler, David. *Jesus Christ, Sun of God: Ancient Cosmology and Early Christian Symbolism*. Wheaton, IL: Quest, 1993.

Fillmore, Charles, and Theodosia DeWitt Schobert. *Metaphysical Bible Dictionary*. Unity Village, MO: Unity School of Christianity, 1931.

Finegan, Jack. *Light from the Ancient Past: The Archaeological Background of the Hebrew-Christian Religion* (Vol. 1). 1946. Princeton, NJ: Princeton University Press, 1974 ed.

Finger, Ben, Jr. *Concise World History*. New York, NY: Philosophical Library, 1959.

Fischer, Carl. *The Myth and Legend of Greece*. Dayton, OH: George A. Pflaum, 1968.

Flew, Antony. *A Dictionary of Philosophy*. New York, NY: St. Martin's Press, 1979.

Flinn, Frank K. (ed). *Encyclopedia of Catholicism*. New York, NY: Facts on File, 2007.

Foley, John P. (ed.). *The Jeffersonian Cyclopedia*. New York, NY: Funk and Wagnalls, 1900.

Foote, G. W., and W. P. Ball (Madalyn Murray O'Hair ed.). *The Bible Handbook*. 1983. Cranford, NJ: American Atheist Press, 1986 ed.

Ford, Guy Stanton (ed.-in-chief). *Compton's Pictured Encyclopedia*. 1922. Chicago, IL: F. E. Compton and Co, 1957 ed.

Ford, Marvin (as told to Dave Balsiger and Don Tanner). *On the Other Side*. Plainfield, NJ: Logos, 1978.

Forman, Samuel Eagle (ed.). *The Life and Writings of Thomas Jefferson*. Indianapolis, IN: Bobbs-Merrill Co., 1900.

Forrest, M. Isidora. *Offering to Isis: Knowing the Goddess Through Her Sacred Symbols*. St. Paul, MN: Llewellyn, 2005.

Fouard, Constant Henri. *The Christ, the Son of God: A Life of Our Saviour Jesus Christ*. 2 vols. Cambridge, MA: John Wilson and Son, 1890.

Fox, Matthew. *The Coming of the Cosmic Christ : The Healing of Mother Earth and the Birth of a Global Renaissance*. New York, NY: Harper and Row,

1988.

——. (ed.) *Western Spirituality: Historical Roots, Ecumenical Routes.* Santa Fe, NM: Bear and Co., 1981.

Fox, Robin Lane. *Pagans and Christians.* New York, NY: Knopf, 1986.

——. *The Unauthorized Version: Truth and Fiction in the Bible.* New York, NY: Knopf, 1991.

Frazer, Sir James George. *The Golden Bough: A Study in Comparative Religion* (1st edition). 2 vols. London, UK: Macmillan and Co., 1890.

——. *The Golden Bough: A Study in Magic and Religion* (2nd edition) 3 vols. London, UK: Macmillan and Co., 1909.

——. *The Golden Bough: A Study in Magic and Religion* (3rd edition) 12 vols. London, UK: Macmillan and Co., 1922.

——. *Folklore in the Old Testament.* New York, NY: Tudor Publishing, (abridged) 1923.

Freke, Timothy, and Peter Grandy. *The Jesus Mysteries: Was the Original Jesus a Pagan God?* New York, NY: Three Rivers Press, 1999.

——. *Jesus and the Lost Goddess: The Secret Teachings of the Original Christians.* New York, NY: Three Rivers Press, 2002.

Freud, Sigmund. *Totem and Taboo.* 1918. New York, NY: Vintage, 1946 ed.

——. *The Future of an Illusion.* 1928. New York, NY: W. W. Norton, 1961 ed.

——. *New Introductory Lectures Psychoanalysis.* Lecture no. 35: "A Philosophy of Life," 1932.

Frye, Albert Myrton, and Albert William Levi. *Rational Belief: An Introduction to Logic.* New York, NY: Harcourt, Brace and Co., 1941.

Furnas, J. C. *The Americans: A Social History of United States* (1587-1914). New York, NY: G. P. Putnam's Sons, 1969.

Gantz, Jeffrey (trans.). *Early Irish Myths and Sagas.* 1981. Harmondsworth, UK: Penguin, 1988 ed.

Gardner, Dr. James. *Jesus Who? Myth Vs. Reality In the Search for the Historical Jesus.* Bangor, ME: Booklocker, 2006.

Gardner, Martin. *Science: Good, Bad, and Bogus.* New York, NY: Avon, 1981.

——. *The New Age: Notes of a Fringe Watcher.* Buffalo, NY: Prometheus, 1988.

Gaskell, G. A. *Dictionary of All Scriptures and Myths.* 1960. New York, NY: Julian Press, Inc., 1973 ed.

Gaskin, Stephen. *Mind at Play.* Summertown, TN: The Book Publishing Co., 1980.

Gaster, Theodor. *Myth, Legend and Custom in the Old Testament.* New York, NY: Harper and Row, 1969.

Gelling, Peter, and Hilda Ellis Davidson. *The Chariot of the Sun and Other Rites and Symbols of the Northern Bronze Age*. New York, NY: Frederick A. Praeger, 1969.

George, Llewellyn. *A to Z Horoscope Maker and Delineator: A Text Book of Astrology*. 1910. St. Paul, MN: Llewellyn, 1969 ed.

Gibbon, Edward. *Memoirs of My Life*. 1788-1791. Harmondsworth, UK: Penguin, 1990 ed.

——. *The Decline and Fall of the Roman Empire* (abridged version). 1776-1788. Harmondsworth, UK: Penguin, 1985 ed.

——. *The Decline and Fall of the Roman Empire*. Vol. 1. 1776-1788. Chicago, IL: Encyclopedia Britannica, 1952 (1989 ed).

Gimbutas, Marija Alseikait. *The Goddesses and Gods of Old Europe: Myths and Cult Images*. 1974. Berkeley, CA: University of California Press, 1992 ed.

——. *The Civilization of the Goddess: The World of Old Europe* (Joan Marler, ed.). New York, NY: HarperCollins, 1991.

Glyn, Anthony. *The British: Portrait of a People*. New York, NY: G. P. Putnam's Sons, 1970.

Godfrey, Laurie R. (ed.). *Scientists Confront Creationism*. New York, NY: W. W. Norton, 1983.

Golas, Thaddeus. *The Lazy Man's Guide to Enlightenment*. 1971. New York, NY: Bantam, 1980 ed.

Goldenberg, Naomi. *The Changing of the Gods: Feminism and the End of Traditional Religions*. Boston, MA: Beacon Press, 1979.

Goldsmith, Martin. *The Zodiac By Degrees: 360 New Symbols*. York Beach, ME: Red Wheel, 2004.

Goodspeed, Edgar J. *The Apocrypha: An American Translation*. 1938. New York, NY: Vintage, 1959 ed.

Goodrich, Norma Lorre. *Medieval Myths: Great Myths of the Middle Ages, From Beowulf to the Cid*. New York, NY: American Library, 1977.

Gordon, Richard Stuart. *The Encyclopedia of Myths and Legends*. 1993. London, UK: Headline, 1994 ed.

Goring, Rosemary (ed.). *Larousse Dictionary of Beliefs and Religions*. 1992. Edinburgh, Scotland: Larousse, 1995 ed.

Gould, Stephen Jay. *Ever Since Darwin*. New York, NY: W. W. Norton, 1977.

——. *Hen's Teeth and Horse's Toes*. New York, NY: W. W. Norton, 1983.

——. *Bully for Brontosaurus*. New York, NY: W. W. Norton, 1991.

Graham, Lloyd M. *Deceptions and Myths of the Bible*. 1975. New York, NY:

Citadel Press, 1990 ed.

Grant, Michael, and John Hazel. *Who's Who in Classical Mythology*. 1973. New York, NY: Oxford University Press, 1993 ed.

Graves, Kersey. *The World's Sixteen Crucified Saviors, or, Christianity Before Christianity: Containing New, Startling, and Extraordinary Revelations in Religious History, which Disclose the Oriental Origin of All the Doctrines, Principles, Precepts, and Miracles of the Christian New Testament, and Furnishing a Key for Unlocking Many of Its Sacred Mysteries, Besides Comprising the History of Sixteen Heathen Crucified Gods*. Boston, MA: Colby and Rich, 1876.

Graves, Robert. *The White Goddess: A Historical Grammar of Poetic Myth*. 1948. New York, NY: Noonday Press, 1991 ed.

——. *The Greek Myths*. 1955. Harmondsworth, UK: Penguin, 1992 combined ed.

Graves, Robert, and Raphael Patai. *Hebrew Myths: The Book of Genesis*. 1964. New York, NY: Anchor, 1989 ed.

Gray, John. *Near Eastern Mythology: Mesopotamia, Syria, and Palestine*. London, UK: Hamlyn, 1963.

Green, John Richard. *A Short History of the English People* (Vol. 1). London, UK: Macmillan and Co., 1892.

Greenberg, Gary. *101 Myths of the Bible: How Ancient Scribes Invented Biblical History*. Naperville, IL: Sourcebooks, 2000.

Grimal, Pierre. *The Penguin Dictionary of Classical Mythology* (A. R. Maxwell-Hyslop, trans.). 1951. Harmondsworth, UK: Penguin, 1990 ed.

Grotjahn, Martin. *The Voice of the Symbol*. Los Angeles, CA: Mara Books, 1971.

Grun, Bernard. *The Timetables of History*. New York, NY: Touchstone, 1975.

Grusin, Richard A. *Transcendentalist Hermeneutics: Institutional Authority and the Higher Criticism of the Bible*. Durham, NC: Duke University Press, 1991.

Gruss, Edmond C. *What Every Mormon Should Know*. 1975. Denver, CO: Accent, 1976 ed.

Guerber, Hélène Adeline. *Myths and Legends of the Middle Ages: Their Origins and Influence on Literature and Art*. Honolulu, HI: University Press of the Pacific, 2003.

Guignebert, Charles. *The Christ*. 1943. New York, NY: Citadel, 1968 ed.

——. *Ancient, Medieval and Modern Christianity*. New York, NY: University Books, 1961.

Guthrie, William K. C. *The Greeks and Their Gods*. Boston, MA: Beacon Press,

1955.

Hadas, Moses (ed.). *A History of Rome*. Garden City, NY: Doubleday Anchor, 1956.

Haining, Peter. *Witchcraft and Black Magic*. New York, NY: Grosset and Dunlap, 1972.

Hall, Eleanor L. *The Moon and the Virgin: Reflections on the Archetypal Feminine*. New York, NY: Harper and Row, 1980.

Hall, Judy. *The Astrology Bible: The Definitive Guide to the Zodiac*. New York, NY: Sterling, 2005.

Hall, J. R. Clark. *A Concise Anglo-Saxon Dictionary*. 1894. Toronto, Canada: University of Toronto Press, 1996 ed.

Hall, Manly P. *The Secret Teachings of All Ages*. 1925. Los Angeles, CA: The Philosophical Research Society, 1989 ed.

Halliday, William Reginald. *Greek and Roman Folklore*. New York, NY: Cooper Square, 1963.

Hamilton, Edith. *The Greek Way*. 1930. New York, NY: Mentor, 1959 ed.

——. *The Roman Way*. 1932. New York, NY: Mentor, 1961 ed.

——. *Mythology: Timeless Tales of Gods and Heroes*. 1940. New York, NY: Mentor, 1963 ed.

Hardon, John A. *Pocket Catholic Dictionary*. 1980. New York, NY: Image, 1985 ed.

Harnack, Adolf. *The Mission and Expansion of Christianity in the First Three Centuries*. 2 vols. New York, NY: G. P. Putnam's Sons, 1908.

Harpur, Tom. *For Christ's Sake*. 1986. Toronto, Ontario, Canada: McClelland and Stewart, 1993 ed.

——. *The Pagan Christ: Recovering the Lost Light*. New York, NY: Walker and Co., 2005.

——. *The Pagan Christ: Is Blind Faith Killing Christianity?* New York, NY: Walker and Co., 2006.

Harris, Eleanor L. *Ancient Egyptian Divination and Magic*. York Beach, ME: Samuel Weiser, 1998.

Harris, Marvin. *Our Kind*. New York, NY: Harper and Row, 1989.

Harrison, Jane Ellen. *Ancient Art and Ritual*. New York, NY: Henry Holt and Co., 1913.

Harrison, Michael. *The Roots of Witchcraft*. Secaucus, NJ: Citadel Press, 1974.

Haskins, Susan. *Mary Magdalene: Myth and Metaphor*. New York, NY: Harcourt Brace and Co., 1993.

Hassnain, Fida, and Dahan Levi. *The Fifth Gospel: New Evidence from the Tibetan, Sanskrit, Arabic, Persian and Urdu Sources About the Historical Life of Jesus*

Christ After the Crucifixion. 1998. Nevada City, CA: Blue Dolphin, 2008 ed.

Hawking, Stephen William. *A Brief History of Time: From the Big Bang to Black Holes*. New York, NY: Bantam, 1988.

Hazama, Dorothy. *The Ancient Hawaiians: Who Were They? How Did they Live?* Honolulu, HI: Hagarth Press, n.d.

Hazlitt, W. Carew. *Faiths and Folklore of the British Isles* (two vols.). New York, NY: Benjamin Blom, 1965.

Heidel, Alexander. *The Gilgamesh Epic and Old Testament Parallels*. Chicago, IL: University of Chicago Press, 1949.

Heindel, Max. *Nature Spirits and Nature Forces*. Oceanside, CA: Rosicrucian Fellowship, 1937.

Hellweg, Paul. *The Insomniacs Dictionary: The Last Word on the Odd Word*. 1986. New York, NY: Ivy, 1989 ed.

Helms, Randel. *Gospel Fictions*. Buffalo, NY: Prometheus, 1988.

Herbermann, Charles G., Edward A. Pace, Condé B. Pallen, Thomas J. Shahan, and John J. Wynne (ed.). *The Catholic Encyclopedia: An International Work of Reference on the Constitution, Doctrine, Discipline, and History of the Catholic Church*. 15 vols. New York, NY: The Encyclopedia Press, 1912.

Herm, Gerhard. *The Celts: The People Who Came Out of the Darkness*. New York, NY: St. Martin's Press, 1976.

Hertz, Joseph H. *Sayings of the Fathers ("Pirke Aboth")*. New York, NY: Behrman House, 1945.

Hesiod. *Theogonia*; *Erga kai Hemerai* (Martin Litchfield West, trans.). In English: *Theogony* and *Work and Days*. C. 8th Century BC. Oxford: Oxford University Press, 1988, 1991 ed.

Hinnells, John R. (ed.). *Persian Mythology*. London, UK: Hamlyn, 1973.

——. *The Penguin Dictionary of Religions: From Abraham to Zoroaster*. 1984. Harmondsworth, UK: Penguin, 1986 ed.

Hinsie, Leland E., and Robert Jean Campbell. *Psychiatric Dictionary*. 1940. New York, NY: Oxford University Press, 1970 ed.

Hitching, Francis. *The Mysterious World: An Atlas of the Unexplained*. 1978. New York, NY: Holt, Rinehart and Winston, 1979 ed.

Hodson, Geoffrey. *The Hidden Wisdom in the Holy Bible*. Vol. 1. 1967. Wheaton, IL: Quest, 1978 ed.

——. *The Hidden Wisdom in the Holy Bible*. Vol. 2. 1967. Wheaton, IL: Quest, 1978 ed.

Hoeller, Stephan A. *Jung and the Lost Gospels: Insights into the Dead Sea Scrolls and the Nag Hammadi Library.* 1989. Wheaton, IL: Quest, 1990 ed.

Hoffer, Eric. *The True Believer.* New York, NY: Harper, 1951.

Hoffman, R. Joseph. *Jesus Outside the Gospels.* Buffalo, NY: Prometheus, 1984.

Holroyd, Stuart. *The Arkana Dictionary of New Perspectives.* Harmondsworth, UK: Arkana, 1989.

Hooke, S. K. *Middle Eastern Mythology: From the Assyrians to the Hebrews.* 1963. Harmondsworth, UK: Penguin, 1991 ed.

Hopfe, Lewis M. *Religions of the World.* 1976. New York, NY: Macmillan, 1987 ed.

Houghton, Louise Seymour. *Hebrew Life and Thought: Being Interpretive Studies in the Literature of Israel.* Chicago, IL: University of Chicago Press, 1907.

Howell, F. Clark. *Early Man.* 1965. New York, NY: Time-Life, 1971 ed.

Hughes, Philip. *A Popular History of the Catholic Church.* New York, NY: Macmillan, 1962.

Hutchinson, Richard Wyatt. *Prehistoric Crete.* 1962. Harmondsworth, UK: Penguin, 1968 ed.

Hutton, Ronald. *The Pagan Religions of the Ancient British Isles: Their Nature and Legacy.* 1991. Oxford, UK: Blackwell, 2000 ed.

Huxley, Francis. *The Way of the Sacred.* New York, NY: Doubleday, 1974.

Ide, Arthur Frederick. *Yahweh's Wife: Sex in the Evolution of Monotheism (A Study of Yahweh, Asherah, Ritual Sodomy and Temple Prostitution).* Las Colinas, TX: Monument Press, 1991.

Inman, Thomas. *Ancient Faiths and Modern: A Dissertation Upon Worships, Legends and Divinities in Central and Western Asia, Europe, and Elsewhere, Before the Christian Era.* New York, NY: J. W. Bouton, 1876.

Jackson, John G. *Christianity Before Christ.* Austin, TX: American Atheist Press, 1985.

James, Peter, and Nick Thorpe. *Ancient Inventions.* New York, NY: Ballantine, 1994.

Jenkins, Philip. *Hidden Gospels: How the Search for Jesus Lost its Way.* Oxford, UK: Oxford University Press, 2001.

John Paul II, Pope. *Crossing the Threshold of Hope.* New York, NY: Alfred A. Knopf, 1994.

Johns, June. *Black Magic Today.* London, UK: New English Library, 1971.

Johnson, Robert A. *She: Understanding Feminine Psychology.* 1976. New York, NY: Perennial, 1977 ed.

Jonas, Hans. *The Gnostic Religion: The Message of the Alien God and the Beginnings of Christianity*. 1958. Boston, MA: Beacon Press, 2001 ed.

Jones, Gwyn. *A History of the Vikings*. 1968. Oxford, UK: Oxford University Press, 1984 ed.

Jones, Prudence, and Nigel Pennick. *A History of Pagan Europe*. London, UK: Routledge, 1995.

Josephus: Complete Works (William Whiston, trans.). Circa 1st to 2nd Centuries. Grand Rapids, MI: Kregel Publications, 1960, 1980 ed.

Julian of Norwich. *Revelations of Divine Love*. 1373. Harmondsworth, UK: Penguin, 1966 ed.

Jung, Carl Gustav. *Man and His Symbols*. 1964. New York, NY: Dell, 1968 ed.

Jung, Emma, and Marie-Louise von Franz. *The Grail Legend*. New York, NY: G. P. Putnam's Sons, 1970.

Keightly, Thomas. *Secret Societies of the Middle Ages*. London, UK: Charles Knight and Co., 1875.

Keller, Werner. *The Bible as History: A Confirmation of the Book of Books*. 1956. New York, NY: Bantam, 1980 ed.

Kelly, Sean, and Rosemary Rogers. *Saints Preserve Us!: Everything You Need to Know About Every Saint You'll Ever Need*. New York, NY: Random House, 1993.

Kelsey, Morton T., and Barbara Kelsey. *Sacrament of Sexuality: The Spirituality and Psychology of Sex*. Warwick, NY: Amity House, 1986.

Kirk, G. S. *The Nature of the Greek Myths*. 1974. Harmondsworth, UK: Penguin, 1978 ed.

Klein, Peter (ed.). *The Catholic Source Book*. Dubuque, IA: Brown-Roa, 2000.

Knight, Richard Payne. *A Discourse On the Worship of Priapus, and Its Connection With the Mystic Theology of the Ancients*. London, UK: privately printed, 1865 ed.

———. *The Symbolic Language of Ancient Art and Mythology*. New York, NY: J. W. Bouton, 1892.

Kramer, Heinrich, and Jakob Sprenger. *Malleus Maleficarum*. 1486. New York, NY: Dover, 1971.

Kramer, Samuel Noah. *History Begins at Sumer: Thirty-Nine Firsts in Recorded History*. 1956. Philadelphia, PA: University of Pennsylvania Press, 1981 ed.

Kuhn, Alvin Boyd. *A Rebirth for Christianity*. 1970. Wheaton, IL: Quest, 2005.

Lacy, Norris J. (ed.). *The Arthurian Encyclopedia*. New York, NY: Garland Publishing, 1986.

Laistner, Max Ludwig Wolfram. *Christianity and Pagan Culture in the Later Roman Empire*. Ithaca, NY: Cornell University Press, 1951.

Lamsa, George M. *The Holy Bible: From Ancient Eastern Manuscripts*. 1933. Philadelphia, PA: A. J. Holman, 1968 ed.

Lange, Johann Peter. *The Life of Jesus Christ: A Complete Critical Examination of the Origin, Contents, and Connection of the Gospels*. 4 vols. Edinburgh, Scotland: T and T. Clark, 1872.

Langford, Norman F. *Fire Upon the Earth: The Story of the Christian Church*. Philadelphia, PA: Westminster Press, 1950.

Lao-Tsu. *Tao Te Ching*. New York, NY: Vintage Books, 1972.

LaVey, Anton Szandor. *The Satanic Bible*. New York, NY: Avon, 1969.

——. *The Satanic Rituals*. New York, NY: Avon, 1972.

Layton, Bentley. *The Gnostic Scriptures: Ancient Wisdom for the New Age*. 1987. New York, NY: Anchor, 1995 ed.

Leakey, Richard E., and Roger Lewin. *Origins Reconsidered: In Search of What Makes Us Human*. New York, NY: Doubleday, 1992.

Lee, Philip J. *Against the Protestant Gnostics*. Oxford, UK: Oxford University Press, 1987.

Leedom, Tim C. (ed.). *The Book Your Church Doesn't Want You To Read*. N.p.: Truth Seeker, 2001 ed.

Leeming, David Adams. *The World of Myth*. 1990. Oxford, UK: Oxford University Press, 1992 ed.

Legge, Francis. *Forerunners and Rivals of Christianity* (two vols.). New York, NY: University Books, 1964.

Leishman, Thomas Linton. *Our Ageless Bible: From Early Manuscripts to Modern Versions*. 1939. New York, NY: Thomas Nelson and Sons, 1962 ed.

——. *The Continuity of the Bible: The Gospels*. Boston, MA: Christian Science Publishing Society, 1976.

LeLoup, Jean-Yves. *The Gospel of Mary Magdalene*. Rochester, VT: Inner Traditions, 2002.

——. *The Gospel of Philip: Jesus, Mary Magdalene, and the Gnosis of Sacred Union*. Rochester, VT: Inner Traditions, 2004.

——. *The Gospel of Thomas: The Gnostic Wisdom of Jesus*. Rochester, VT: Inner Traditions, 2005.

Lenz, Frederick. *Lifetimes: True Accounts of Reincarnation*. New York, NY: Fawcett Crest, 1979.

Lerner, Gerda. *The Creation of Patriarchy*. 1986. Oxford, UK: Oxford University Press, 1987 ed.

Lessa, William A., and Evon Z. Vogt. *Reader in Comparative Religion: An*

Anthropological Approach. New York, NY: Harper and Row, 1979.

Levi. *The Aquarian Gospel of Jesus the Christ: The Philosophic and Practical Basis of the Religion of the Aquarian Age of the World and of the Church Universal*. Marina Del Ray, CA: DeVorss and Co., 1982.

Lewis, Harvey Spencer. *Mansions of the Soul: The Cosmic Conception*. 1930. San Jose, CA: Ancient Mystical Order Rosae Crucis (AMORC), 1969 ed.

———. *The Secret Doctrine of Jesus*. 1937. San Jose, CA: Rosicrucian Press, 1954 ed.

Lillie, Arthur. *Buddhism in Christendom, or Jesus, the Essene*. London, UK: Kegan Paul, Trench and Co., 1887.

Lindsay, Jack. *The Origins of Astrology*. New York, NY: Barnes and Noble, 1971.

Lockyer, Herbert. *All the Women of the Bible*. Grand Rapids, MI: Zondervan, n.d.

Loetscher, Lefferts A. (ed.-in-chief). *Twentieth Century Encyclopedia of Religious Knowledge* (2 vols). Grand Rapids, MI: Baker Book House, 1955.

Ludlow, Daniel H. (ed.). *Encyclopedia of Mormonism: The History, Scripture, Doctrine, and Procedure of the Church of Jesus Christ of Latter-Day Saints*. New York, NY: Macmillan, 1992.

Lurker, Manfred. *The Gods and Symbols of Ancient Egypt*. 1974. New York, NY: Thames and Hudson, 1984 ed.

———. *Dictionary of Gods and Goddesses, Devils and Demons* (G. L. Campbell, trans.). 1984. London, UK: Routledge, 1988 ed.

MacCana, Proinsias. *Celtic Mythology*. London, UK: Hamlyn, 1970.

MacGregor, Geddes. *Reincarnation in Christianity: A New Vision of Rebirth in Christian Thought*. 1978. Wheaton, IL: Quest, 1989 ed.

Mack, Burton L. *Who Wrote the New Testament?: The Making of the Christian Myth*. New York, NY: HarperOne, 1996.

MacLysaght, Edward. *The Surnames of Ireland*. 1985. Dublin, Ireland: Irish Academic Press, 1999 ed.

Malachi, Tau. *Gnosis of the Cosmic Christ: A Gnostic Christian Kabbalah*. St. Paul, MN: Llewellyn, 2005.

———. *Living Gnosis: A Practical Guide to Gnostic Christianity*. St. Paul, MN: Llewellyn, 2005.

———. *St. Mary Magdalene: The Gnostic Tradition of the Holy Bride*. St. Paul, MN: Llewellyn, 2006.

Mangasarian, Mangasur M. *The Truth About Jesus: Is He a Myth?* Chicago, IL: Independent Religious Society, 1909.

Mann, Nicholas R. *The Isle of Avalon: Sacred Mysteries of Arthur and Glastonbury*.

London, UK: Green Magic, 2001.

Marciniak, Barbara. *Bringers of the Dawn: Teachings from the Pleiadians.* Santa Fe, NM: Bear and Co., 1992.

Marcus, Rebecca B. *Prehistoric Cave Paintings.* New York, NY: Franklin Watts, 1968.

Maspero, Gaston. *Popular Stories of Ancient Egypt.* New York, NY: University Books, 1967.

Massey, Gerald. *The Historical Jesus, and the Mythical Christ: Natural Genesis and Typology of Equinoctial Christolatry.* 1883. New York, NY: Cosimo, 2006 ed.

——. *Ancient Egypt: The Light of the World* (twelve vols.). London, UK: T. Fisher Unwin, 1907.

Matthews, Caitlín and John. *The Encyclopedia of Celtic Wisdom: A Celtic Shaman's Sourcebook.* Rockport, MA: Element, 1994.

Matthews, John. *The Winter Solstice: The Sacred Traditions of Christmas.* Wheaton, IL: Quest, 2003.

McCannon, Tricia. *Jesus: The Explosive Story of the 30 Lost Years and the Ancient Mystery Religions.* Charlottesville, VA: Hampton Roads Publishing, 2010.

McClelland, Norman C. *Encyclopedia of Reincarnation and Karma.* Jefferson, NC: McFarland and Co., 2010.

McColman, Carl. *The Big Book of Christian Mysticism: The Essential Guide to Contemplative Spirituality.* Charlottesville, VA: Hampton Roads Publishing, 2010.

McConkie, Bruce R. *Mormon Doctrine.* 1966. Salt Lake City, UT: Bookcraft, 1992 ed.

McKenzie, John L. *Dictionary of the Bible.* New York, NY: Collier, 1965.

McKinsey, C. Dennis. *The Encyclopedia of Biblical Errancy.* Amherst, NY: Prometheus, 1995.

McLean, Adam (ed.). *A Treatise on Angel Magic: Magnum Opus Hermetic Sourceworks.* 1989. York Beach, ME: Weiser, 2006 ed.

Mead, Frank Spencer, and Samuel S. Hill. *Handbook of Denominations in the United States.* 1951. Nashville, TN: Abingdon Press, 1989 ed.

Mead, George Robert Stow. *Thrice-Greatest Hermes: Studies in Hellenistic Theosophy and Gnosis.* London, UK: Theosophical Publishing Society, 1906.

——. *The Mysteries of Mithra.* London, UK: Theosophical Publishing Society, 1907.

Meredith, Joel. *Meredith's Book of Bible Lists.* Minneapolis, MN: Bethany

House, 1980.

Merivale, Patricia. *Pan the Goat-God*. Cambridge, MA: Harvard University Press, 1969.

Meurois-Givaudan, Anne and Daniel. *The Way of the Essenes: Christ's Hidden Life Remembered*. Rochester, VT: Destiny, 1992.

Miles, Clement A. *Christmas Customs and Traditions*. New York, NY: Dover, 1976.

Metford, J. C. J. *Dictionary of Christian Lore and Legend*. London, UK: Thames and Hudson, 1983.

Metzger, Bruce M., and Michael D. Coogan (eds.). *The Oxford Companion to the Bible*. New York, NY: Oxford University Press, 1993.

Meyer, Marvin. *The Gnostic Gospels of Jesus: The Definitive Collection of Mystical Gospels and Secret Books About Jesus of Nazareth*. New York, NY: HarperCollins, 2005.

Miller, Robert J. (ed.). *The Complete Gospels* (annotated scholars version). 1992. New York, NY: Polebridge Press, 1994.

Mills, A. D. *Oxford Dictionary of English Place-names*. 1991. Oxford, UK: Oxford University Press, 1998 ed.

Mollenkott, Virginia Ramey. *The Divine Feminine: The Biblical Imagery of God as Female*. New York, NY: Crossroad Publishing, 1993.

Milman, Henry Hart. *The History of Christianity, From the Birth of Christ to the Abolition of Paganism in the Roman Empire*. 3 vols. London, UK: John Murray, 1840.

Monaghan, Patricia. *The Book of Goddesses and Heroines*. 1990. St. Paul, MN: Llewellyn, 1991 ed.

Monroe, Douglas. *The 21 Lessons of Merlyn: A Study in Druid Magic and Lore*. St. Paul, MN: Llewellyn, 1992.

Montagu, Ashley. *The Natural Superiority of Women*. 1952. New York, NY: Collier, 1992 (new and revised) ed.

Morehead, Albert H. (ed.). *The Illustrated World Encyclopedia*. 1954. Woodbury, NY: Bobley Publishing, 1977 ed.

Morgan, Elaine. *The Descent of Woman*. 1972. New York, NY: Bantam, 1973 ed.

Murdock, D. M. (a.k.a. Acharya S.). *The Christ Conspiracy: The Greatest Story Ever Sold*. Kempton, IL: Adventures Unlimited Press, 1999.

——. *Suns of God: Krishna, Buddha and Christ Unveiled*. Seattle, WA: Stellar House, 2004.

——. *Christ in Egypt: The Horus-Jesus Connection*. Seattle, WA: Stellar House, 2009.

——. *Jesus as the Sun Throughout History*. Seattle, WA: Stellar House, n.d.

Murray, Margaret Alice. *The Witch-Cult in Western Europe*. London, UK: Oxford University Press, 1921.

Nelson, Thomas (pub.). *Nelson's New Compact Illustrated Bible Dictionary*. 1964. Nashville, TN: Thomas Nelson, 1978 ed.

Neumann, Erich. *The Great Mother: An Analysis of the Archetype*. New York, NY: Pantheon, 1955.

Newall, Venetia. *The Encyclopedia of Witchcraft and Magic*. New York, NY: A and W Visual Library, 1974.

New Larousse Encyclopedia of Mythology. 1959. London, UK: Hamlyn, 1976 ed.

Nolloth, Charles Frederick. *The Rise of the Christian Religion: A Study in Origins*. London, UK: Macmillan and Co., 1917.

Norton, Andrew. *The Evidences of the Genuineness of the Gospels*. Boston, MA: American Unitarian Association, 1868.

Notovitch, Nicolas. *The Unknown Life of Jesus Christ*. 1894. Chicago, IL: Indo-American Book Co., 1907 ed.

Odent, Michael. *Water and Sexuality*. Harmondsworth, UK: Arkana, 1990.

O'Flaherty, Wendy Doniger. *Hindu Myths*. Harmondsworth, UK: Penguin, 1975.

Olson, Carl (ed.). *The Book of the Goddess, Past and Present: An Introduction to Her Religion*. New York, NY: Crossroad, 1983.

Orme, A. R. *Ireland* (from "The World's Landscapes" series, James M. Houston, ed). Chicago, IL: Aldine, 1970.

Osborne, John. *Britain*. New York, NY: Time-Life, 1963.

Pagels, Elaine. *The Gnostic Paul: Gnostic Exegesis of the Pauline Letters*. 1975. Harrisburg, PA: Trinity Press International, 1992 ed.

——. *The Gnostic Gospels*. 1979. New York, NY: Vintage, 1981 ed.

——. *Adam, Eve, and the Serpent: Sex and Politics in Early Christianity*. 1988. New York, NY: Vintage, 1989 ed.

——. *The Origin of Satan: How Christians Demonized Jews, Pagans, and Heretics*. New York, NY: Random House, 1995.

——. *Beyond Belief: The Secret Gospel of Thomas*. New York, NY: Random House, 2003.

Patai, Raphael. *The Hebrew Goddess*. 1967. Detroit, MI: Wayne State University Press, 1990 ed.

Paulsen, Kathryn. *The Complete Book of Magic and Witchcraft*. 1970. New York, NY: Signet, 1980 ed.

Pearson, Carol S. *Awakening the Heroes Within: Twelve Archetypes to Help Us Find Ourselves and Transform Our World*. New York, NY: HarperCollins,

1991.

Pennick, Nigel. *The Pagan Book of Days: A Guide to the Festivals, Traditions, and Sacred Days of the Year*. Rochester, VT: Destiny, 1992.

Perowne, Stewart. *Roman Mythology*. 1969. Twickenham, UK: Newnes Books, 1986 ed.

Picknett, Lynn. *The Secret History of Lucifer and the Meaning of the True Da Vinci Code*. New York, NY: Carroll and Graf, 2006.

Picknett, Lynn, and Clive Prince. *The Templar Revelation: Secret Guardians of the True Identity of Christ*. New York, NY: Touchstone, 1998.

Pinch, Geraldine. *Egyptian Mythology: A Guide to the Gods, Goddesses, and Traditions of Ancient Egypt*. Oxford, UK: Oxford University Press, 2004.

Porter, Stanley E., and Stephen J. Bedard. *Unmasking the Pagan Christ: An Evangelical Response to the Cosmic Christ Idea*. Toronto, Canada: Clements Publishing, 2006.

Potter, Charles Francis. *The Lost Years of Jesus Revealed*. 1958. New York, NY: Fawcett, 1962 ed.

Prahbupada, A. C. Bhaktivedanta Swami. *Beyond Birth and Death*. Los Angeles, CA: The Bhaktivedanta Book Trust, 1979.

Price, Robert M. *Deconstructing Jesus*. Amherst, NY: Prometheus, 2000.

Pritchard, James B. *Palestinian Figurines in Relation to Certain Goddesses Known Through Literature*. New Haven, CT: American Oriental Society, 1943.

Prophet, Elizabeth Clare. *The Lost Years of Jesus: Documentary Evidence of Jesus' 17-Year Journey to the East*. Gardiner, MT: Summit University Press, 1988.

———. *Reincarnation: The Missing Link In Christianity*. Gardiner, MT: Summit University Press, 1997.

———. *Mary Magdalene and the Divine Feminine: Jesus' Lost Teachings on Woman - How Orthodoxy Suppressed Jesus' Revolution for Woman and Invented Original Sin*. Gardiner, MT: Summit University Press, 2005.

Qualls-Corbett, Nancy. *The Sacred Prostitute: Eternal Aspect of the Feminine*. Toronto, Canada: Inner City Books, 1988.

Raftery, Barry. *Pagan Celtic Ireland: The Enigma of the Irish Iron Age*. London, UK: Thames and Hudson, 1994.

Ramm, Bernard L. *Hermeneutics*. 1967. Grand Rapids, MI: Baker Book House, 1988 ed.

Reaney, P. H. *Oxford Dictionary of English Surnames*. 1958. Oxford, UK: Oxford University Press, 1997 ed.

Reed, David A., and John R. Farkas. *Mormons Answered Verse By Verse*. 1992. Grand Rapids, MI: Baker Book House, 2000 ed.

Reed, Ellen Cannon. *Circle of Isis: Ancient Egyptian Magic for Modern Witches*. Franklin Lakes, NJ: Career Press, 2002.

Regula, deTraci. *The Mysteries of Isis: Her Worship and Magick*. 1995. St. Paul, MN: Llewellyn, 2001 ed.

Reilly, Patricia Lynn. *A God Who Looks Like Me: Discovering a Woman-Affirming Spirituality*. New York, NY: Ballantine, 1995.

Renan, Ernest. *Life of Jesus* (five vols.). 1887-1894. Boston, MA: Little, Brown, and Co., 1915 ed.

Roberts, R. Philip. *Mormonism Unmasked: Confronting the Contradiction Between Mormon Beliefs and True Christianity*. Nashville, TN: Broadman and Holman, 1988.

Robertson, John M. *Christianity and Mythology*. London, UK: Watts and Co., 1900.

——. *A Short History of Christianity*. London, UK: Watts and Co., 1902.

——. *Pagan Christs: Studies in Comparative Hierology*. London, UK: Watts and Co., 1903.

——. *Pagan Christs*. 1966. New York, NY: Dorset Press, 1987 ed.

Robinson, James M (ed.). *The Nag Hammadi Library in English*. 1978. San Francisco, CA: HarperCollins, 1990 ed.

Rocco, Sha. *Sex Mythology*. 1898. Austin, TX: American Atheist Press, 1982 ed.

Rufus, Anneli S., and Kristan Lawson. *Goddess Sites: Europe*. New York, NY: HarperCollins, 1991.

Rule, Lareina. *Name Your Baby*. 1963. New York, NY: Bantam, 1978 ed.

Runciman, Steven. *A History of the Crusades: Vol. 1, The First Crusade and the Foundation of the Kingdom of Jerusalem*. 1951. New York, NY: Harper Torchbooks, 1964 ed.

Runes, Dagobert D. (ed.). *Dictionary of Judaism*. 1959. New York, NY: Citadel Press, 1991 ed.

Russell, Bertrand. *Why I Am Not a Christian*. New York, NY: Touchstone, 1957.

Rutherford, Ward. *Celtic Mythology: The Nature and Influence of Celtic Myth—from Druidism to Arthurian Legend*. New York, NY: Sterling, 1990.

Salmonson, Jessica Amanda. *The Encyclopedia of Amazons: Women Warriors from Antiquity to the Modern Era*. New York, NY: Paragon House, 1991.

Schonfield, Hugh Joseph. *The Passover Plot: A New Interpretation of the Life and*

Death of Jesus. 1965. New York, NY: Bantam, 1969 ed.

——. *Those Incredible Christians*. New York, NY: Bernard Geis, 1968.

——. *The Jesus Party*. New York, NY: Macmillian, 1974.

——. *The Essene Odyssey: The Mystery of the True Teacher and the Essene Impact on the Shaping of Human Destiny*. Shaftesbury, UK: Element Books, 1984.

——. *The Original New Testament: A Radical Translation and Reinterpretation*. New York, NY: HarperCollins, 1985.

Scott, George Ryley. *Phallic Worship: A History of Sex and Sexual Rites*. London, UK: Senate, 1996.

Schwartz, Howard. *Gabriel's Palace: Jewish Mystical Tales*. New York, NY: Oxford University Press, 1993.

——. *Tree of Souls: The Mythology of Judaism*. Oxford, UK: Oxford University Press, 2004.

Schweitzer, Albert. *The Quest of the Historical Jesus*. 1906. London, UK: Adam and Charles Black, 1910 ed.

——. *The Mystery of the Kingdom of God: The Secret of Jesus' Messiahship and Passion*. New York, NY: Dodd, Mead and Co., 1914.

——. *Out of My Life and Thought: An Autobiography*. 1933. New York, NY: Henry Holt and Co., 1949 ed.

Scranton, Laird. *The Science of the Dogon: Decoding the African Mystery Tradition*. Rochester, VT: Inner Traditions, 2006.

Seabrook, Lochlainn. *Carnton Plantation Ghost Stories: True Tales of the Unexplained from Tennessee's Most Haunted Civil War House!* 2005. Franklin, TN, 2016 ed.

——. *Nathan Bedford Forrest: Southern Hero, American Patriot*. 2007. Franklin, TN, 2010 ed.

——. *Abraham Lincoln: The Southern View*. 2007. Franklin, TN: Sea Raven Press, 2013 ed.

——. *The McGavocks of Carnton Plantation: A Southern History - Celebrating One of Dixie's Most Noble Confederate Families and Their Tennessee Home*. 2008. Franklin, TN, 2011ed.

——. *A Rebel Born: A Defense of Nathan Bedford Forrest*. 2010. Franklin, TN: Sea Raven Press, 2011 ed.

——. *A Rebel Born: The Screenplay* (for the film). 2011. Franklin, TN: Sea Raven Press.

——. *Everything You Were Taught About the Civil War is Wrong, Ask a Southerner!* 2010. Franklin, TN: Sea Raven Press, revised 2014 ed.

——. *The Quotable Jefferson Davis: Selections From the Writings and Speeches of the*

Confederacy's First President. Franklin, TN: Sea Raven Press, 2011.

———. *The Quotable Robert E. Lee: Selections From the Writings and Speeches of the South's Most Beloved Civil War General.* Franklin, TN: Sea Raven Press, 2011 Sesquicentennial Civil War Edition.

———. *Lincolnology: The Real Abraham Lincoln Revealed In His Own Words.* Franklin, TN: Sea Raven Press, 2011.

———. *The Unquotable Abraham Lincoln: The President's Quotes They Don't Want You To Know!* Franklin, TN: Sea Raven Press, 2011.

———. *Honest Jeff and Dishonest Abe: A Southern Children's Guide to the Civil War.* Franklin, TN: Sea Raven Press, 2012.

———. *Encyclopedia of the Battle of Franklin - A Comprehensive Guide to the Conflict that Changed the Civil War.* Franklin, TN: Sea Raven Press, 2012.

———. *The Quotable Nathan Bedford Forrest: Selections From the Writings and Speeches of the Confederacy's Most Brilliant Cavalryman.* Spring Hill, TN: Sea Raven Press, 2012.

———. *Forrest! 99 Reasons to Love Nathan Bedford Forrest.* Spring Hill, TN: Sea Raven Press, 2012.

———. *Give 'Em Hell Boys! The Complete Military Correspondence of Nathan Bedford Forrest.* Spring Hill, TN: Sea Raven Press, 2012.

———. *The Constitution of the Confederate States of America Explained: A Clause-by-Clause Study of the South's Magna Carta.* Spring Hill, TN: Sea Raven Press, 2012 Sesquicentennial Civil War Edition.

———. *The Great Impersonator: 99 Reasons to Dislike Abraham Lincoln.* Spring Hill, TN: Sea Raven Press, 2012.

———. *The Old Rebel: Robert E. Lee As He Was Seen By His Contemporaries.* Spring Hill, TN: Sea Raven Press, 2012 Sesquicentennial Civil War Edition.

———. *The Quotable Stonewall Jackson: Selections From the Writings and Speeches of the South's Most Famous General.* Spring Hill, TN: Sea Raven Press, 2012 Sesquicentennial Civil War Edition.

———. *Saddle, Sword, and Gun: A Biography of Nathan Bedford Forrest for Teens.* Spring Hill, TN: Sea Raven Press, 2013.

———. *The Alexander H. Stephens Reader: Excerpts From the Works of a Confederate Founding Father.* Spring Hill, TN: Sea Raven Press, 2013.

———. *The Quotable Alexander H. Stephens: Selections From the Writings and Speeches of the Confederacy's First Vice President.* Spring Hill, TN: Sea Raven Press, 2013 Sesquicentennial Civil War Edition.

———. *Give This Book to a Yankee! A Southern Guide to the Civil War for Northerners.* Spring Hill, TN: Sea Raven Press, 2014.

———. *The Articles of Confederation Explained: A Clause-by-Clause Study of America's*

First Constitution. Spring Hill, TN: Sea Raven Press, 2014.

——. *Confederate Blood and Treasure: An Interview With Lochlainn Seabrook.* Spring Hill, TN: Sea Raven Press, 2015.

——. *Nathan Bedford Forrest and the Battle of Fort Pillow: Yankee Myth, Confederate Fact.* Spring Hill, TN: Sea Raven Press, 2015.

——. *Everything You Were Taught About American Slavery War is Wrong, Ask a Southerner!* Spring Hill, TN: Sea Raven Press, 2015.

——. *Confederacy 101: Amazing Facts You Never Knew About America's Oldest Political Tradition.* Spring Hill, TN: Sea Raven Press, 2015.

——. *The Great Yankee Coverup: What the North Doesn't Want You to Know About Lincoln's War!* Spring Hill, TN: Sea Raven Press, 2015.

——. *Slavery 101: Amazing Facts You Never Knew About America's "Peculiar Institution."* Spring Hill, TN: Sea Raven Press, 2015.

——. *Confederate Flag Facts: What Every American Should Know About Dixie's Southern Cross.* Spring Hill, TN: Sea Raven Press, 2016.

——. *Nathan Bedford Forrest and the Ku Klux Klan: Yankee Myth, Confederate Fact.* Spring Hill, TN: Sea Raven Press, 2016.

——. *Seabrook's Bible Dictionary of Traditional and Mystical Christian Doctrines.* Spring Hill, TN: Sea Raven Press, 2016.

——. *Everything You Were Taught About African-Americans and the Civil War is Wrong, Ask a Southerner!* Spring Hill, TN: Sea Raven Press, 2016.

——. *Nathan Bedford Forrest and African-Americans: Yankee Myth, Confederate Fact.* Spring Hill, TN: Sea Raven Press, 2016.

——. *Women in Gray: A Tribute to the Ladies Who Supported the Southern Confederacy.* Spring Hill, TN: Sea Raven Press, 2016.

——. *Lincoln's War: The Real Cause, the Real Winner, the Real Loser.* Spring Hill, TN: Sea Raven Press, 2016.

——. *The Unholy Crusade: Lincoln's Legacy of Destruction in the American South.* Spring Hill, TN: Sea Raven Press, 2017.

——. *Abraham Lincoln Was a Liberal, Jefferson Davis Was a Conservative: The Missing Key to Understanding the American Civil War.* Spring Hill, TN: Sea Raven Press, 2017.

——. *All We Ask is to be Let Alone: The Southern Secession Fact Book.* Spring Hill, TN: Sea Raven Press, 2017.

——. *The Ultimate Civil War Quiz Book: How Much Do You Really Know About America's Most Misunderstood Conflict?* Spring Hill, TN: Sea Raven Press, 2017.

——. *Rise Up and Call Them Blessed: Victorian Tributes to the Confederate Soldier, 1861-1901.* Spring Hill, TN: Sea Raven Press, 2017.

——. *Victorian Confederate Poetry: The Southern Cause in Verse, 1861-1901*. Spring Hill, TN: Sea Raven Press, 2018.

——. *The Way of Holiness: The Evolution of Religion—From the Cave Bear Cult to Christianity*. Franklin, TN: Sea Raven Press, unpublished manuscript.

——. *The Goddess Encyclopedia of Secret Words, Names, and Places*. Franklin, TN: Sea Raven Press, unpublished manuscript.

——. *Seabrook's Complete Encyclopedia of Deities*. Franklin, TN: Sea Raven Press, unpublished manuscript.

——. *The Unauthorized Encyclopedia of the Bible*. Franklin, TN: Sea Raven Press, unpublished manuscript.

——. *The Complete Dictionary of Christian Mythology*. Franklin, TN: Sea Raven Press, unpublished manuscript.

——. *Aphrodite's Daughters: The True Story of Prostitution*. Franklin, TN: Sea Raven Press, unpublished manuscript.

——. *Mothers and Bachelors: Ending the Battle of the Sexes: A Radical New Look at Marriage and the Family, Based on the Sciences of Anthropology, Primatology, and Sociobiology*. Franklin, TN: Sea Raven Press, unpublished manuscript.

Seznec, Jean. *The Survival of the Pagan Gods*. Princeton, NJ: Princeton University Press, 1953.

Shaw, Ian (ed.). *The Oxford History of Ancient Egypt*. 2000. Oxford, UK: Oxford University Press, 2002 ed.

Simons, Gerald. *Barbarian Europe* (from the *Great Ages of Man* series). New York, NY: Time-Life, 1968.

Sinnett, Alfred Percy. *The Occult World*. London, UK: Theosophical Publishing Society, 1906.

Sjöö, Monica, and Barbara Mor. *The Great Cosmic Mother: Rediscovering the Religion of the Earth*. New York, NY: Harper and Row, 1987.

Skelton, Robin, and Margaret Blackwood. *Earth, Air, Fire, Water: Pre-Christian and Pagan Elements in British Songs, Rhymes and Ballads*. Harmondsworth, UK: Arkana, 1990.

Smith, Andrew Phillip. *The Gnostics: History, Tradition, Scriptures, Influence*. London, UK: Watkins, 2008.

Smith, John Holland. *The Death of Classical Paganism*. New York, NY: Charles Scribner's Sons, 1976.

Smith, Lacey Baldwin. *This Realm of England: 1399 to 1688*. 1966. Lexington, MA: D. C. Heath and Co., 1983 ed.

Smith, Morton. *Jesus the Magician*. San Francisco, CA: Harper and Row, 1978.

Smith, William. *Smith's Bible Dictionary* (Francis N. Peloubet and Mary A. Peloubet, eds.). Circa 1880s. Nashville, TN: Thomas Nelson, 1986 ed.

Sobol, Donald J. *The Amazons of Greek Mythology.* Cranbury, NJ: A.S. Barnes and Co., 1972.

Soltau, Wilhelm. *The Birth of Jesus Christ.* London, UK: Adam and Charles Black, 1903.

Spalding, Baird Thomas. *Life and Teachings of the Masters of the Far East.* 5 vols. 1924. Marina Del Rey, CA: DeVorss and Co., 1964-1976 ed.

Spence, Lewis. *Ancient Egyptian Myths and Legends.* 1915. New York, NY: Dover, 1990 ed.

——. *An Encyclopedia of Occultism.* 1920. New York, NY: Citadel Press, 1993 ed.

——. *The History and Origins of Druidism.* 1949. New York, NY: Samuel Weiser, 1971 ed.

Starbird, Margaret. *The Goddess in the Gospels: Reclaiming the Sacred Feminine.* Rochester, VT: Bear and Co., 1998.

——. *Magdalene's Lost Legacy: Symbolic Numbers and the Sacred Union in Christianity.* Rochester, VT: Bear and Co., 2003.

Stark, Rodney. *Discovering God: The Origins of the Great Religions and the Evolution of Belief.* New York, NY: HarperCollins, 2007.

Stein, Diane. *The Goddess Book of Days.* 1988. Freedom, CA: Crossing Press, 1992 ed.

Stokes, McNeill. *Missing Links to Jesus: Evidence in the Dead Sea Scrolls.* Graham, NC: Plowpoint Press, 2008.

Stone, Merlin. *When God Was a Woman.* San Diego, CA: Harvest, 1976.

——. *Ancient Mirrors of Womanhood: A Treasury of Goddess and Heroine Lore from Around the World.* 1979. Boston, MA: Beacon Press, 1990 ed.

Strauss, David Friedrich. *The Life of Jesus Critically Examined* (Marian Evans, trans.) New York, NY: Calvin Blanchard, 1860.

——. *The Old Faith and the New: A Confession* (Mathilde Blind, trans.). London, UK: Asher and Co., 1874.

Streep, Peg. *Sanctuaries of the Goddess: The Sacred Landscapes and Objects.* Boston, MA: Bullfinch Press, 1994.

Strong, James. *Strong's Exhaustive Concordance of the Bible.* 1890. Nashville, TN: Abingdon Press, 1975 ed.

Stuart, J. P. (ed.). *Popery Adjudged; or, The Roman Catholic Church Weighed in the Balance of God's Word and Found Wanting.* Boston, MA: Redding and Co., 1854.

Stuart, Micheline. *The Tarot: Path to Self Development*. Boulder, CO: Shambhala, 1977.

Sturluson, Snorri. *The Prose Edda*. Berkeley, CA: University of California Press, 1954.

Suarès, Carlo. *The Cipher of Genesis: The Original Code of the Qabala as Applied to the Scriptures*. Berkeley, CA: Shambala, 1970.

Swindoll, Cynthia (ed.). *Abraham: Friend of God*. 1986. Fullerton, CA: Insight for Living, 1988 ed.

Sykes, Egerton. *Who's Who in Non-Classical Mythology* (Alan Kendall, ed.). 1952. New York, NY: Oxford University Press, 1993 ed.

Szekely, Edmond Bordeaux. *The Essene Gospel of Peace*. 1971. Nelson, British Columbia, Canada: International Biogenic Society, 1981 ed.

Tabor, James D. *The Jesus Dynasty: The Hidden History of Jesus, His Royal Family, and the Birth of Christianity*. New York, NY: Simon and Schuster, 2007.

Taylor, Rev. Robert. *The Diegesis; Being a Discovery of the Origin, Evidences, and Early History of Christianity*. Boston, MA: Abner Kneeland, 1834.

Temple, Robert. *The Sirius Mystery: New Scientific Evidence of Alien Contact 5,000 Years Ago*. Rochester, VT: Destiny, 1998.

——. *The Sphinx Mystery: The Forgotten Origins of the Sanctuary of Anubis*. Rochester, VT: Inner Traditions, 2009.

Tenney, Merrill C. (gen. ed.). *Handy Dictionary of the Bible*. Grand Rapids, MI: Lamplighter, 1965.

Terapeut. *The Crucifixion, By an Eye-Witness: A Letter Written Seven Years After the Crucifixion, By a Personal Friend of Jesus in Jerusalem, to an Esseer [Essene] Brother in Alexandria*. 1907. Chicago, IL: Indo-American Book Co., 1911 ed.

Teresa, Saint (of Avila). *The Interior Castle, or the Mansions*. 1588. New York, NY: Benziger Brothers, 1912 ed.

Testimonies of the Life, Character, Revelations and Doctrines of Mother Ann Lee, and the Elders With Her. Albany, NY: Shaker Heritage Society, 1888.

The Dhammapada: The Sayings of Buddha. 6th Century BC. "Rendering" by Thomas Byrom. New York, NY: Vintage, 1976.

The Diamond Sutra, and The Sutra of Hui Neng. Berkeley, CA: Shambala (The Clear Light Series), 1973 ed.

The Epic of Gilgamesh (N. K. Sandars, ed.). Circa 3000 BC. Harmondsworth, UK: Penguin, 1960 (1972 ed.).

The Fossil Record and Evolution. Collected articles from *Scientific American*. San Francisco, CA: W. H. Freeman and Co., 1982 ed.

242 CHRISTMAS BEFORE CHRISTIANITY

The Golden Treasury of Myths and Legends (adapted by Anne Terry White). New York, NY: Golden Press, 1959.

The Herder Symbol Dictionary. 1978. Wilmette, IL: Chiron Publications, 1990 ed.

The Lost Books of the Bible and the Forgotten Books of Eden. Nashville, TN: World Bible Publishers, 1926.

The New American Desk Encyclopedia. 1977. New York, NY: Signet, 1984 ed.

The New Encyclopedia Britannica: Knowledge in Depth. 1768. Chicago, IL/London, UK: Encyclopedia Britannica, 1975 ed.

The Oxford English Dictionary (compact edition, 2 vols.). 1928. Oxford, UK: Oxford University Press, 1979 ed.

The Urantia Book: Revealing the Mysteries of God, the Universe, World History, Jesus, and Ourselves. 1955. Chicago, IL: Urantia Foundation, 2010 ed.

Thompson, James Westfall, and Edgar Nathaniel Johnson. *An Introduction to Medieval Europe: 300-1500*. New York, NY: W. W. Norton, 1937.

Thorburn, Thomas James. *The Mythical Interpretation of the Gospels: Critical Studies in the Historic Narratives*. New York, NY: Charles Scribner's Sons, 1916.

Thorsten, Geraldine. *God Herself: The Feminine Roots of Astrology*. New York, NY: Avon, 1981.

Tille, Alexander. *Yule and Christmas: Their Place in the Germanic Year*. London, UK: David Nutt, 1899.

Towns, Elmer L. *The Names of Jesus*. Denver, CO: Accent, 1987.

Traupman, John C. *The New College Latin and English Dictionary*. 1966. New York, NY: Bantam, 1988 ed.

Trevelyan, George Macaulay. *History of England: Vol. 1, From the Earliest Times to the Reformation*. 1926. Garden City, NY: Anchor, 1952 ed.

Tripp, Edward. *History of England: Vol. 2, The Tudors and the Stuart Era*. 1926. Garden City, NY: Anchor, 1952 ed.

——. *The Meridian Handbook of Classical Mythology*. 1970. Harmondsworth, UK: Meridian, 1974 ed.

Turcan, Robert. *The Cults of the Roman Empire*. 1992. Oxford, UK: Blackwell, 2000 ed.

Tutalo, Gia (ed.). *What Will We Call the Baby?* Boca Raton, FL: Globe Communications, 1995.

Udry, J. Richard. *The Social Context of Marriage*. 1966. Philadelphia, PA: J. B. Lippincott, 1974 ed.

Van De Mieroop, Marc. *A History of the Ancient Near East, ca. 3000-323 BC*. 2004. Oxford, UK: Blackwell, 2007 ed.

Vermaseren, Maarten J. *Cybele and Attis*. London, UK: Thames and Hudson, 1977.

Vermes, Geza (ed.). *The Dead Sea Scrolls in English*. 1962. Harmondsworth, UK: Penguin, 1987 ed.

Viola, Frank, and George Barna. *Pagan Christianity? Exploring the Roots of Our Church Practices*. 2002. Carol Stream, IL: BarnaBooks, 2008 ed.

von Daniken, Erich. *Chariots of the Gods?: Unsolved Mysteries of the Past* (Michael Heron, trans.). 1968. New York, NY: Bantam, 1973 ed.

——. *Gods from Outer Space: Return to the Stars*, or *Evidence for the Impossible*. 1968. New York, NY: Bantam, 1974 ed.

Wace, Henry, and Philip Schaff (eds.). *A Select Library of Nicene and Post-Nicene Fathers of the Christian Church*. 14 vols. Oxford, UK: Parker and Co., 1890.

Walker, Barbara G. *The Woman's Encyclopedia of Myths and Secrets*. San Francisco, CA: Harper and Row, 1983.

——. *The Crone: Woman of Age, Wisdom, and Power*. San Francisco, CA: Harper and Row, 1985.

——. *The Woman's Dictionary of Symbols and Sacred Objects*. San Francisco, CA: Harper and Row, 1988.

Wallis, Wilson Dallam. *Messiahs: Christian and Pagan*. Boston, MA: Gorham Press, 1918.

Walum, Laurel Richardson. *The Dynamics of Sex and Gender: A Sociological Perspective*. Chicago, IL: Rand McNally College Publishing, 1977.

Washington, Henry Augustine (ed.). *The Writings of Thomas Jefferson*. 9 vols. Washington, D.C.: Taylor and Maury, 1854.

Watts, Alan. *Behold the Spirit: A Study in the Necessity of Mystical Religion*. 1947. New York, NY: Random House, 1971 ed.

——. *The Supreme Identity: An Essay on Oriental Metaphysic and the Christian Religion*. New York, NY: Pantheon, 1950.

——. *The Wisdom of Insecurity: A Message For an Age of Anxiety*. New York, NY: Pantheon, 1951.

——. *Myth and Ritual in Christianity*. 1954. Boston, MA: Beacon Press, 1968 ed.

——. *The Way of Zen*. 1957. New York, NY: Vintage, 1989 ed.

——. *This Is It, and Other Essays on Zen and Spiritual Experience*. 1958. New York, NY: Vintage, 1973 ed.

——. *Does It Matter?: Essays on Man's Relation to Materiality*. 1971. Novato, CA: New World Library, 2007 ed.

——. *In My Own Way: An Autobiography*. 1972. Novato, CA: New World

Library, 2001 ed.

Way, George, and Romilly Squire. *Scottish Clan and Family Encyclopedia.* Glasgow, Scotland: HarperCollins, 1994.

Webster's Biographical Dictionary. Springfield, MA: G. and C. Merriam, 1943.

Webster's Ninth New Collegiate Dictionary. Springfield, MA: Merriam-Webster, 1984.

Weigall, Arthur. *The Life and Times of Akhnaton: Pharaoh of Egypt.* London, UK: W. Blackwood and Sons, 1910.

——. *Wanderings in Anglo-Saxon Britain.* New York, NY: George H. Doran, 1926.

——. *The Paganism in Our Christianity.* New York, NY: G. P. Putnam's Sons, 1928.

Wells, George Albert. *Did Jesus Exist?* Amherst, NY: Prometheus, 1987.

——. *The Historical Evidence for Jesus.* Amherst, NY: Prometheus, 1988.

——. *The Jesus Legend.* Chicago, IL: Open Court, 1996.

White, Jon Manchip. *Ancient Egypt: Its Culture and History.* 1952. New York, NY: Dover, 1970 ed.

——. *Everyday Life in Ancient Egypt.* 1963. New York, NY: Perigree, 1980 ed.

White, R. J. *The Horizon Concise History of England.* New York, NY: American Heritage, 1971.

White, Suzanne. *The New Astrology.* 1986. New York, NY: St. Martin's Press.

Whitney, Loren Harper. *A Question of Miracles: Parallels in the Lives of Buddha and Jesus.* Chicago, IL: The Library Shelf, 1908.

Wilde, Lady. *Irish Cures, Mystic Charms, and Superstitions* (compiled by Sheila Anne Barry). New York, NY: Sterling, 1991.

Wilkinson, Gardner. *The Manners and Customs of the Ancient Egyptians.* 5 vols. London, UK: John Murray, 1847.

Wilkinson, Richard H. *The Complete Temples of Ancient Egypt.* London, UK: Thames and Hudson, 2000.

——. *The Complete Gods and Goddesses of Ancient Egypt.* London, UK: Thames and Hudson, 2003.

Wilson, Barrie. *How Jesus Became a Christian.* New York, NY: St. Martin's Press, 2008.

Wilson, Ian. *Jesus: The Evidence.* Washington, D.C.: Regnery, 2000.

Wilson, Stuart, and Joanna Prentis. *The Essenes: Children of the Light.* Huntsville, AR: Ozark Mountain, 2005.

Wind, Edgar. *Pagan Mysteries in the Renaissance.* New York, NY: W. W. Norton, 1968.

Winks, Robin W., Crane Brinton, John B. Christopher, and Robert Lee Wolff. *A History of Civilization, Vol. 1: Prehistory to 1715.* 1955. Englewood Cliffs, NJ: Prentice Hall, 1988 ed.

Witt, Reginald Eldred. *Isis in the Ancient World.* 1971. Baltimore, MD: John Hopkins University Press, 1997.

Yogananda, Paramahansa. *Autobiography of a Yogi.* 1946. Los Angeles, CA: Self-Realization Fellowship, 1972 ed.

———. *The Second Coming of Christ: The Resurrection of the Christ Within You.* 2 vols. Los Angeles, CA: Self-Realization Fellowship, 2004.

Young, Dudley. *Origins of the Sacred: The Ecstasies of Love and War.* 1991. New York, NY: Harper Perennial, 1992 ed.

Young, G. Douglas (gen. ed.). *Young's Compact Bible Dictionary.* 1984. Wheaton, IL: Tyndale House, 1989 ed.

Zaehner, R. C. (ed.) *Encyclopedia of the World's Religions.* 1959. New York, NY: Barnes and Noble, 1997 ed.

Zimmerman, J. E. *Dictionary of Classical Mythology.* New York, NY: Bantam, 1964.

Zondervan (publisher). *Zondervan Compact Bible Dictionary.* 1967. Grand Rapids, MI: Zondervan, 1993 ed.

Zugibe, Frederick T. *The Crucifixion of Jesus: A Forensic Inquiry.* New York, NY: M. Evans, 2005.

INDEX

129, 130, 149, 160, 242
Medieval period 10, 95, 119, 135, 159, 169, 174
Mediterranean basin 52
Mediterranean Sea 29, 157
megalithic pillar worship 164
Melchior 103
Mendes, Egypt 158
Mennonites 140
Menorah 186
menstrual blood 105, 151, 182, 184
menstrual cycle 156
Mer 31, 42, 46, 48, 73, 82, 119, 123, 154, 178, 216, 228, 298
merchants 119, 178
Mercia, England 73
Mercury 42
mercy 31
Meri 2, 3, 6, 9-11, 31, 36, 37, 46, 48, 49, 51, 54, 69, 82, 83, 95, 96, 122, 131, 135, 136, 139, 145, 152, 154, 171, 175, 177, 178, 182, 185, 209, 210, 212, 214, 216, 220-223, 227, 233-238, 241, 242, 244, 295, 296
mermaid 82, 88
merman 88
Merovech 29, 295
Merovee 29
Merovingian dynasty 29, 295

Merry Christmas, greeting 163
merrymaking 185
Mesha 49
Mesopotamia 42, 95, 123, 170, 216, 224
Mesopotamians 123
messiah 14, 26, 29, 72, 77, 149
messiahs 180, 243
Messiah's heraldic star 100
messiah-savior-Sun-gods 77
messianic prophecy 89
metaphysicist 188
meteor 93
Methodists 24
Mexico 184
Micah 49, 186
Middle Ages 55, 127, 147, 210, 214, 218, 223, 224, 228
Middle East 154
Midsummer 38, 52, 130, 144, 166
midsummer bonfires 130
Midsummer Day 52
Midsummer Solstice 144
midwinter fire celebrations 129
midwinter fires 169
Midwinter Solstice 144
Mikado 74
Milan, Italy 111
milk 130, 165
mince pie 10, 163, 164
mince pies 68, 113, 164
mind/body/spirit 105
Minerva 8, 42, 120
Minoans, the 22

MEET THE AUTHOR

LOCHLAINN SEABROOK, a Kentucky Colonel and the winner of the prestigious Jefferson Davis Historical Gold Medal for his "masterpiece," *A Rebel Born: A Defense of Nathan Bedford Forrest*, is a neo-Victorian, unreconstructed Southern historian, award-winning author, Civil War scholar, Bible authority, and traditional Southern Agrarian of Scottish, English, Irish, Welsh, German, and Italian extraction.

A child prodigy, Seabrook is today a true Renaissance Man whose occupational titles also include encyclopedist, lexicographer, musician, artist, graphic designer, genealogist, photographer, and award-winning poet. Also a songwriter and a screenwriter, he has a 40 year background in historical nonfiction writing and is a member of the Sons of Confederate Veterans, the Civil War Trust, and the National Grange. Due to similarities in their writing styles, ideas, and literary works, Seabrook is often referred to as the "new Shelby Foote," the "Southern Joseph Campbell," and the "American Robert Graves" (his English cousin).

Colonel Lochlainn Seabrook, award-winning historian, author, and Bible authority, is America's most popular and prolific pro-South author. His spiritual works have introduced hundreds of thousands to the truth about Jesus and the Bible.

A cousin of King James (whose Medieval English translation of the Bible is still the world's most popular version) and a descendant of both the Grail King Merovech (Frankish founder of the Merovingian dynasty) and Tiberius Caesar (emperor of Rome during the time of Jesus, Luke 3:1), Seabrook is the grandson of an Appalachian coal-mining family, a seventh-generation Kentuckian, co-chair of the Jent/Gent Family Committee (Kentucky), founder and director of the Blakeney Family Tree Project, and a board member of the Friends of Colonel Benjamin E. Caudill. Seabrook's literary works have been endorsed by leading authorities, museum curators, award-winning historians, bestselling authors, celebrities, noted scientists, well respected educators, TV show hosts and producers, renowned military artists, esteemed Southern organizations, and distinguished academicians from around the world.

Seabrook has authored over 50 popular adult books on the American Civil War, American and international slavery, the U.S. Confederacy (1781), the Southern Confederacy (1861), religion, theology and thealogy, Jesus, the Bible, the Apocrypha, the Law of Attraction, alternative health, spirituality, ghost stories, the paranormal, ufology, social issues, and cross-cultural studies of the family and marriage. His Confederate biographies, pro-South studies, genealogical monographs, family histories, military encyclopedias, self-help guides, and etymological dictionaries have received wide acclaim.

Seabrook's eight children's books include a Southern guide to the Civil War, a biography of Nathan Bedford Forrest, a dictionary of religion and myth, a rewriting of the King Arthur legend (which reinstates the original pre-Christian motifs), two bedtime stories for preschoolers, a naturalist's guidebook to owls, a worldwide look at the family, and an examination of the Near-Death Experience.

Of blue-blooded Southern stock through his Kentucky, Tennessee, Virginia, West Virginia, and North Carolina ancestors, he is a direct descendant of European royalty via his 6th great-grandfather, the Earl of Oxford, after which London's famous Harley Street is named. Among his celebrated male Celtic ancestors is Robert the Bruce, King of Scotland, Seabrook's 22nd great-grandfather. The 21st great-grandson of Edward I "Longshanks" Plantagenet), King of England, Seabrook is a thirteenth-generation Southerner through his descent from the colonists of Jamestown, Virginia (1607).

The 2nd, 3rd, and 4th great-grandson of dozens of Confederate soldiers, one of his closest connections to the War for Southern Independence is through his 3rd great-grandfather, Elias Jent, Sr., who fought for the Confederacy in the Thirteenth Cavalry Kentucky under Seabrook's 2nd cousin, Colonel Benjamin E. Caudill. The Thirteenth, also known as "Caudill's Army," fought in numerous conflicts, including the Battles of Saltville, Gladsville, Mill Cliff, Poor Fork, Whitesburg, and

Leatherwood.

Seabrook is a descendant of the families of Alexander Hamilton Stephens, John Singleton Mosby, William Giles Harding, and Edmund Winchester Rucker, and is related to the following Confederates and other 19th-Century luminaries: Robert E. Lee, Stephen Dill Lee, Stonewall Jackson, Nathan Bedford Forrest, James Longstreet, John Hunt Morgan, Jeb Stuart, P. G. T. Beauregard (approved the Confederate Battle Flag design), George W. Gordon, John Bell Hood, Alexander Peter Stewart, Arthur M. Manigault, Joseph Manigault, Charles Scott Venable, Thornton A. Washington, John A. Washington, Abraham Buford, Edmund W. Pettus, Theodrick "Tod" Carter, John B. Womack, John H. Winder, Gideon J. Pillow, States Rights Gist, Henry R. Jackson, John Lawton Seabrook, John C. Breckinridge, Leonidas Polk, Zachary Taylor, Sarah Knox Taylor (first wife of Jefferson Davis), Richard Taylor, Davy Crockett, Daniel Boone, Meriwether Lewis (of the Lewis and Clark Expedition) Andrew

Jackson, James K. Polk, Abram Poindexter Maury (founder of Franklin, TN), William Giles Harding, Zebulon Vance, Thomas Jefferson, George Wythe Randolph (grandson of Jefferson), Felix K. Zollicoffer, Fitzhugh Lee, Nathaniel F. Cheairs, Jesse James, Frank James, Robert Brank Vance, Charles Sidney Winder, John W. McGavock, Caroline E. (Winder) McGavock, David Harding McGavock, Lysander McGavock, James Randal McGavock, Randal William McGavock, Francis McGavock, Emily McGavock, William Henry F. Lee, Lucius E. Polk, Minor Meriwether (husband of noted pro-South author Elizabeth Avery Meriwether), Ellen Bourne Tynes (wife of Forrest's chief of artillery, Captain John W. Morton), South Carolina Senators Preston Smith Brooks and Andrew Pickens Butler, and famed South Carolina diarist Mary Chesnut.

Seabrook's modern day cousins include: Patrick J. Buchanan (conservative author), Cindy Crawford (model), Shelby Lee Adams (Letcher County, Kentucky, portrait photographer), Bertram Thomas Combs (Kentucky's fiftieth governor), Edith Bolling (wife of President

Woodrow Wilson), and actors Robert Duvall, Reese Witherspoon, Lee Marvin, Rebecca Gayheart, Andy Griffith, Riley Keough, and Tom Cruise.

Seabrook's screenplay, *A Rebel Born*, based on his book of the same name, has been signed with acclaimed filmmaker Christopher Forbes (of Forbes Film). It is now in pre-production, and is set for release in 2017 as a full-length feature film. This will be the first movie ever made of Nathan Bedford Forrest's life story, and as a historically accurate project written from the Southern perspective, is destined to be one of the most talked about Civil War films of all time.

Born with music in his blood, Seabrook is an award-winning, multi-genre, BMI-Nashville songwriter and lyricist who has composed some 3,000 songs (250 albums), and whose original music has been heard in film (*A Rebel Born, Cowgirls 'n Angels, Confederate Cavalry, Billy the Kid: Showdown in Lincoln County, Vengeance Without Mercy, Last Step, County Line, The Mark*) and on TV and radio worldwide. A musician, producer, multi-instrumentalist, and renown performer—whose keyboard work has been variously compared to pianists from Hargus Robbins and Vince Guaraldi to Elton John and Leonard Bernstein—Seabrook has opened for groups such as the Earl Scruggs Review, Ted Nugent, and Bob Seger, and has performed privately for such public figures as President Ronald Reagan, Burt Reynolds, Loni Anderson, and Senator Edward W. Brooke. Seabrook's cousins in the music business include: Johnny Cash, Elvis Presley, Billy Ray and Miley Cyrus, Patty Loveless, Tim McGraw, Lee Ann Womack, Dolly Parton, Pat Boone, Naomi, Wynonna, and Ashley Judd, Ricky Skaggs, the Sunshine Sisters, Martha Carson, and Chet Atkins.

Colonel Seabrook lives with his wife and family in historic Middle Tennessee, the heart of Forrest country and the Confederacy, where his conservative Southern ancestors fought valiantly against Liberal Lincoln and the progressive North in defense of Jeffersonianism, constitutional government, and personal liberty.

If you enjoyed this book you will be interested in Colonel Seabrook's other popular related titles:

☛ SEABROOK'S BIBLE DICTIONARY OF TRADITIONAL & MYSTICAL CHRISTIAN DOCTRINES
☛ JESUS & THE GOSPEL OF Q: CHRIST'S PRE-CHRISTIAN TEACHINGS AS RECORDED IN THE NEW TESTAMENT
☛ CHRIST IS ALL & IN ALL: REDISCOVERING YOUR DIVINE NATURE & THE KINGDOM WITHIN
☛ JESUS & THE LAW OF ATTRACTION: THE BIBLE-BASED GUIDE TO CREATING PERFECT HEALTH, WEALTH, & HAPPINESS

Available from Sea Raven Press and wherever fine books are sold

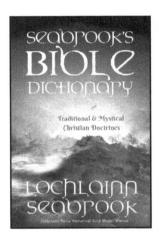
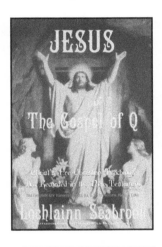

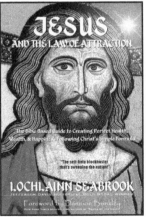

ALL OF OUR BOOK COVERS ARE AVAILABLE AS 11" X 17" POSTERS, SUITABLE FOR FRAMING.

≈© **SeaRavenPress.com** ©≈

Printed in the USA
CPSIA information can be obtained
at www.ICGtesting.com
LVHW091231261124
797558LV00005B/1037